Time-Limited Art Psy

Time-Limited Art Psychotherapy: Developments in theory and practice comes at a watershed in the provision of art psychotherapy in public services. The increase in 'payment by results', clinical throughput and evidence-based practice, as well as the changing NHS context means there is an increasing need to provide effective therapeutic treatments within brief time limits where appropriate.

The book brings together the developments in theory and practice in time-limited working strategies emerging in the field. The contributors, all practising therapists, examine the practice of time-limited art psychotherapy with different clients in a range of settings, with a variety of approaches, showing how they react and adapt to the changing face of mental health services.

Time-Limited Art Psychotherapy will be essential reading to art psychotherapists, trainers and trainees in art psychotherapy and other schools of psychotherapy who integrate creative approaches within their practice. It will also form a useful contribution to the continuing professional development for a range of psychological therapists and practitioners of integrated psychotherapies such as CAT and mentalization-based therapies amongst others.

Rose Hughes is an HCPC registered art psychotherapist and UKCP registered psychotherapist, working in private practice and in the NHS. She has worked primarily in adult mental health since 1983.

Time-Limited Art Psychotherapy

Developments in theory and practice

Edited by Rose Hughes

Routledge
Taylor & Francis Group

LONDON AND NEW YORK

First published 2016
by Routledge
2 Park Square, Milton Park, Abingdon, Oxon OX14 4RN

and by Routledge
711 Third Avenue, New York, NY 10017

Routledge is an imprint of the Taylor & Francis Group, an informa business

British Library Cataloguing in Publication Data
A catalogue record for this book is available from the British Library

Library of Congress Cataloging-in-Publication Data
A catalog record for this book has been requested

Cover image: *The Conversation:* Ink on Paper.
Copyright Rose Hughes

ISBN: 978-0-415-83476-6 (hbk)
ISBN: 978-0-415-83477-3 (pbk)
ISBN: 978-1-315-72613-7 (ebk)

Typeset in Times
by Apex CoVantage, LLC

Printed and bound by CPI Group (UK) Ltd, Croydon, CR0 4YY

This book is dedicated to all those who learn to live with and survive mental health difficulties, their courage in the face of traumatic histories are born out in their challenging internal narratives.

In Memory of Thomas
Rose Hughes
June 2014

Contents

Figures

Contributors

Rose Hughes is an HCPC registered art psychotherapist and UKCP registered psychotherapist, working in private practice and in the NHS. She has worked primarily in adult mental health since 1983.

Michael Atkins trained in Audio Visual Studies at West Surrey College of Art and Design and qualified as an art therapist in 1989, studying in Sheffield. He went on to complete the Advanced Training in Art Psychotherapy Diploma at Goldsmiths. Michael has worked in child and adolescent mental health services since 1998, adding skills in solution focused practice and more recently interpersonal psychotherapy. In recent years Michael has fulfilled the role of regional co-ordinator for his local regional art therapy group and been team leader. Michael has provided clinical placements for art therapy trainees and has provided supervision for colleagues in art and play therapy.

Rosalyn Doyle has been an art and design lecturer in a college for 12 years, working with students from a range of learning abilities and ages. She is also a qualified art therapist, currently working in mental health, in an NHS Foundation Health Trust community day centre, as an honorary art psychotherapist. She is the librarian for BAAT region 4.

Lynne Francis is an HPC registered art therapist and a practising artist. Lynne currently works as a studio manager and art therapist at Studio Upstairs in Bristol and in private practice. In her art therapy practice, Lynne brings together mindfulness and art therapy and she also runs training courses in mindfulness and art therapy for the British Association of Art Therapists. Lynne has extensive experience of working with a diverse range of individuals and groups in both healthcare and individual settings, holds qualifications in both general and mental health nursing and is a qualified secondary school teacher.

Sheila Grandison is currently the Training & Workforce Development Lead for Arts Therapies in the East London NHS Foundation Trust, and a former Head of Arts Therapies for Adult Services in the same trust. Sheila is a past chair of BAAT and since 2008 has worked in partnership with Tate Modern, London, developing training programmes related to social justice, mental health and art.

She is an executive member of ISPS UK (International Society for Psychological and Social Approaches to Psychosis) and holds an honorary lecturership in the School of Health Studies, City University, London.

Marian Liebmann has worked in art therapy with offenders, women's groups, community groups, and for 19 years in the Inner City Mental Health Team in Bristol, where she developed work on anger issues, and worked with asylum seekers and refugees. She lectures on art therapy at several universities in the UK and Europe. She also works in restorative justice, mediation and conflict resolution, and has run workshops on art, conflict and anger in many countries. She has written/edited 12 books, including *Art Therapy and Anger*. In 2010 she was awarded her PhD by publications from Bristol University, and in 2013 she was awarded an OBE for services to art therapy and mediation.

Kate Rothwell is currently the Head of Arts Therapies for the Forensic Directorate of the East London Foundation Trust and clinically assigned to the Specialist Learning Disabilities service working with adult offenders in a locked environment. Kate is an art psychotherapist at HMP Grendon and was a senior lecturer on the MA Art Therapy programme at the University of Hertfordshire. She is a private practitioner, educator, clinical supervisor and published author.

Gillian Solomon is an HCPC registered art and cognitive psychotherapist specialising in the use of imagery. She has worked for the NHS and in private practice with adults, couples and families, practising in Africa and the UK since 1990.

Neil Springham is a consultant art therapist at Oxleas NHS Foundation Trust, London, and has practised for 27 years in adult mental health, addictions and now specialises in personality disorder treatment. He was a course leader at the Unit of Psychotherapeutic Studies, Goldsmiths College, co-founded the UK Art Therapy Practice Research Network and was twice elected chair of the British Association of Art Therapists. He holds a PhD in Psychology and founded ResearchNet as a network of linked service user and provider collaborative groups which use co-produced research and experience based co-design to create change within mental health services. He has published and lectured internationally on issues in co-production research and in art therapy.

David Thorne is an art therapist with 13 years in the Barnet, Enfield and Haringey Mental Health Trust and 18 years of experience working as an art therapist within mental health. He has lectured on the MA and Foundation Courses in art therapy at the University of Hertfordshire and has given numerous talks. He has been developing a mentalization-based art therapy service for the Enfield Personality Disorder Service, and this is where the work represented here has been developed.

Chris Wood is part of the Art Therapy Northern Programme, which is a base for art therapy training and research in Sheffield. As a research fellow at the University of Sheffield she works to support arts therapists engaged in PhD research. She also works as an art therapist.

Acknowledgements

This book would not have been possible without the hard work and enthusiasm of all the contributors. The authors have sensitively described in their chapters diversity of approaches not previously presented in the art psychotherapy literature.

Thanks to Val Huet, Chief Executive Officer of BAAT, who has supported this project from her standing as the national professional lead.

Thanks to David Thorne for his editorial support with the Introduction to this book and chapter 3.

Thanks to Emer Douglas, art psychotherapist, for her generous technical support preparing this book for publication.

I would like to thank the NHS and other clinical organisations that have supported the clinical work of the authors that have led to this new theory and practice.

Finally thanks to all at Routledge, Taylor & Francis Group for believing in this book and bearing with us as it grew.

Foreword

Val Huet, BAAT CEO

I write this foreword with a feeling of excitement and a sense of relief, as this long overdue book is finally published. My feeling of excitement comes not only from seeing the impressive quality of the art therapy practice described here but also from the fact that a rich diversity of theoretical approaches has been included. The sense of relief comes from knowing that countless art therapists will find good and solid advice on time-limited art therapy practice, an issue that has been rather absent till now from a lot of our literature and training.

A look back at how time-limited or 'brief' art therapy was described is rather illuminating: when I qualified as an art therapist in 1986, 'brief therapy' described any work that lasted less than nine months to a calendar year. It was not unusual for clients to be in any type of therapy for periods of up to two to three years and this within the public health or social care sectors. Art therapists then would some-times see clients for brief interventions but mostly, these cases did not involve several agencies and severe issues. Additionally, the culture of art therapy educa-tion was also different: a variety of models and skills were taught that included structured themes workshops, dream work, mask and make up sessions, etc., as well as non-directive experiential groups. Therefore many art therapists, includ-ing trainees, felt able to be interactive with clients which suited short-term work well.

A confluence of events changed this: large scale cuts within the NHS in the 1990s introduced a wave of service rationing. At the same time, a growing call for evidence-based practice became fused and confused with pressures on service commissioning (Parry, 1997). Open-ended, long-term therapy was challenged and so was the assumption that length equated quality of outcome. Increasingly, time limits for all types of psychotherapy were introduced within services. For many art therapists, time-limited therapy became perceived as a necessary but regret-table compromise that had to be made in order to survive in this new culture. Parallel events within art therapy were also significant: from the late eighties, a non-directive psychoanalytic culture had steadily been adopted as a quasi 'gold standard' of art therapy practice. It was not long before an active or interactive stance became confused with 'acting out': anything else than a completely non-directive approach was seen as regrettable and leading to second-class therapy.

Therefore many art therapists tried, at least for a time, to do time-limited art therapy in a non-directive way, an unhappy and ultimately futile pursuit. Many ended up abandoning this approach and developing some excellent practice adaptions (Huet, 1997) and some, including Rose Hughes (the editor of this book), went on to do further therapy trainings on time-limited interventions. A few publications focusing on time-limited art therapy, notably Wood's on a single art therapy session within palliative care (1990) and Luzzato's (1997) on short-term art therapy groups on an acute ward, were positive examples of time-limited art therapy and Hughes on integrating time limited CAT into art psychotherapy Inscape (2007).

Increasingly, art therapists are developing and sharing a diversity of approaches as well as claiming this as 'proper' art therapy (Springham, 2013). Psychoanalysis has much to offer that is valuable and congruent to our work: for instance, the roots of Mentalization-Based Therapy are firmly within psychoanalysis. However, other theories and approaches can also be extremely helpful and since they also have a lot of empirical evidence, they should not be ignored: understanding what works how and why remains a central issue for all psychotherapies (Roth & Fonagy, 1996).

This book is a valuable contribution towards opening up a professional horizon that was in danger of becoming limited and limiting. Above all, it shows that time-limited art psychotherapy is a valuable therapeutic intervention.

References

Huet, V. (1997). Challenging professional confidence: Arts therapies and psychiatric rehabilitation. *Inscape*, *2* (1), 14–19.

Hughes, R. (2007). An enquiry into an integration of cogntivie analytic therapy with art therapy. *International Journal of Art Therapy: Inscape*, *12* (1), 28–38.

Luzzatto, P. (1997). Short-term art therapy on the acute psychiatric ward: The open session as a psychodynamic development of the studio-based approach. *Inscape*, *2* (1), 2–10.

Parry, G. (1997). Bambi fights back: Psychotherapy research and service improvement. *Inscape*, *2* (1), 11–13.

Roth, A. & Fonagy P. (1996). *What works for whom: A critical review of psychotherapy research (2nd edition)*. London: Guildford Press.

Springham, N. (2013). Art therapy Amnesty. *Newsbriefing, December 2013*, 11–15.

Wood, M. (1990). Art therapy in one session. *Inscape, Winter*, 27–33.

Introduction

Rose Hughes

> The Link between time and reality is insoluble. We can divorce ourselves from
> time only by undoing reality or from reality only by undoing the sense of time.
> Categorical time is measured by clocks and calendars; existential time is that
> which is experienced, lived in, rather than observed. Each moment is the fruit
> of forty thousand years. The minute winning days, like flies, buzz home to
> death, and every moment is a window on all time.
>
> (Thomas Wolfe, cited by Mann 1973, p 3)

Time is thought about and experienced in many different ways derived from reli-
gious, cultural, scientific and embodied standpoints typically associated with age
and consciousness. Time is a commodity in that we sell or buy time by the hour
during our working lives. This objective use of time is a gradual process from
infancy with its embodied illusion of timelessness. Children in non-traumatised
environments will have little sense of time until the age of around their sixth year.
For babies and young children time is like an endless ocean into which they are
immersed, as one with, until they are awakened into structured time at an increasing rate from birth. It can be witnessed in the child's inability to frame time and to
attend to it, to get dressed for school, to prepare to go to bed and the like. Adults
hold time for them and help them to adjust to existential time as they begin their
relational journey from birth. Part of this learning is through the disillusionment
of ideal care, by the essential and inevitable failure of caregivers. Time's link to
reality is cultural and political too.

Similarly economic production has direct links with time in terms of wages and
production and with the life cycle of the population. Health care has undergone
reframing from its person-centred, social and nonprofit-based practice spear-
headed by the post WWII labour government, the Beverage Report and Health
Minister Aneurin Bevan's inception of our NHS. That this system developed in
the UK was because post-war optimism and recognition that the people of the
nation form a social community having fought two world wars and created great
economic wealth through the first industrial revolution in the world and the development of the first mass working class. People's human value and collective responsibility for care was seen as something naturally shared. Our allies in WWII, the

Soviet Union and other nations trying at that time to socialise their economies and social practices, were seen as essentially human centred in principal. This ideology also had roots in other nations and in forms derived from their circumstances. For some social collective acts are perceived differently by peoples who feel controlled and limited by it and who see collective activity as, falsely, in my view, evidence of lack of individual personal responsibility. For example, in nations occupied to suppress residual fascism in the years after the war and the defeat of fascism. Also, in other nations with an individualistic 'pioneering' belief linked to a partly mythologised and romanticised past, such as the gold rush in the USA.

Today in the UK, health care and public services are pivotally costed as commodities and pricing commodities takes some of its value from time, time to deliver, produce and the increasing centricity of this approach inevitably compromises the NHS human centre. The NHS is now open to seek a profitable economic market place for the private sector and reducing wages, staffing levels and nationally owned hospital premises, to create wealth for the new providers of infrastructure and services is but another facet of this. This practice creates austerity for the majority. As one of the richest nations it is the most precious things that should be preserved and workers in the NHS and other services under the same cultural attack are trying to make sense of the situation and maintain standards of care at a clinical and professional level, despite the culling that is increasingly rampant.

Clinicians and clients are increasingly subject to the government's so-called 'efficiency savings'. Deficit in funding due to changes in infrastructure and service providers is being 'charged' to the public services and this includes mental health provision. That these monies cannot be found where the consequence is less anti-social and calamitous is a question that begs to be answered, if it were not so clear that the NHS is a great new market place for businessmen, replacing the old investment in factories and the like of our former industrial times.

The prevailing hegemony is that the 'inefficiency' exists not only in funding but in the clinician and indeed, the service user! The staff should do 'more for less' and the public should have less access to services, because the government wants to spend tax revenues elsewhere and provide services that have minimalised cost to the competing 'providers'. Karl Marx and Friedrich Engels developed historical research into the development of modern society through dialectical and historical material analysis; thesis, antithesis, synthesis.

They described how ancient people shared ownership of land throughout the world and that village communities were found to be a primitive form of communistic society. They speak of how the dissolution of these primaeval societies began to be differentiated in to separate and finally antagonistic classes (Marx and Engels, 1965).

In a sense we can see that in mental health care we mostly try to create a safe container for our clients and this we can liken to the ancient village community where each person's efforts are to assist one another. It is therefore not surprising that two things happen in our professional group as in society. We, like the new societies described by Marx and Engels, compete and treasure our roles and identities in part, in a quest for survival on these class derived principles and a larger part we struggle for the principles upon which the NHS was founded, to care for the people's health from the 'cradle to the grave'. In the East Staffordshire NHS we have observed lately how compromising this central tenet can lead to depersonalisation and poor staff practice and poor care. In day-to-day context of over-stretched use of time, in which the gentleness of compassion can be buried and trodden upon, we as clinicians wish to conserve the child space and child time long enough to support effective clinical work, be it nursing through to art psychotherapy. This is the aim of facilitating an environment that Winnicott framed in his pioneering work with children in the NHS (Winnicott, 1990). This is the environment where new understandings and emotional processing can support improved sense of self in the world.

Art psychotherapy emerged in the asylums of the late Victorian era and World War I trauma wards and tuberculosis sanatoria during the epidemic of the early to mid-1900s. Artists began to take art materials to patients to assist them through a healing process of body and mind. Adrian Hill and Edward Adamson are well-known early pioneers in the sanatoria and psychiatric asylums respectively in England.

Art is a vehicle to travel through time, to enable us to leave the moment or to view it close up or at a distance as best suits the emotional need or reflection of distress. We travel through time in images and their narratives. Art process and image can take us to the formlessness of childhood, to be lost in the moment and the imaginal reverie. Art can create a safe space to look back to trauma and view it alongside the art psychotherapist or shared with the art psychotherapy group. Art materials can empower where lives are diminished and crushed through the 'potential space' of the paper or the lump of clay and create a voice for clients as well as an embodied connection to their own efficacy. This is worked through by their manipulation of the art materials and their managing in the object that which was previously unmanageable psychologically.

In *The Time Machine*, H. G. Wells speaks of the time traveller as returning to chronological time in a traumatised state.

> He was in an amazing plight. His coat was dusty and dirty and smeared with green down the sleeves; his hair disordered, and as it seemed to me to be greyer-either with dust and dirt or because its colour had actually faded. His face was ghastly pale; his chin had a brown cut on it-a cut half healed; his expression was haggard and drawn, as by intense suffering.
>
> (Wells, 2002, p 13)

Internal conflicts as we witness and encounter them in the art psychotherapy room can be very much in this felt sense of trauma illustrated by Wells' traveller. Like the child grown up, returning to the child place can be a journey of exploration and cathexis of trauma by its capacity to be changed in the art psychotherapy image and new experience of others, and of the therapist, in a new and better representation of the suffering and chaotic feelings our past self, reworked and left once again in a more manageable and less intrusive form. Marion Milner, pioneer art psychotherapist wrote in her book 'On Not Being Able To Paint' of her experience of being soothed by seeing Picasso's painting on exhibition in which a trauma she identified with was depicted and communicated in such a way as to make it more manageable, even humorous and kind (Milner, 1957).

Michael Edwards (2010, p 69), Jungian art psychotherapist, wrote of his observation:

> Anxiety is often a fear of chaos. The same can be true of the empty stage, the unplayed musical instrument. The arts can thus remind us of the frightening aspects of our personal relation to chaos [chaos emerging out of personal and social phenomenon in our internal worlds.] However they can also moderate this experience by providing a suitable image on which to project our fantasies.

Art psychotherapy facilitates time travel as an internal journey into the self. Associated impressions and our ancestors' representations emerge through the stories that clients share in art psychotherapy. Art can reveal the profound impoverishment of the deprived child as adult and offer a space to substantiate the underprivileged self, to add to the sense of self in an explicit and visual process of artistic creation. It can create a new starting point in time, beyond the traumas that hold the moment frozen on many levels of experience. Trauma and other states brought to art psychotherapy are most often repetitious and this is very distressing for the client. However, within this lays the potential to review and rework past times impact thereby allowing new potential and generativity to follow into future time. Art making and the creative impetus can help with this. It can be a safe space to grieve for all of this.

There are those who arrive with elaborate defences to face the world, others, themselves and their life's journey. In these cases it is often so that their experiences have been so unbearable that these new aspects of self are set to preserve the child self. To protect the child from current or historical world experienced as peopled with neglecting, abusing and shaming enactments from others. If these defences seem acceptable to the person they are not likely to seek therapy but for many they are unable to contain and support the challenges they seek to defeat, and that serve to inadvertently add to their repetition and so the person begins to breakdown in various ways. Jerome S. Bernstein (2005, p 91) explores and analyses this in his book *Living in the Borderland: The Evolution of Consciousness and the Challenge of Healing Trauma*. He names it the trauma portal.

In his eloquent and penetrating work, *The Inner World of Trauma*, Jungian psychoanalyst Donald Kalsched, discusses 'trauma' in children as any experience that causes the child unbearable pain or anxiety. He goes on to say that 'unbearable experiences' are those that 'overwhelm the usual defensive measures' and that the distinguishing feature of such trauma is what Heinz Kohut calls a 'disintegration anxiety', an 'unnameable dread associated with the threatened dissolution of a coherent self' (Kalsched, cited by Berstein 2005).

He speaks of how the psyche creates an alternate world peopled by archetypal defences that rescue the personality when trauma strikes. Kalsched sees this emerging in the internal world whereas Bernstein (2005) sees this as a connection to nature he observes in the 'borderland personality', being those who use nature and art in an new experiential, symbolic, ritual and profound way to manage trauma.

In this nameless dread that besets the distressed and traumatised person there is something important to be said about time-limited art psychotherapy as it provides an expectation of progress through the sessions by creating a clear time boundary. By so doing it supports greater or lesser degrees of reintegration out of the amorphousness of the anxiety state. It therefore recruits a healthy part of the client sooner whilst not being too brief that there is no time to begin 'working through' (similar to the grief process) in the time shared with the therapist. Time-limited art psychotherapy can help to integrate this trauma and with it increase access to nurturing in the inner world, whilst most time-limited models of therapy assist the person to access their internal archetypes, their object relations found in their imaginal inner world of thought and image. This can occur in therapy in ways that nourish and sustain ongoing connection between self and other. In such cases of trauma the relation to time has taken a route out of lived reality into a frozen traumatised place from which creativity and time have been lost or stagnated. The role of time-limited therapy is to help the individual harness and clearly rediscover, through the therapy, the seeds of resilience and generativity. This emergence in time-limited art psychotherapy is deeply moving and worthy of proper value and credit as individuals emerge out of most shocking beginnings and subsequent experiences.

Another factor of time that impresses most forcefully on the therapist in the NHS and other clinical settings of this period is the shift in the symbolic relation to time as a cultural phenomenon. In Freud's time the symbolic material of his patients were represented by the development of the industrial age. The phallic symbolisation of railway trains in dream material is a well-known example of this. We are now in the digital age, some say the late digital age. We are expected to work at speeds of the digital media. Our potency is measured by this. We have hand-held computers, email and electronic diaries that can be administered electronically by managers, framing time for us. A phone salesman told me recently of wrist watches that will soon have all the media functions for email, internet and the like. Eye spectacles with built in computer screens have arrived. Speed and multi tasking is the new production line.

There are targets to account for the ever-increasing number of tasks that the Quality Care Commission want those of us in public services to adhere to and account for electronically and digitally. Now we are in an age no longer moving at the speed of the old steam train but travelling at the speed of light and there about. Human beings have viewed their own speed as evidence of effectiveness from the school system through to factory production.

In his book *About Time: From Sundials to Quantum Clocks, How the Cosmos Shapes Our Lives – And We Shape The Cosmos*, Adam Frank (2012) explores the impact of time on successive generations. He speaks of cosmology and physicists evolving theories of how time began. In the social history of lived time we learn of the radical changes of the Industrial Revolution and Newton's discoveries radically impacting on human lives in the 1700s. Though clocks were invented in the fourteenth century it was three hundred years later before the minute hand was invented! Prior to this we relied on bells and candles to measure and mark out time. Frank talks of the evolution of culture emerging in the end of the last ice age as new forms of social organisation led to new ways of thinking and the beginning of a new evolutionary trajectory. As culture emerged so did sense of self; we invented ourselves so to speak.

Of time and its pressures, which are linked to economic forces and productivity of the individual, Adam Frank describes the current increase in pressure as part of this evolutionary, economic and political process.

> It was through a direct, embodied engagement with the material world – what we made, how we made it and how that changed the way we organised ourselves – that time itself changed. Each culture shaped its day to day life through the technologies it built and through its 'Institutional facts' – the invented social reality the technologies allowed and supported.
>
> (Frank, 2012, p xviii)

Whilst this book is a celebration of new developments in time-limited art psychotherapy, it is also a response to the pressures in the clinical setting to provide effective treatments where there are increased time restraints linked to productivity and demand as more people require help from the travails of life and their internal worlds. But, it would be a collusion with these pressures of time if due note is not made of the oppressive experience of ever-increasing speed. Paul Virilo in his book, *The Administration of Fear*, describes the conflictual impact time as a measure of speed has upon us. 'Phenomenology has been unable to explain that speed is not a phenomenon but the relationship between phenomena. Speed is relativity and relativity is politics!' (Virilo, 2012, p 26).

In the digital age there is constant pressure to consume at speed and to be productive at an ever-increasing pace. As the dreams of early analyses were representative of the speed and motion of their times and their symbolic content, for example, the dream material represented in Freuds writings, so, too, are we profoundly impacted upon by the digital age and the pressure for almost instantaneous processing and action of so many things and in ever increasing ways. People now feel the burden of yet one more work task which will '*take just a minute*' as if therefore the minutes don't add up to a grand and increasing total, as if we are not over-consumed by this pace of time and its devaluation of relationship in work culture. Keeping up with pace is the new fashion, first and foremost, so that technology leads the cultural zeitgeist and people follow its values in a pervasive hegemony, where young people can't find employment but have neural pathways trained to work technology at great speed. Speeding up time is fashionable, it is the winner! Not keeping up on the treadmill of digital speed is over looked or rejected, vilified or hidden. It is the rejected aspect of a pervasive industry and the new productivity.

Virilo describes this in his book as;

> . . . we have left the acceleration of history and entered the acceleration of reality. When we speak of live events, of real time, we are talking about the acceleration of reality and not the acceleration of history. The classical definition of acceleration of history is the passage from horses to trains, from trains to propeller planes and from planes to jet aircraft. They are within speeds that are controlled and controllable . . . We have reached the limits of instantaneity, the limits of human thought and time.
>
> (Virilo, 2012, p 33)

However, there is great joy in recovering from distress, of boxing more cleverly with life, of learning to be on your own side and learning to make sense of others both in greatness and their shadow, so that we can live effectively in the interpersonal world and in our internal worlds. This is our aim for clients who come for time-limited art psychotherapy. It is a journey with acceptance and challenge, without the excesses of focus on unsavoury elements of the unconscious that Freud and Klein interpreted as the toxic heart of clients. These viewed by some as the immovable object. In turn the 'otherness' of the therapist becomes potentially toxic in it imperiousness. Time-limited therapy frees people whilst giving a potent sense of being held. Time-limited therapy is hopeful and none pathologising in its understanding and relationship to clients.

Time-limited art psychotherapy is explored in the chapters of this book from the perspective that each authors brings to this domain at this time. The book was conceived out of a feeling of marginalisation against the traditional backdrop of long-term analytic art psychotherapy practice and value systems that I felt alongside my positive regard for time-limited therapy. However it was an assumption that long-term treatment implied better therapeutic outcome and this made new approaches unappealing to the profession in many cases. It has been a delight editing this book. On this journey I met the authors whose work you find here. They are based across the breadth and depth of England. Some have worked in teams specialising in time-limited treatments and have adapted and grown their practice in this context. Others have worked alone or with a small group of peers to develop art psychotherapy in time-limited models. Others have researched effective time-limited treatment evaluations and time-limited art psychotherapy pathways in the recovery model, using resources effectively and imaginatively. There is no one time-limited approach that is promoted above others, but a range of approaches to art psychotherapy practice. This is I feel evidence of the cusp of change, where there is exploration and a momentum response to the shared experiences of our social and economic environment. There are a wide variety of clinical settings in which these practice shifts have been evolving as new theories about change emerge and we respond creatively to the needs of art psychotherapy clients. It will be interesting to see if this variety will become part of the identity of art psychotherapy, or if one or more approaches will be favoured. Whilst for the trainee therapist these developments may need more theory and practice to get heads around, it is in most cases grounded on traditional art psychotherapy understandings integrated into new effective methods and understandings of self.

The authors are all HCPC and BAAT registered Art Psychotherapists or Art Therapists. Both titles are accredited to professionals recognised by these professional bodies. Which title is used by the authors in this book depends on a number of factors, for some it is based on their post title where they are employed, for others it is to hold the emphasis in certain ways that are meaningful to them. For example a perceived emphasis on the term 'art' rather than the enlargement of the term therapy into psychotherapy. Others wish for the psychotherapeutic nature of art psychotherapy to be explicit in their use of title. Others have additional psychotherapy and other related trainings and this may also influence the choice they make. So, throughout the book both terms are used. Also, there is some debate about the definition of 'time-limited' therapy. My definition of this subject is that 'time-limited' refers to a course of therapy whereby the number of sessions and therefore the anticipated ending date is agreed with the client early in the treatment. This framework has useful therapeutic implications for the internal process of therapy as it moves the therapeutic relationship in some measure from a context for dependency longings to be met, towards an active empowerment of the individual in a collaborative alliance. Some authors use the term 'brief therapy'; this, unlike 'time limited', indicates something of the number of sessions available. This may vary from around six to fourteen sessions. Others use the term 'Time sensitive' by which their process is not time-limited in the way I have described it and neither is it necessarily brief. However, it aims to be sensitive and as brief as possible. It would therefore not come under the category of longer-term therapy in most instances.

The following are points that the authors have made about the about why they feel time-limited art psychotherapy is effective. The chapter titles give a clear indication of the areas explored.

- It is effective in conjunction with effective multidisciplinary working in hospital settings.
- It works best in carefully designed care pathways so that time-limited art psychotherapy is offered at the right time.
- Time-limited art psychotherapy offers continuity of provision by positioning the therapist correctly in the service and the client's journey from acute to recovery.
- It works explicitly towards what comes next after therapy ends.
- It meets the client's preference.

- It can have disproportionally good effect as therapeutic gains happen early in treatment.
- It can be a useful model for clients moving between services or leaving hospital.
- It recognises the realities of life, that we don't have limitless time, our time is rationed.
- It can have a particular role as part of longer-term mental health work.
- It can make a real difference to a person's life.
- It can lend focus to the work of therapy.
- Clients and therapists know where they are within the therapy work – this can be reassuring for clients and therapists.
- It can fit within a service and avoids being 'cut across' by other aspects of a treatment journey. Clients are socialised into the therapy process sooner.
- Clients are encouraged to be more active participants in their therapy. It thereby enhances capabilities over deficits.
- Clients recognise their difficulties more clearly and the reasons for these difficulties alongside need to change.
- It leads to a heightened sense of personal mastery and the capacity and potential for change.

References

Bernstein, J. S. (2005) *Living in the Borderland: The Evolution of Consciousness and the Challenge of Healing Trauma*. Routledge Taylor and Francis Group. UK, USA and Canada.

Edwards, M. (2010) *A Jungian Circumambulation of Art and Therapy: Ornithology for the Birds*. Insider Art Publishers UK p 69.

Frank, A. (2012) *About Time: From Sundials to Quantum Clocks, How the Cosmos Shapes Our Lives – And We Shape the Cosmos*. One World Publications UK.

Kalsched, D. (2000) *The Inner World of Trauma: Archetypal Defences of the Personal Spirit* p 36–40. Routledge, Taylor and Francis Group, London.

Kohut, H. (1984) How Does Analysis Cure? Ed A. Goldberg, University of Chicago Press.

Mann, J. MD (1973) *Time-Limited Psychotherapy*. Harvard University Press: Cambridge, Massachusetts and London, England.

Marx, K. and Engels, F. (1965) *Manifesto of the Communist Party*. Foreign Languages Press: Peking, China.

Milner, M. (1957) *On Not Being Able to Paint*. William Heinemann Publishers ltd. Second edition.

Virilo, P. (2012) *The Administration of Fear*. Semiotext(e) Invention series 10. The MIT Press, USA and England.

Wells, H. G. (2002) *The Time Machine An Invention*. Modern Library paperback edition. (1895) New York, USA.

Winnicott, W. D. (1990) *The Maturational Process and the Facilitating Environment*. Karnac Book: London, England.

Chapter 1

Time-limited art psychotherapy

Theory from practice and teaching

Neil Springham

Teaching is an excellent way to learn. I began teaching a time-limited art psychotherapy course (hereafter referred to as TLAPC) titled Brief Art Therapy in 2002, and I hope to represent here what I have learnt about the subject by doing so over that time. My learning has been particularly rich because the TLAPC was offered as continuing professional development for qualified art therapists. Having practising art therapists bring their clinical experience to the training allows in-depth exploration of the relationship between therapeutic principles and their application in the real world. The TLAPC has a specific four day 'sandwich' structure for just that reason: day one and two are taught together and six weeks later day three and four likewise. Principles are introduced, field tested and then brought back for review in the second part of the TLAPC.

The long-term learning from teaching that resulted from TLAPC was an unexpected outcome for me. I started teaching it as a short-term venture because I assumed time-limited principles must inevitably become mainstream in professional theory and so a specific course in that subject would become redundant. My assumption was wrong. Since 2002 I have taught regularly, two or three cohorts a year, and offered additional one-day sessions to larger groups and teams. I am astonished to estimate that this amounts to approaching 500 art therapists. The popularity of the training seems likely to point to a persistent deficit of time-limited art psychotherapy theory relative to its practice in the field. For example, all art therapists' clinical experience in training is within a time-limited framework. Most art psychotherapy is paid for either by the public purse or charities, which are limited funds, so it is likely that most qualified art therapists also work with time limits. This indicates substantial practice and knowledge in the field that has not been reflected in the literature. I argue that this practice-theory divide makes an already demanding clinical practice harder. In light of this, the present book is very much needed.

This chapter aims to address the time-limited art psychotherapy practice-theory divide by exploring the principles that art therapists attending TLAPC have consistently described as useful to the real-world of their work. By way of illustration I start with a description of my own clinical experience of working in a six-week time frame, just as I do in the training. I then hope to represent a more general picture of art therapists' practice drawn from the many experiences we have worked on in the TLAPC over the twelve years as a means of moving inductively to a hypothesis. The theory that results from the long dialectic between theory and practice on the TLAPC therefore should be described as co-produced with those art therapists generous enough to offer their experience for exploration.

Theorise a six-week model art psychotherapy

My own relationship with time-limited art psychotherapy began in a NHS addiction treatment program in the late 1980s (Springham, 1992). This programme involved partial hospitalisation with a range of groups (of which art psychotherapy was one), with individual session run concomitantly. Service users would join and leave the programme at different times and so the art psychotherapy group rarely had the same membership from one week to the next. The programme itself was positioned in a context where the service user would move through a pathway. Our point in that pathway was termed stage one, which involved a physical detoxification period and service user education, re-assessment and brief psychosocial input. Stage two would be a longer psychosocial treatment, often called 'rehab', where issues could be worked through more thoroughly. Stage three would be recovery in the sense of ongoing vigilance and peer support in the community. The aim of stage one treatment was to assess and move a high volume of service users to the appropriate stage two setting. Our time limit at stage one was six weeks.

The gap between art psychotherapy theory and real-world practice was an issue for me from the start. I felt unprepared for the work by the therapeutic models I had encountered in training. At that time, art psychotherapy was at the height of being influenced by psychoanalysis. This had strengthened its practice by theorising the role of the therapeutic relationship, with a particular emphasis on working through transference. However that emphasis presented challenges to the notion of time limited in art psychotherapy because working through is a lengthy process. In exploring psychoanalysis further, it was apparent that it had its own debates about time limits which had begun from an early point. Those debates merit some exploration at this point because developments made in time-limited psychoanalysis have direct bearing on the same in art psychotherapy.

It has been observed that Freud's own approach began as a brief model, which became longer as his theory of insight and transference developed (Messer, 2001). Whilst this was its founder's stated trajectory (Freud, 1937/1959), a subset of the psychoanalytic movement questioned the assumptions about the duration of treatment. Arguably, such debates were productive because the consideration of therapy as a time-limited process forced questions about what agent of change should be prioritised in its practice. For example, Ferenzi (1921) became interested in developments in behavioural sciences that emphasised 'doing' and questioned the passive stance of the therapist. Alexander proposed that insight was not the only mechanism in psychoanalysis by suggesting the lived encounter with the therapist was itself 'corrective emotional experience' (Alexander & French, 1946). Mann (1973) was interested in the effect of endings in therapy as a means of foregrounding separation and existential issues for processing within the therapy. He recommended setting a time limit from the start in order to expedite that effect. Others suggested that a time limit obliged the therapist and service user to formulate a shared sense of the problem and the goals of therapy more actively to the benefit of the therapeutic alliance (Malan, 1963; Davanloo, 1980; Sifneos, 1972). In terms of group approaches Yalom's (1970) work with acute psychiatric inpatient wards deserves special mention for formulating the concepts of considering each group as having a life in one session, high levels of therapist-led structure intervention and a firm 'here and now' focus.

Attempts to utilise time limits in psychoanalysis have been without criticism. In responding to Otto Rank's attempt to shorten therapy, Freud suggested his motivation was merely an effort to 'suit the rush of American life' (1937/1959, p. 317). It is significant that this reference followed Freud's unloved visit to America, the place where the principle of 'time is money' was first coined. Freud's criticism frames the time limit as a compromise to financial restraints implying the therapy may be second rate. More latterly it is evident that some time-limited interventions may have potential to harm. For example, the UK National Institute for Clinical Excellence guidelines for psychological therapy for borderline personality disorder does not recommend a time limit that is too brief. Too many service users reported difficulties arising from having been offered multiple brief interventions from therapists and counsellors. This may initially be confusing to therapists aiming to offer brief models to service users with related conditions. However, central to understanding that harm is the role of the attachment process involved in therapy. Interventions that use the therapeutic relationship to bring about change, such as transference-based therapy, are particularly demanding when the therapist is the primary attachment figure for the service user. Brief interventions in this model can hyper-stimulate the service user's attachment system only to be catastrophically followed by their abandonment as the therapy ends. In such circumstances the recommendation is for more structured approaches that hold that attachment vulnerability in mind. Indeed, the capacity required to cope with the demands of therapy are clearly accounted for in time-limited psychoanalytic models. This is a summary of the entry criteria for brief psychodynamic therapy:

> The patient is sufficiently uncomfortable with his/her feelings or behaviour to seek help via psychotherapy; has basic trust in the possibility of relief from distress through the therapist-patient relationship; is willing to consider conflicts in interpersonal terms and to examine feelings; can relate to others as separate individuals; allows his or her relationship predisposition to be played out in the therapy relationship and collaboratively examined; is motivated as determined by the extent of the previous characteristics.
>
> (Strupp & Binder, 1984, p. 57–58)

These capabilities represent a sophisticated, well-functioning psychological disposition that none of the service users in my group were likely to have. In fact the kind of psychological resources this entry criterion described looked more like those that addicted service users may eventually hope to develop after the end of a lot of therapy. The demands placed on the attachment system in therapy should be an important consideration for art therapists. At the point I was starting my group the concept of working with transference was becoming central in art psychotherapy theory. The dominant strand of this, influenced by group analysis, emphasised the role of transference and an interpretative, non-directive stance (McNeilly, 1983; Skaife, 1990). These ideas seemed to take on an aura of 'gold standard' in UK art psychotherapy, often being quoted in literature (myself included) and having a profound effect on the way art therapists were trained and discussed their work. This presented me with a dilemma that many art therapists have described in TLAPC: was brief art psychotherapy contra-indicated for my context?

Reflecting on this dilemma has led me to see it as self-created. I suspect that as a newly qualified therapist I was particularly susceptible to the lure of gold standards because I was unconfident and anxious to find models that appeared to offer certainty. But my experience, often replicated in the accounts of those attending the TLAPC, was that in the real, messy world of frontline clinical practice gold standards are a council of perfection. Many describe excellent practice but worry that it may not be 'proper' art psychotherapy. Gold standards can skew a more balanced appraisal of the work undertaken and often devalue it. Good practice in one clinical area looks very different to good practice in another. I found drug and alcohol addicted services users at that stage responded badly to a non-directive stance, viewing it with suspicion and increasing the potential for aggression in the group. When I abandoned it, the group functioned better. This demonstrated to me that therapeutic approaches do not need to always put working through transference as their aim. Many art therapists have described approaches that do not tax the attachment system so heavily but the absence of such models in the literature is a problem.

At the time I found I needed to abandon the idea of a monolithic gold standard and instead adopted a composite approach to theorising my work. Whilst nothing in the literature matched my context exactly, art therapists had begun to explore contexts that had similar practice conditions to mine. Luzzatto (1989) described work with addicted individuals and Sprayagen (1989) with acute inpatients spoke about how art psychotherapy quickly engaged service users in meaningful dialogue through images within a brief time frame. Albert-Puleo (1980) described the advantages of indirect-engagement through images in art psychotherapy for service users who found direct approaches too difficult. Curiously, the literature that spoke most helpfully to my experience was generated by art therapists working in palliative care. For me these writers outlined the challenges and possibilities of working in complex need teams with more relevance to the reality of practice I was experiencing. They described with honesty the need for the art therapist to adapt to fit the context, which included working at the bedside, frank discussions of the present situation (i.e. dying). I suggest such ideas had a level notoriety in the 1980s art psychotherapy culture that they do not now. I wonder if this area became so pioneering because the brute fact of death as the time limit simply made any non-practical ideas redundant. Of particular value to my thinking was Michelle Woods' 1992 paper provocatively entitled 'Art Therapy in One Session.' Woods gave a moving description of just how powerful the process of joint witnessing of artworks linked to the treatment context could be. It helped me to see and value what could be achieved early in art psychotherapy: not complete working through, but powerful and speedy engagement with personal attitudes to emotions.

Yet, whilst the literature of that time offered useful insights into how art may expedite the engagement phase of treatment it offered less in thinking about managing its ending. Endings raise troubling questions: when is someone ready to end and what does that state look like? Recovery from addiction is a long and slow process and I do admit to initially being unsure why stage one was so short, worrying that this period had been set for the benefit of service providers. However, service users consistently said that far from being a brief intervention for them, six weeks seemed an eternity when they first considered it. Many said that they would not have committed to even stage one if it had been longer. Whatever ending I would describe would need to be congruent with the team and organisation's conceptualisation of ending. Attempting to transpose psychoanalytic theory without taking account of the conditions of treatment and the type of service user they aimed to treat had initially confounded me. But I was not comparing like for like when I applied the criteria for their approach to mine. Once on the programme, the clear end date had a powerful focusing effect to the work. The key elements of my practice were that most service users did not choose therapy, but came to it in crisis. In my context I was not the sole, or even the predominant relationship the service user had in the addictions team. The attachment demands were different. There simply would not be time to work through transference in six sessions and neither the service user nor the organisation was asking me to do it: the attempt to do so was a self-imposed impossible task. Description of real-world outcomes in art psychotherapy was, and remains, a deficit in art psychotherapy literature. I found that it helped me to theorise my intervention's end point as determined by its context. This framed my primary task in less ambitious terms, but terms that I argue were not less valuable for being so. I eventually formulated my intervention in the following terms.

Stage one of addiction treatment aimed to detoxify service users and allow them a period of sobriety to reappraise their situation and plan their next stage of treatment. Once the physical detoxification of substances had taken place a large part (though not all) of this task was psychological. Service users came to stage one addiction treatment with highly dysregulated feelings, confusion and a great deal of shame and guilt. These features were both a problematic for the aim of treatment and central risk factors for relapse. Art psychotherapy aimed to provide a means of temporarily managing feelings so that the service user might better reappraise their situation and consider their options. In six weeks the intervention aimed to facilitate an assessment which would motivate and match the service user to an appropriate long term rehab approach.

In practice many service users on the treatment programme would oscillate between despair and denial. These states were described by Orford (1985) as universal symptoms of addiction. Service users could either slip into paralysing despair or deny they had a long-term problem, both of which would confound the treatment task. I conceptualised my task as attempting to support the service user to temporarily manage their feelings specifically in finding a balance between despair and denial. This work happened with the team and relied on formulating a shared understanding of the service user's difficulties. As the art therapist providing group psychotherapy I needed to take an active stance because I was permanently working with service users at an early stage in psychotherapy. Art works were very helpful in identifying and experiencing those feelings safely and convincingly for the service user, particularly for those who found direct relationships difficult. It was essential for me to minimalise unhelpful interpersonal ambiguity and be transparent about the aim of treatment and this helped to reduce psychological distress to a more manageable level. I found I often cited Disraeli's phrase, 'I am prepared for the worst, but hope for the best' in the group to encapsulate the emotional outcome we were aiming for. Reviewing artworks at the end of the six weeks was a powerful way of giving the service user a coherent narrative of their progress and many found this encouraging.

Framing my approach within its context helped me to achieve congruence with the organisation I was employed in. That congruence then acted as a supportive base for the intervention. In this respect time-limited work taught me the value of having a clear model of what followed the psychotherapy. I would argue the issue of 'what next' needs to be addressed before starting time-limited art psychotherapy. Gains made by our service users could only be sustained if they could go on to apply the changes they had encountered in a suitable context. I could only have confidence in my approach if I had confidence in stage two. The personal process of letting go of notions of gold standard art psychotherapy was at times confusing but I was able to conclude that the value of that six-week intervention could be summarised simply: without getting stage one right there would be no stage two.

Generalising to time-limited art psychotherapy theory

Using the basis of my own experience of working in a time-limited frame to developing the TLAPC confronted me with the question of how much could be generalised from one context to another. That which is generalisable is most likely to form the basis of time-limited art psychotherapy theory and so is relevant to this chapter. On the course we attempt to address the issue of context and generalisability by beginning with attendees each describing their work place, its challenges and what the art therapist wishes to gain from the training. The contexts are highly varied and often include: acute adult mental health wards; foster children placements; courts assessing custody; victims of torture; refugees and asylum seekers; women's refuges; child and adolescent mental health; forensic mental health; palliative care; acquired brain injuries; dementia services; learning disability and more. The most important observation here is that work undertaken by art therapists is above all characterised by its diversity. This fact foreshadows any attempt to build generalisable theory. Each environment is different and many will challenge professional confidence. Indeed, what impresses me every time I hear practice described is the needs-led, rather than therapist-led, approach art therapists take in a continuous effort to use art to find ways of delivering quality psychological therapy where there are gaps for those who need it. Moreover, each art therapist has built up a store of condition specific knowledge about the systems they work in and the types of distress they meet. These factors make a monolithic set of procedures as a *one size fits all* theory of time-limited art psychotherapy unlikely. I have argued that the poor results of the Multi-Centre Study of Art Therapy in Schizophrenia (MATISSE), which involved over 800 participants (Crawford et al., 2012) was evidence against monolithic models of art psychotherapy being applied to specific conditions (Springham, 2012). Moreover, not all theory need be conceptualised in terms of procedures. Psychological therapies have been well defined by principles that guide the therapist (Piper & Ogrondniczuk, 1999). This would seem to me to be more appropriate for building a theory of time-limited art psychotherapy. In this way theory might support the art therapist to find their particular solution, for their particular service user, in their particular organisation. In light of the many conversations and debates on the TLAPC, I have attempted to push my thinking to a level of formulation that might identify those principles that appear to be most generalisable. I now formulate this into the following stepwise model (table 1.1).

Table 1.1 Stepwise model

	Art therapist and organisation	Art therapist and service user
Step 1	• Congruence with organisational aims • Therapist's case formulation	• Reducing psychological distress
Step 2		• Shared case formulation • Extending therapeutic learning

In this formulation, the top axis describes two types of activity: one that takes place between the art therapist and the organisation they work in; and the second concerns face-to-face interaction with the service user. Both types of interface were related to therapeutic effectiveness in my experience in the drug and alcohol team and both have proven to be relevant in the discussions with art therapists on the TLAPC. The steps outlined in the side axis prioritise the actions that occur in each interface.

It is noticeable that the majority of activity happens between art therapist and the organisation in step one and the reverse in step two. This is because so much of time-limited psychotherapy requires investment at the front end of treatment for the art therapist in order to set the frame for seeing the service user. For clarity, I now wish to describe the terms used in this stepwise model.

Congruence with organisational aims

Art therapists paid by organisations, rather than directly by the service user (as in private practice), are triangulated between the organisation and service user by that contract. This factor is not always reflected explicitly in art psychotherapy theory, which tends to favour only describing art therapist to service user interaction. Yet nowhere is the presence of the organisation that commissions the art psychother-apy more evident than in decisions about its time limit. Much of our literature gives the impression that the service user and art therapist decide the end point, but this denies the legitimate claim of the organisation to have influence. Commissioned psychotherapy takes place in a process of rationing: time providing service to user A denies time to user B. Rationing is part of the therapeutic relationship and it is in the art psychotherapy room. Therefore the art therapist needs to be able to talk about commissioning to the service user, but this is only possible if they have found their own relationship to their organisation and what it is requiring them to do. In my example of drug and alcohol treatment an initial lack of organisational congru-ence reduced my ability to be present in the art psychotherapy session because I would at some level be anxious about engaging with the service user in issues of time limits. This was because I was myself unconfident about thinking about why that time limit existed and therefore what I imagined my task to be. My ability to explicitly articulate my role within the organisation's primary task took time, but clarity about organisationally congruent aims of my intervention directly helped me deliver art psychotherapy to the service user. It was something of a revelation to me to realise I did not have to get the service user to the kind of outcomes described in long term, private practice psychotherapy within six weeks. My aim at stage one was to develop readiness to use stage two and this was a manageable task in six weeks. This articulation gave me a sense of what the end of psychotherapy should look like too. From clarifying these points I noticed my discourse with the service user became more about their psychological issues, rather than about my low level preoccupation with my fit with the organisations.

Describing end states in art psychotherapy is not easy because of the diversity of organisational contexts it is practiced in. Many service users come to art psy-chotherapy in a state of crisis, deprivation or chaos. Few come from a secure posi-tion after careful consideration. The complex needs of our service users means that social needs, such as housing, or physical care, are required to be put in place. Amongst all those competing needs, it can be confusing for the art therapist to define their role and therefore to define when their work is ended. I would suggest we are hampered by the culture of our professional discourse in this respect, particularly where our language tends not to describe explicitly the practice or its outcomes. This was a result found by Patterson et al. (2011) in interviewing art therapists about practice in MATISSE. I have found that looking beyond psychological therapies has been helpful in this respect. The following definitions, devised by speech and language therapists (table 1.2), outline the aims of a range

Table 1.2 Care aims definitions (alternative labels are in brackets) Malcomess, June 2009, reproduced with permission.[1]

CARE AIM	PRIMARY PREDICTED OUTCOME OF THIS EPISODE OF CARE FOR THIS PERSON
	What is my Duty NOW?
ASSESSMENT (Investigation)	I will have an understanding of the functional impact/future impact of the presenting problem/situation or condition. I will know if I have a duty of care to this service user and I will know the Care Aim.
ANTICIPATORY (Prevention)	The risk of future harm (where predicted harm/functional impact has not yet happened) will have decreased and/or any anticipated difficulties/complications or impacts will have been prevented.
MAINTENANCE (Stabilisation)	Where functional impact/harm is currently unstable or deteriorating, this will have stabilised but not improved, or deterioration/loss of function will have slowed down. This care aim does not apply to stable situations.
ENABLING (Participation)	The functional impact/harm caused by the presenting problem/difficulty/situation or condition will have decreased or will be absent and the service user will be participating more in his/her daily life.
CURATIVE (Resolution)	The condition will be healing, problem resolving and/or skills will be moving towards normal limits (pre-morbid/age-appropriate levels) but I am not expecting a change in functional impact (participation) yet.
REHABILITATION (Improvement)	The condition will have improved, problem will have diminished and/or skills will have increased, but these will be unlikely to reach normal limits in the future. I am not expecting a change in functional impact yet.
SUPPORTIVE (Adjustment)	Readiness for change and/or acceptance of the current situation/condition/impact will have increased as a result of a change in feelings, attitudes and/or insight. I am not expecting a change in function or impact yet.
PALLIATIVE (Comfort)	Comfort will have increased and/or pain will have diminished but the condition/problem or overall impact of these is unlikely to have changed (i.e. the service user will not be participating more actively in daily life.)

of interventions. An advantage of a plain English, non-jargonised description is that it provides clarity that can be shared between art therapists, service users and the organisation. Art therapists attending TLAPC often describe these as applicable and useful to describe the range of their work.

In talking about organisational congruence I do not wish to replace one council of perfection with another. I acknowledge that exploring one's role within the organisation's primary task can lead to difficult realisations. How can the art therapist be free to work with the service user's issues with the ending if they themselves are unsure about the validity, safety or ethicalness of the ending they offer? The following vignette offers an example of this:

> An art therapist offers a service to a user who lives in a care home. The service user improves in art psychotherapy but those gains do not generalise beyond the session. It becomes clear that the poor culture of care in the home is a major factor in the apparent psychological problem which has been attributed to the service user by the original referral. The ethical dilemma for the art therapist then is how to end psychotherapy if it means returning the service user to that culture. The art therapist feels obliged to continue psychotherapy beyond the normal time limit. This then impacts on their case load and other users are denied an art psychotherapy service.

In this case art psychotherapy has become less about a psychological intervention and more about a compensation for an iatrogenic context. On the TLAPC we describe the process of psychotherapy morphing into adoption because that compensatory process forms a non-ending attachment. Is adoption an organisationally congruent aim? It is possible, but unlikely in the contemporary culture that the organisation would be so openly pessimistic to cast the user into an essentially palliative care category. I would argue that the problem is that the organisational congruence issues should be tackled before psychotherapy begins. It is clear that this brings those tough choices forward to the start of psychotherapy: should you go in if you do not have an exit strategy. On the TLAPC a number of art therapists have found they needed to give priority away from face-to-face service delivery to address these organisational issues. In the vignette above, the art therapist may need to spend time with managers at the care home to see if they wish to hear about what psychotherapy has uncovered. For other therapists they may need to address what's next by linking in with local social inclusion initiatives. These need not be carried out by the art therapist, but they must find their relationship to those end processes at the start of psychotherapy. Most starkly of all, if it is not possible for the art therapist to be ethically comfortable with what happens after the art psychotherapy then they may consider not starting. I would suggest that these issues need to be factored into how the particular case is formulated.

One last area of congruence that continuously arises on the TLAPC is that of clinical supervision. Many who attend the first block on the TLAPC return on the second describing feeling more congruent with the practice but *less congruent* with their clinical supervisors. The contention typically concerns the active stance, explicit stance of the therapist in time-limited psychotherapy. By way of illustration the following anonymised supervisory example comes from art psychotherapy on an adult acute mental health ward:

Supervisee: The patient really wanted me to tell him how to use art materials, he was agitated and wanted to know that I knew how they should be used. So I thought it was important to show him how to use them so he could settle.

Supervisor: Don't you think you were being rather unthinking in your response by just telling them how to use materials?

Supervisee: But it seemed to really matter to him that I knew how to use art materials.

Supervisor: Couldn't you have explored it instead? You could have said 'what would it mean if I didn't know how to use them?'

The supervisor's approach conforms to many of the theoretical assumptions of that art psychotherapy I experienced in the 1980s and '90s. It may be that when the service user is mentalizing this questioning approach may open up possibilities in their thinking. But the risk is that the therapist's self-referencing to hypothetical incompetence may be beyond a distressed service user. Distressed minds tend to function more concretely and taking the communication that way would increase fear. Many attendees of the TLAPC report being told by art psychotherapy supervisors that their active stance is a form of 'acting-out'. A distinction needs to be drawn: not all action is acting-out. Conversely, being silent and still in the face of distress can itself be a powerfully damaging form of acting out. This is often more akin to the rabbit stunned in the headlights response. Sometimes this problem occurs because there is a mismatch between the supervisor's assumptions and skills and the task commissioned by the organisation. If left unaddressed this troubling area of incongruence with the organisation will affect practice.

Case formulation

The aim of case formulation is to develop a working hypothesis about how present phenomena may have been influenced by past experience for a particular individual. This process is not to be confused with diagnosis, which in general '. . . is the process of identifying disease and allocating it to a category on the basis of symptoms and signs' (Gelder, Mayou & Cowen, 2001). In 2007 the British Association of Art Therapists attempted to differentiate this from what an art therapist aims to do in assessment and formulation, which is '. . . to increase understanding, and make sense of experience so as to stimulate new thinking and open up possibilities.' Unlike diagnosis, formulation does not seek to ask what is wrong with a person, but asks what has happened to a person and seeks to understand how the detrimental effects of that experience keep reoccurring.

Formulation is not an attempt to create statement or proposition that is regarded as being established, accepted or self-evidently true. The aim is to attempt greater clarity and focus for the therapeutic intervention. Central to case formulation is the principle of a working hypothesis. The Oxford dictionary defines this as 'a supposition or proposed explanation made on the basis of limited evidence as a starting point for further investigation.'

In table 1.1, the stepwise model divides case formulation into two steps. Where the service user is not overly distressed or confused, the procedure is best carried out jointly with them. However, this is not always possible for those with a severe learning disability, acute psychosis or dementia. In this case it should be a starting point for the therapist and ideally the treating team to combine on. The advantage of formulating with the service user is that it forms the basis of contracting the therapeutic alliance, which is what both parties have agreed to come together to do. The alliance is a strong predictor of therapeutic efficacy, particularly when its formulation includes the service user's viewpoint (Bedi, Davis & Williams, 2005). Formulation aims to understand the service user's strengths and weaknesses, not just their deficits. This can be a helpful intervention in itself because often the service user will have some formulation of themselves, consciously or otherwise. In my experience such self-formulation is full of self-blame, lacking mitigating context and predicts ongoing despair and hopelessness.

I was the supervisor of the addictions team for fifteen years. The job of this supervision was to formulate an understanding of the service user so that we could build an alliance with them and take a shared approach as a team. Over that time I realised that the most successful supervision I undertook imposed a structure on the huge amounts of information this process involved. This structure allocated information according to the following three chronological domains:

1   Long-term history/family history.
2   Referral route: 'why now'.
3   First art psychotherapy session: 'how did you feel'.

The rationale for this chronological structure is that case formulation does not solely seek to build a narrative of what happened to a person in their distant past. Although this is very useful in itself, a hypothesis has a more ambitious aim in seeking to look at how that past might predict *ongoing* difficulty for the individual. To this end two other time points offer particularly promising opportunities to identify repeating patterns. I have found the journey a service user takes through services with a specific focus on how staff, who are of course human beings and subject to interpersonal pressure, react beyond employing protocol and procedures in their interaction with the service user and their story. It has always been very illuminating to ask 'why has this person come to art psychotherapy now?' This information can be combined with what is known from the service user's history to begin building a hypothesis. Then, the first encounter with the art therapist repeats this interactive experiment and adds a third dimension to the formulation, allowing a triangulation process.

The first session often contains a great deal of information about attachment style. It is important it include a detailed chronological account of how the session unfolded. Was the patient on time, did they come alone, how did it start, how did they respond to the art materials, what imagery was produced. Again, it is important to press for how the therapist felt during the session, because this will give information about how they were treated by the service user. Some attempt to observe the reflective functioning of the service user is very helpful. Some art therapists have videoed the first session to micro-analyse the level of attunement between art therapist and service user so it can be worked on more effectively to good effect (Evans & Dubowski, 2001).

Case formulation can be done with a supervisor or with a peer and is a highly interactive process. The first service the supervisor/peer provides is to order the mass of information the art therapist gives them. Often information is recalled associatively, rather than linearly, and the role of the supervisor/peer is to let the supervisee talk freely and to allocate information to one of the domains. The next stage is for the supervisor/peer to attempt to describe the patterns they see as repeating from long-term history, through referral route to the first session. In this sense the aim is to put behaviour into attachment pattern context. The final task is to try to build a plain English description of what has been discussed. Whilst this description is likely to change as more is found out, the hypothesis can very much act as an anchor through vicissitudes of treatment. This can be therapeutic because: 'The aim of treatment is to continually present a view of the internal world that is stable and coherent-in order for this to be adopted by client' (Bateman & Fonagy, 2004, p. 34).

Reducing psychological distress

This should be the first aim of any face-to-face intervention because it is not possible to attempt any other kind of therapeutic work if a service user is hyper-aroused, full of fear, anger or confusion. Attempting a highly interpretative complex process prematurely can make matters worse. Ami Woods and I have explored this more fully in looking at service user experience on acute mental health wards (Woods & Springham, 2011). We found that when service users are highly distressed, they often need an approach that works with the concrete state of mind that accompanies that distress. In this and many other respects our research very much supports the ideas of mentalization-based therapy (Bateman & Fonagy, 2004).

Mentalization is a common mechanism of change and so is applicable to art psychotherapy. Although the mentalization has been most developed in the area of borderline personality disorder, its scope is being widened as 'a compass for treatment' for a range of conditions (Allen, Bleiberg & Haslam-Hopwood, 2013). Synthesising psychoanalytic, neurobiological and attachment theory perspectives, the mentalization approach works from the premise that: 'The brain's first and most powerful approach to affect regulation is via social proximity and interaction' (Coan, 2008, p. 260). Mentalization approaches lead with the therapist actively '. . . taking a genuine stance of not knowing but attempting to find out' (Bateman & Fonagy, 2004, p. 315). Explicit perspective taking can activate neurologically based mirroring processes. Being seen and understood triggers the release of oxytocin and this then has a related effect of affect regulation through serotonin and reward through dopamine (Zak, 2012).

It is possible that art psychotherapy can make unique contributions to supporting mentalizing and reducing distress. The artwork itself enhances mirroring. As an art psychotherapy service user, Findlay described how hard it is to begin with words after trauma. Art psychotherapy provided a means to represent and see what she felt (Springham, Findlay, Woods & Harris, 2012). Making art is calming possibly because it accesses processing pathways between hand and the brain (Elbrecht, 2013). Shared attention on that artwork, already highlighted by Woods (1992), has been explored by Isserow (2008, 2013), extends these benefits. These examples give us hopeful glimpses of how art psychotherapy can reduce distress and indicate the potential for more research.

Extending therapeutic learning

This principle is self-consciously placed in stage two of the stepped model. This assumes a level of mentalizing has been achieved so that more abstract work can take place such as utilising the beneficial potential of endings processes. Again art psychotherapy shares features with other approaches that can be used, but also offers unique procedures for practice.

Winnicott (1971) has theorized the exchange of material between mothers and infants in terms of his notion of the transitional object. Transitional objects act as concrete *aid de memoire*s supporting representational links with the absent attachment figure. Many therapies have explored how benefits can be extended beyond the reliance on the often elusive processes of memory. Cognitive analytic therapy has pioneered the use of therapeutic letters written in sessions and carried by the service user in their life, much like a transitional object (Ryle, 1995). Cognitive behavioural therapy has employed audio-recording of sessions on the basis the service user can repeatedly revisit the learning from the psychotherapy in a calmer state (Shepherd et al., 2009). Art therapists have a unique range of procedures at their disposal in this regard. Reviews of artworks have been a standard feature of art psychotherapy for many decades. Artworks form a powerful record of progress and so can support the ending process. Latterly art therapists have combined this with recording techniques. Hosea (2006) used video recordings of mothers and their children making art together as a way of envisaging and reinforcing attachment processes between them. Art therapists have been extending the review of artworks by recording the conversation and rendering this into an audio-image recording format that is given to the service user at end of treatment. This has already demonstrated benefits in helping service users to manage the ending of psychotherapy (Springham & Brooker, 2013).

Conclusion

To conclude then, time-limited art psychotherapy is a major practice that has not been definitively theorised. All theory is provisional and subject to change if new evidence comes to light. Future research will help us to find new ways to practice to better help those who come to art psychotherapy for help. That should not delay attempts to make explicit statements about what we do based on the evidence now, because those statements help us to test our assumption and generate new understanding. Theory put forward here is limited because it is my formulation as a single person recounting many conversations from teaching. However, the TLAPC and the art therapists who have attended have afforded me a uniquely privileged opportunity to formulate my thinking around that practice into explicit statements. Like me, many would perhaps not have initially chosen time-limited psychotherapy as their preferred mode. Many describe an external imperative for enrolling, as needing principles to help them to respond to complex situations within a short time frame as demanded by their employing organisations. Yet at the end of the TLAPC we often discuss the value of having explored all that a time limit to psychotherapy raises. Indeed a simple reversal of the proposition proves the point: what would we say about a psychotherapy that does not end? That ending obliges us to address the most fundamental questions about art psychotherapy: what are we aiming for, how do we make it happen and how can we know when we are there? Increasing confidence in these areas mutually benefits all involved in the art psychotherapy project, be they in roles of service users, commissioners or psychotherapy providers.

Note

1   Malcomess, K. (2009) Care Aims and Definitions, received from personal correspondence with kind permission to reproduce in this chapter.

Bibliography

Albert-Puleo, N. (1980) Modern psychoanalytic art therapy and its implications to drug abuse. *The Arts in Psychotherapy* 17: 43–52.

Alexander, F., & French, T. (1946) *Psychoanalytic Therapy: Principles and Application.* New York: Ronald Press.

Allen, J., Bleiberg, E., & Haslam-Hopwood, T. (2013) *Mentalizing as a Compass for Treatment,* extracted from http://mentalizacion.com.ar/images/notas/Mentalizing%20as%20 a%20Compass%20for%20Treatment.pdf on 1 June 2013.

Bateman, A., & Fonagy, P. (2004) *Psychotherapy of Borderline Personality Disorder: Mentalisation Based Treatment.* Oxford: Oxford University Press.

Bedi, R., Davis, M., & Williams, M. (2005) Critical incidents in the formation of the therapeutic alliance from the client's perspective. *Psychotherapy: Theory, Research, Practice, Training* 42(3): 311–323.

British Association of Art Therapists (2007) *Statement on Diagnosis,* extracted 18th May 2013 www.baat.org/members/ATDiagnosisstatement.pdf

Coan, J. (2008). Toward a neuroscience of attachment. In J. Cassidy & P. R. Shaver (Eds.), *Handbook of Attachment: Theory, Research, and Clinical Applications* 2nd ed., (pp. 241–265). New York: Guilford Press.

Crawford, M., Killaspy, H., Kalaitzaki, E., Barnes, T., Byford, S., Clayton, K, & Waller, D. (2012) The MATISSE study: a randomised trial of group art therapy for people with schizophrenia. *British Medical Journal* 344: e846.

Davanloo, H. (1980) *Short Term Dynamic Psychotherapy.* New York: Jason Aronson.

Elbrecht, C. (2013) *Trauma Healing at the Clay Field: A Sensorimotor Art Therapy Approach.* London and New York: Sage.

Evans, K., & Dubowski, J. (2001) *Art Therapy with Children on the Autistic Spectrum: Beyond Words.* London: Jessica Kingsley Publishers.

Ferenzi, S. (1994) *Final Contributions to the Problems & Methods of Psycho-Analysis.* London: Karnac Books (originally published in 1921).

Freud, S. (1937/1959) Analysis terminable and interminable. In J. Stachey (Ed.), *Collected Papers* (Vol 5, pp. 316–357). New York: Basic books (originally published in 1937).

Gelder, M., Mayou, M., & Cowen P. (2001) *Oxford Textbook of Psychiatry.* Oxford: Oxford University Press.

Hosea, H. (2006) 'The brushes footmarks': parents and infants paint together in a small community art therapy group. *International Journal of Art Therapy: Inscape* 11(2): 69–79.

Isserow, J. (2008) Looking together: joint attention in art therapy. *International Journal of Art Therapy: Inscape* 13(1, June): 34–42.

Isserow, J. (2013) Between water and words: reflective self-awareness and symbol formation in art therapy. *International Journal of Art Therapy: Inscape* 18(3, December): 112–131.

Luzzatto, P. (1989) Drinking problems and short term art therapy: images of withdrawal and clinging. In A. Gilroy & T. Dalley (Eds.), *Pictures at an Exhibition* (pp. 207–231). London: Routledge.

Malan, D. (1963) *A Study of Brief Psychotherapy.* New York: Plenum.

Malcomess, K. (2001) The reason for care. *Royal College of Speech and Language Therapy Bulletin* (November): 12–14.

Malcomess, K. (2009) Care Aims and Definitions. Personal correspondence.

Mann, J. (1973) *Time-Limited Psychotherapy.* Cambridge, MA: Harvard University Press.

McNeilly, G. (1983) Directive and non-directive approaches to art therapy. *The Arts in Psychotherapy* 10: 216–219.

Messer, B. (2001) What makes brief psychodynamic psychotherapy time efficient. *Clinical Psychology: Science and Practice* 8(1): 5–22.

Orford, J. (1985) *Excessive Appetites: A Psychological View of Addictions.* London: J. Wiley & Sons.

Oxford English Dictionary (2013) *Definition of Hypothesis,* extracted from http://oxforddictionaries.com/definition/english/hypothesis?q=hypothesis on 4 April 2013.

Patterson, S., Crawford, M., Ainsworth, E., & Waller, D. (2011) Art Therapy for people diagnosed with schizophrenia: therapists' views about what changes, how and for whom. *International Journal of Art Therapy: Inscape* 16(2): 70–80.

Piper, W., & Ogrondniczuk, J. (1999) Therapy manuals and dilemmas of dynamically orientated therapist and researchers. *American Journal of Psychotherapy* 53(4): 467–482.

Ryle, A. (1995) *Cognitive Analytic Therapy: Developments in Theory and Practice.* Chichester: John Wiley.

Shepherd, L., Salkovskis, P., & Morris, M. (2009) Recording therapy sessions: an evaluation of patient and therapist reporting behaviours, attitudes and preferences. *Behavioural and Cognitive Psychotherapy* 37: 141–150.

Sifneos, P. (1972) *Short Term Psychotherapy and Emotional Crisis.* Cambridge, MA: Harvard University Press.

Skaife, S. (1990) Self determination in group analytic art therapy. *Group Analysis* 23: 237–244.

Sprayagen, B. (1989) Brief inpatient groups: a conceptual design for art therapists. *American Journal of Art Therapy* 28: 34–45.

Springham, N. (1992) Short-term group processes in a group for drug and alcohol patients *Inscape* (Winter): 14–19.

Springham, N. (2012) Editorial. *International Journal of Art Therapy: Inscape* 17(3): 88–89.

Springham, N., & Brooker, J. (2013) The reflect interview using audio-image recording: development and feasibility study. *International Journal of Art Therapy: Inscape* 18(2): 54–66.

Springham, N., Findlay, F., Woods, A., & Harris, J. (2012) How can art therapy contribute to mentalization in borderline personality disorder? *International Journal of Art Therapy: Inscape* 17(3): 115–130.

Strupp, H., & Binder, J. (1984) *Psychotherapy in a New Key.* New York: Basic Books.

Winnicott, D. (1958/71) Transitional objects and transitional phenomena. In *Playing and Reality* (pp. 1–34). London: Tavistock.

Woods, A., & Springham, N. (2011) On learning from being the inpatient. *International Journal of Art Therapy: Inscape* 16(2): 60–68.

Woods, M. (1992) Art therapy in one session. *Inscape* (Spring): 12–17.

Yalom, I. (1970) *The Theory and Practice of Group Psychotherapy.* New York: Basic Books.

Zak, P. (2012) *The Moral Molecule.* New York: Dutton Publishers.

Chapter 2

Quick sketches and snapshots for brief art therapy

As a time-limited approach

Chris Wood

People referred to services often have difficult lives and complex needs, yet mental health professionals are increasingly asked to work with people for shorter periods of time. In the midst of a world economic crisis there are increased pressures on services, on the people providing them and on the people using them. Perhaps as a result, the research about time-limited therapy is growing. Some of the pressures are undoubtedly economic and others concern widening access and social inclusion.

Many of the realities behind providing shorter periods of work are uncomfortable to think about and this may be why there are so many different models and names for work that is both brief and time-limited. One pragmatic approach to resolving the issue of what to call the work is to consider usage and look at what is visible in electronic databases. There are many more uses in both art therapy and psychotherapy literature of the prefix 'brief', than of the prefix 'time-limited'. Similarly it is easier to find more examples in the huge range of global data, of careful studies of 'art therapy', than of equally careful studies of 'art psychotherapy'. Consequently this chapter mainly uses the phrase 'brief art therapy' and qualifies it occasionally with the phrases 'time-limited' and 'short term', because studies named 'brief art therapy' seem currently to be those included in the global dialogue.

There are responsibilities provoked by offering any form of brief work. These are to ensure that there is collaboration with other services, with Service User movements, and with community groups: because it is important not to leave people feeling abandoned at the end of time-limited work. Towards the end of this chapter there is a discussion of the diagram by Huet and Springham (2010). The diagram suggests a way of shaping approaches to brief art therapy so they can be part of a collaborative system of mental health work aimed at maximum social inclusion.

There are a huge range of potential approaches to short-term work in general. This chapter is written from the perspective that it will be possible to integrate forms of work from some of these approaches for different models of brief art therapy. It seems possible for example, to learn and integrate from approaches like: cognitive analytic therapy; cognitive therapy; mentalization; time-limited psychodynamic psychotherapy; and various forms of counselling, but this will require coherent linking of theory and practice and more research. This chapter aims to produce a modest overview of possibilities.

People who use art therapy

A wide range of people use art therapy. They are not identifiable in their physical appearance as people who have mental health concerns. Yet, they are often those adults, young people and children, who might not, because of the weight of social exclusion, be offered other forms of psychological intervention or psychotherapeutic work. They include older people struggling with emotional issues provoked by the passage of time; people with complex mental health problems; many adults and children with hard living circumstances and difficult histories of attachment. They might be people with: dementia; people who are homeless; people who use drugs and alcohol; and refugees who are often caught up in wars and natural disasters.

A range of disciplines works in the interests of mental health and given the range of complex needs that people bring to services, this is appropriate. There are occasions when stand-alone art therapy is appropriate, but in a climate where services are under strain, those people who might do well with a stand-alone therapeutic intervention are less likely to be accepted for the mental health services. That they are not accepted for stand-alone work is not always appropriate, but it is understandable given that many people who now use art therapy have complex and difficult lives and often tend to need more than one service intervention.

Recently the work of those studying the health of populations, e.g. Wilkinson and Pickett (2006, 2009) and Marmot (2010) point to the physical and mental health difficulties created for everyone as a result of increasing levels of income inequality. There are more examples of unnecessary early mortality, more teenage pregnancy, higher levels of obesity, higher infant mortality, higher levels of addiction and higher numbers of people in prison. International studies posted on the Equality Trust website point to evidence that inequalities influence the overall ability of people in *all* income groups to feel trust in their neighbours and society in general. They also point to decreases overall in social mobility. Obviously these issues have an effect on mental health: which is increasingly understood to be a complicated combination of environmental circumstances and individual difficulties.

During difficult times it is not easy to witness the extent of need and then contemplate short-term therapeutic work. Maybe a helpful starting point for the therapist is to remember the powerful impact of simply paying attention to what people say. People using a range of mental and physical health services report feelings (in different media) that they do not always feel heard by staff, but that they feel empowered when efforts are made to show them that they are being heard and taken seriously. Service scandals seem to begin (e.g. Francis, 2013) with a decline in respect shown to service users. Showing people who use services that their concerns are taken seriously can help them engage. In art therapy, this includes paying them the fundamental respect necessary in all services, but in particular it involves careful attention and acknowledgement of what is shared in their artwork.

A general history of limited time

Rawson (2002) puts forward the idea that the history of psychological therapies contains a number of points when ideas about short-term work are rediscovered and elaborated. She points to Malan's observation (1963) that the early work of analysts was often brief and successful and then gradually the length of analysis grew, so much so, that it acquired the popular impression of being interminable.

During this history various lists about who should not be offered brief therapy have been written. It has tended to be ruled out for people who are actively suicidal; heavily addicted; or who have poor impulse control (e.g. quick to anger, or act out aggressively or sexually). Dryden and Feltham (1992) however, whilst agreeing that there are people who may not find brief work helpful, suggest that it is possible to be less strictly selective (1992: 5). They point to some of the difficulties of being so selective using the work of Holmes and Lindley (1989) who claim that although brief work might be more appealing to working-class clients, they suggest that at the time they were writing, working-class clients were unlikely to be offered it because their distress might (initially at least) be articulated in addiction and suicidal ideas.

Repeatedly in the history of brief work it has been suggested that it is not appropriate for people who are not actively disturbed, yet repeatedly it seems possible to find examples of brief work done successfully with people who are on the lists of exceptions. People with disrupted early attachments, for example, may only be able to bear a little therapy at a time and so a short-term therapy approach may be of use to them. In some circumstances brief art therapy approaches might be particularly appropriate because of the way the art making can provide protection from some talking. However, funding constraints on service provision mean that people in a range of disciplines are often trying to work briefly with people and situations that are complicated and difficult. Increasingly, professionals have to make judgements about the appropriateness of attempting a short-term intervention whether in social, educational, medical or therapeutic settings. Often they will feel they have little choice: and yet even in very difficult circumstances a brief intervention might empower the client with a tangible sense of being able to sustain themselves and make useful changes.

In circumstances of economic strain, ongoing support from any one intervention is unlikely. It is important to plan systems of care and therapy that try to connect a range of services. Shepherd, Boardman and Slade (2008) describe this as a recovery approach, whereas Huet and Springham (2010) discuss social inclusion. In this climate there may be a need for art therapists to hone negotiating and advocacy skills. Also they might occasionally think it wise to inform their colleagues that were it possible they would recommend a longer period of art therapy, when actually what they can propose is a short period of work with the prospect of the client being able to return for a further short period.

There are many versions of what constitutes brief therapy. Rawson's critical analysis (2002) sifts through the literature on different approaches to brief psychodynamic psychotherapy. Salient features from a range of models are highlighted and carefully considered.

The early part of her analysis points to how much shared thinking there is about ways of engaging the client. She describes the significance of the following points:

In each case:

- the importance of the first sessions;
- the importance of being in tune;
- the flexibility of the therapist;
- the helpfulness of the brevity of time available; and
- the teaching role of the therapist.

The following were identified in two out of three cases:

- checking out with the client re focus; and
- the use of immediacy in response (challenge).

(Rawson, 2002: 37)

The overall conclusion of Rawson and of many others in related fields (e.g. Aked and Thompson, 2011; Feltham and Dryden, 1992; Hughes, 2007; Mann, 1973; Ryle and Kerr, 2002; Springham, 2010) is that the client's involvement and hope is central. Inviting people who use art therapy to make artwork is a very particular way of invoking collaborative agency and hope (Hughes, 2007; Springham, 2010; Kalmanowitz and Lloyd, 2002 and 2005).

In time-limited work efforts are made to quickly establish alliance and quickly respond to negative transference in ways that do not perpetuate it (e.g. Aveline, 2001: 380). This is also discussed by Mann (1973) and by Kerr and Ryle (2002).

Overview of brief art therapy as a time-limited approach

There have been a steadily increasing number of case studies of brief work published in international art therapy literature since the 1970s. Although there are too many to list here, they describe a wide range of approaches and contexts for brief art therapy. For example, one uses a brief eight-session planned intervention with good results with an adolescent male (Stanley et al., 1993). Another account with adolescents is of a brief intervention using visual art and poetry on a psychiatric ward (Atlas et al., 1992). Laura Richardson summarises some of the different models being used by art therapists:

> . . . use a range of time frames from Michel Wood's (1990) 'Art therapy in one session,' to interventions bounded by in-patient stays, and where possible and appropriate more open-ended work. Approaches include the psychodynamic (McClelland, 1992; Springham, 1992; Wood, 1990) cognitive behavioural (Loth-Rozum and Malchiodi, 2003), and integrative (Luzzatto, 1997; Atlas et al., 1992; Riley, 1999). Adapting to the context, Luzzatto (1997) integrates Hill's (1948) open studio model with a Foulksian (1964) emphasis on accommodating diversity, and Springham (1992) describes his Yalom (1975) influenced time-limited closed group in a detoxification programme setting. McClelland (1992) stresses the particular importance of team ownership when using a process-oriented approach. By contrast, Loth-Rozum and Malchiodi (2003), are influenced by cognitive behavioural therapy (Beck, 1976; Ellis, 1993) using a primarily educational focus, whilst Riley (1999), Riley and Malchiodi (2003) recommend solution-focused brief models (Shazer, 1988), where strengths rather than problems are the focus. The aim is to reduce young people's shame about needing help, with the time limit itself offering hope of recovery . . . All the writers stress the care needed in calibrating an appropriate depth for vulnerable individuals, suggesting a thorough assessment process.
>
> (Richardson, 2011: 39)

Deena Northover (2011) describes the particular structuring of a model she names brief dynamic art psychotherapy:

> A model influenced by Mark Aveline's approach (2001) when faced with mounting waiting lists. Aveline reminds us of the enduring contributions of psychoanalysis,

> > '. . . that tend to be forgotten when under attack for being 'endless in time and endless in goal' . . . careful attention to meaning, the importance of complex motivation and psychological conflict in determining behaviour, the distortion through use of mental mechanisms of reality perception (self and others) and the crucial importance of childhood experience in development' (2001: 380).

> Assessment and formulation are fundamental. With time constraints, the therapist and patient are often more actively involved in agreeing the core

issues and the issues to exclude. The frame (focus, structure, time-limits and materials) is then set out and agreed. Focus:

> 'together with the urgency confirmed by the constraint of a time-limit, form the two principal ingredients in the demonstrated success of this approach . . . successful outcome correlates with early positive therapeutic alliance . . . therapist activity, the prompt addressing of negative transference and focused work with intra-psychic and interpersonal conflicts of central importance to the patient' (Aveline, 2001: 375).

Working with these principles and the use of art materials enables the patient to re-address past trauma from a focus on present day issues and problems. Focus and the structure of the session is negotiated and agreed at the beginning of each session, but the art making is usually non-directive. The disposal of the image also forms an essential component of the therapy.

Early on patients are invited to think about how the abusive, traumatic event(s) they have endured affect their behaviour in their present internal and external worlds and relationships, and how these may be unwittingly repeated and enacted. As Aveline puts it, 'The stern demand of explorative psychotherapy is to see and accept one's own contribution to problems in living and to make changes' (2001: 378).

(Northover, 2011: 40–1)

In regular training courses for BAAT, Neil Springham presents important aims of brief art therapy as being towards calming and improved orientation for the client about their current distress. He suggests a mentalizing checklist for the therapist:

- Focus on the image making in a manner of the client's choice
- A genuine stance of not knowing
- Enquiries about the client's understanding of the motives of others
- Reflections aim to represent the client's internal world in a modified form
- When the client has 'affect storms' a dialogue is maintained throughout, but not linked to the therapeutic work until the storm has receded.

The American art therapist and author Judith Rubin (2001) points to the wide range of theoretical standpoints now existing in art therapy and suggests that all of these might be adapted for brief art therapy. Rubin does not discuss how this might be done and in a sense this is ongoing work for the profession. Students often necessarily work for time-limited periods on placement and work that is relevant to adaptation for briefer approaches is often considered and explored by them in their case studies.

A more specific description of a time-limited art therapy is provided by Hughes (2007). She provides a careful account of her experience of integrating a cognitive analytic approach within art therapy. She includes two illustrative vignettes, showing the elements of practice. The profession would make good use of more papers like this, because it shows how to adapt and integrate art therapy with another model.

Research and randomised control trials (RCTs) about 'time-limited', 'short term' and 'brief art therapy'

That art therapy will be served by adapting from general models of time-limited psychological work seems supported by evidence from global data. The number of references about brief therapeutic approaches in electronic data bases has greatly increased. For example, in 2011 there were some 6,000 generic references, yet within two years the number increased to 15,000. Database references about brief art therapy are small in comparison; they did increase between 2011 and 2013, but from approximately 20 to 60.

In 2013 using the specific search phrase 'brief art therapy', when looking in Cinahl, Medline and PsychInfo, gave some 177 references with about half being relevant: whereas the phrase 'time-limited art therapy' gave six references with only two relevant. A similar search using the phrases 'time-limited psychotherapy' gave 1,700 references and 'brief psychotherapy' gave some 14,000. This simply makes the point again about the effects of nomenclature on visibility within a global dialogue.

Within contemporary art therapy research there are a small number of randomised control trials concerning brief art therapy. These include short-term individual art therapy (ten sessions) for women who are depressed (Thyme et al., 2007); 12 sessions of group art therapy for people with a diagnosis of schizophrenia (Richardson et al., 2007); and five sessions of individual sessions of brief art therapy for women with breast cancer (Öster et al., 2007). The Swedish trials of art therapy for women both have clear trial protocols aimed at testing brief work that is time-limited. Whereas, the Richardson trial (2007) tested a 12-week brief art therapy group approach as a result of funding constraints.

That trial (Richardson et al., 2007) had protocols involving rigorous preparatory work for clients with a diagnosis of schizophrenia, in order to help them understand their participation in group art therapy. They joined groups which used an adapted version of Waller's group interactive art therapy with a time-limited frame of 12 weeks. The trial results suggested that the brief group art therapy had some impact on the negative symptoms of schizophrenia. These results are different from those in the Matisse trial (Crawford et al., 2012) of group art therapy for people with the same diagnosis. However, the Matisse trial (Crawford et al., 2012) did not apparently include preparatory work, because clients waited an average of 60 days between being told of the trial and joining a group. Nor did the trial adapt Waller's group method to respond to the needs of people with a diagnosis of schizophrenia (Wood, 2013).

The trial by Thyme et al. (2007) for women who were referred from psychiatric services because of their depression: compared ten sessions of short-term art therapy with ten sessions of short-term verbal psychotherapy. Both arms of the comparison were reported to be effective. The measures included self-rating scales, symptom check lists and both the Beck Depression Inventory and the Hamilton Rating Scale of Depression. The trial therapists included three experienced psychotherapists and two experienced art therapists. Clients had either some ten therapy sessions, with verbal psychotherapy lasting 45 minutes, or ten art therapy lasting 60 minutes (the difference in time allowed for the art making).

The verbal psychotherapy was given according to Mann (1973). The brief art therapy in the trial using ideas from Schaverien's book *The Revealing Image* (1991) employed a reflective approach to scribble work (Cane, 1951; Betensky, 1995). The women were asked to try making their scribble work on large pieces of paper pinned to a wall to enable them to move freely during the time of drawing. This was with the aim of enabling the clients to be more conscious of the effects of depression on their bodies. They were also on occasion asked to make some scribbles with their eyes closed to encourage a feeling of an 'alert inactivity state' found in sleeping infants, as described by Wolff in his infant observations work in 1959. It is not completely clear what the Swedish art therapists were hoping for here, but Wolfe's paper proposes that there are self-organising systems at play for human beings, even at the level of musculature. The Swedish art therapists must in some sense have been hoping to awaken these processes in their depressed clients. Maybe this was with the aim of helping clients gain a sense of immediacy and focus in the present.

One vignette in the study describes a brief art therapy session with a 19-year-old woman.

> With her scribble, she expressed how tired and stressed she was with every-thing in her life that disturbed her. It showed her yawning and half-asleep while her legs were running around . . . During her art therapy, she strength-ened her beliefs in herself and her plans for the future. These examples illus-trates that in art therapy, the paper is used to 'contain' and 'hold' the pictures in 'a present moment' approach (Stern, 2004) while they are processed in art psychotherapy. Schaverien (1991) suggests that the picture is like a scape-goat, it becomes embodied and empowered and is since disposed of, and that this may draw attention to inner conflicts. The process is thought to encour-age the patient and enables an altered sense of self to come forth.
>
> (Thyme et al., 2007: 253)

In the Öster et al. trial (2007), five sessions of art therapy were found to help women with breast cancer experience an improved quality of life. These five ses-sions were spread over the five weeks the women attended the hospital for their cancer treatments. This trial also employed Betensky's approach to helping clients articulate what they see in their artwork. Clients were initially invited to begin by making scribbled artwork. Then they were asked to elaborate answers in images and words to the question: 'What do I see?' (Betensky, 1995).

The Svensk et al. paper in 2009 forms part of a larger project on art therapy for women with breast cancer. In associated papers (Öster et al., 2007: 286) it was argued that:

> the focus on the women's own experience in art therapy created opportunities to elaborate, and in a setting that gave legitimacy to their own interpretations. This is in contrast to a large body of mono-vocal medical discourse, which often makes women's own stories invisible.

Several elements of brief art therapy were highlighted as significant in these randomised control trials.

- The careful preparation of the client for the therapy by the art therapist: in the Richardson et al. (2007) trial. Strenuous efforts were made to prepare clients by the art therapist, with him making home visits with colleagues to people with long-term mental health diagnosis; this was to help clients understand the group in which they would participate. Replicating the equivalent of this (not necessarily in home visits), in different circumstances could provide early opportunities for forging a therapeutic alliance.
- The preparation of the client from the beginning to expect a specific time-limited number of art therapy sessions.
- The clarity of the structure of the therapy from beginning to end. So for example, in the Thyme et al. (2007) trial with women experiencing depression, there was a plan for each of the ten sessions.
- The focus on working with the art making meant that there was a potential to bring the focus of the work into the present. The art making was introduced using a combination of prescribed art tasks, free association, and non-directed art making.
- The use of art by clients enabled them to conceive of themselves and their difficulties from a different perspective. This was seen in the breast cancer trial to be empowering of the client's own agency and affirming of their identity.

What was not tested by these trials was the potential use of 'homework' (maybe including things like keeping a scrapbook or doing additional artwork) within a time-limited frame. Nor was the idea tested of a review being used a little time after the end of the therapy (as described by Hughes, 2007).

The use of art making

In reading both the case study and the systematic research accounts it seems important to wonder about the function of the art made in brief art therapy. The title for this paper refers to quick sketches and snapshots. Watching someone make a quick sketch when it works well is powerful. Looking across the centuries to the great line drawings of Albrecht Dürer (1471–1528), or Leonardo da Vinci (1452–1519), we can see their lasting impact, although some we are told, were the work of moments. The use of snapshots ranges from a treasured few old black and white Kodak prints in shoe boxes; to the millions snapped daily on phones. Photographic work though often made briefly can have huge emotional impact.

Long-drawings (perhaps another way of conceiving painting) might take one session or several sessions. These might be over a few weeks or they might take much longer to complete. In this way one painting done over several weeks might be the main focus a brief art therapy intervention.

The absorption in making art might mean time is forgotten. Absorption can be the opposite of alienation and making art has the potential to re-engage a person in their own agency and life (Wood, 2007 and 2011). Repeatedly in art therapy literature, efforts made to articulate the ways in which people find less threatening pathways into the therapeutic relationship through making art. 'The plastic and written art opportunities offered them a transitional experience between utter isolation and feared interpersonal closeness through which their demons or worries could be externalised, exorcised or communicated' (Atlas et al., 1992: 293).

Aldridge (1998) describes the way a family uses art during five sessions spread over ten months. Their use of art (individually and collectively) helped them understand the very different perspectives from which they had experienced a serious trauma. In the final family art therapy session they made art in a manner that enacted a healing ritual that maybe helped in leaving the trauma in the art room. 'They had been able to reconnect as a family. In achieving this, the artwork and image-making were paramount in the externalising and controlling the disturbing memory of trauma, and in providing the opportunity and means for understanding its effects on the whole family' (Aldridge, 1998: 140–1).

Kalmanowitz and Lloyd write about brief work on a spectrum from 'engaged art' to art therapy depending on the circumstances. In a paper (1999) about experience in the former Yugoslavia, they describe different circumstances in which they try to structure sessions for brief periods (intensive work over a few weeks) for adults and children coping with the extreme consequences of war. These might include loss of home, migration, injury and loss of loved ones: all of these might threaten a person's sense of identity and have consequences for mental health.

They point to the ways in which even fragments of art making can be part of the struggle for life. They show the extraordinary example of refugee children building and drawing artworks about their different ideas of home. Some 'homes' were lovingly and collectively made with found objects in the town rubbish dump, and also in the surrounding forests wherever the children found materials with which to build. Repeatedly racism against the refugees meant that local children knocked down these structures, but the careful advanced planning for the sessions meant that it was possible for the therapeutic work to continue. This seems related to ideas about using art in ways that enable seeing oneself from a different perspective, and using art and relationship to find a sense of agency and empowerment.

Of course parts of the work with people traumatised by the war are painful. Of these Kalmanowitz and Lloyd write what seems germane to all brief work.

We found at both Hrastnik and Prvic an extreme situation in which art played a role as a subtle intervention. The pervading sense of emptiness which existed particularly at Prvic was extremely difficult to work and live with and yet it became increasingly clear to us that the art sessions could not and should not attempt to fill this, despite the constant discomfort we experienced at not being good enough or offering enough. In both places, the art sessions, nevertheless attempted to provide a space in which a seed could be planted which would have a life after we left and upon which each individual could build.

(1999: 24–5)

In art therapy the focus on the artwork is important. The act of making artwork can focus the attention. The artefact itself might capture something essential about the client's issues. Also (perhaps most importantly) the artwork might enable the client to have their feelings in the company of the therapist. This may surprise some insight for both client and therapist. It may also provide a metaphor that can be worked on in the present, elaborated and changed in the future and in the memory.

However, some pieces may shock and these need attention even if the issues they provoke do not seem to be part of the brief therapy focus. Although in general it seems wise to follow the client's lead in relation to their imagery: in brief work the therapist might decide not to respond so expansively. Nevertheless, focus on the artwork can help the client to find their own path: '. . . the hands will often know how to solve a riddle, with which the mind has long wrestled' (Jung cited in Chodorow and Miller, 2004: 171).

The context of practice

Since 2010, during courses for the British Association of Art Therapists on brief art therapy approaches, Neil Springham has emphasised the importance of thinking about the history of the client's referral as a way of understanding the context of the client's distress. He has also stressed the idea that the art therapist needs to be clear about what they are offering and how they present art therapy. This is to try to ensure that their work is understandable in the context. Students working in a range of settings for example, have recognised that in some contexts it might be helpful to use the term 'art therapy' and in others 'art psychotherapy'.

In the legal framework of the Health and Care Professions Council (HCPC) the two names for the profession are interchangeable. Yet it is clear that in some settings, perhaps in schools or with young people for example, some might respond with more understanding to the term 'art therapy'. In one assertive outreach team in which I work there is an empowered Service User influence and they simply don't appreciate anything with the term 'psycho' in it! In another setting of a psychiatric outpatient clinic, one woman client told me that the name 'art psychotherapy' helped her understand what was being offered. This might also be true for other clients referred by GPS, although in one trial of time-limited work in in a GP surgery (Wilson, 2008), the name 'art therapy' was used. The range of usage and understanding in different contexts shows the usefulness to therapists of having two protected titles.

In brief therapy: collaboration between client and therapist is essential. In brief work in particular, it seems appropriate that both assessment and summary are agreed with the client. This is to suggest something simpler than the Reformulation Letters described by cognitive analytic or CAT therapists, although their literature provides helpful examples of collaborative work.

A humorous CAT reformulation example letter is written to Gromit of 'Wallace and Gromit' fame by Brighton Therapy works on their website. This shows how much detail is used by cognitive analytic therapists. Rose Hughes also provides clear examples of integrating such reformulations into art therapy (Hughes, 2007).

It seems helpful to agree what comes out of early therapy meetings as a focus for the work with the client. The focus or aims then need to be written up in language that is accessible to both client and members of other professions who may have made the referral. Early documentation about the aims of therapy that includes the client and the client's language can be empowering and help the client engage in the therapeutic work. Similarly summaries written collaboratively with the client where possible, mean that the client has a lasting record of what they have achieved *so far*. An important aspect of change for everyone is our sense that incremental steps can be taken.

In a paper by the Jungian analyst Renos Papadopoulos (2011) there is a powerful example of providing therapeutic care within two to three individual sessions spread over several months in a refugee camp. Writers like Papadopoulos (2007) are responding to extreme need by proposing ideas about empowerment in the form of 'adversity activated development'. In art therapy Kalmanowitz, Lloyd et al. (1997, 1999, 2002 and 2005) are also responding to people in extreme situations by adapting a range of brief art therapy approaches appropriate to the context. In one of their papers (1999) they cite Tanja Franciskovic's pyramid of intervention in post-war situations: this illustrates the need to adapt to context. Much of Franciskovic's writing and research are about the effects of trauma upon citizens of the former Yugoslavia. One piece of research (2008) shows how practical the first steps towards recovery might be, because her research indicates that many people cannot begin to recover until they can be housed. This is sobering and a check on the reality of what can be offered by psychological services in general.

An evidence-based approach to mental health (Five Ways to Wellbeing) that perhaps wryly uses the notion of 'five a day' (pieces of fruit and vegetable) in physical health, has has been described by Aked and Thompson writing for New Economics Foundation (2011). The five elements of well-being proposed are: connect; be active; take notice; keep learning; and give. All of these elements have been used in scoping exercises in different areas of the UK and have demonstrably been found to help with a sense of well-being for individuals and groups. The element of taking notice in particular seems relevant to a brief art therapy perspective.

> Be curious. Catch sight of the beautiful. Remark on the unusual. Notice the changing seasons. Savour the moment, whether you are walking to work, eating lunch or talking to friends. Be aware of the world around you and what you are feeling. Reflecting on your experiences will help you appreciate what matters to you.
>
> (Aked and Thompson, 2011: 8)

The lives of some people who use art therapy are hard and complex, yet it may be that the measures used in this policy initiative could help in supporting the case for art therapy. As conditions change there is a need to develop new ways of thinking. Papadopoulos and Hilderbrand in writing about conditions post-war suggest:

> In other words, as yet we have not developed a model comparable to that of divorce, which would enable us to normalise the suffering due to war (which includes the refugee experience) without diminishing its disruptive effects as well as its abhorrent nature. Thus, it appears as an unavoidable consequence that the stories that are told about refugees by themselves and by professionals tend to be formulated within the context of a pathology and deficit paradigm.
>
> (1997: 209)

Different language with fewer pathological connotations might be better able to account for human difficulties. This, with real cause, is the constant demand of Service User movements in both physical and mental health services.

What next for the client?

At the beginning of this chapter it is acknowledged that the circumstances in which people in many professions are offering short-term work are hard. In the inspiring book by Jo Wilding *Don't Shoot the Clowns: Taking a Circus to the Children of Iraq* (2006), Wilding repeatedly writes about having been asked if what the children of Iraq needed was a circus. She records that in the beginning she often had doubts and that she knew that much more was also needed. Yet it is clear from the stories told in the book that even when the circus stayed only briefly, people in different areas of war torn Iraq benefited. The circus enabled children and adults alike to remember how to play. In offering brief art therapy it may sometimes similarly feel that it is inappropriate and even like taking a circus into a war zone. Yet it may also be, that brief but intensive periods of art therapy and the memories of play they engender, help people *begin* to sustain themselves.

At the BAAT AGM held in Edinburgh in 2010 Val Huet and Neil Springham showed the diagram, Figure 2.1.

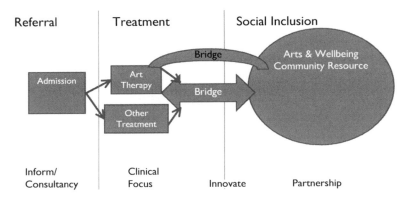

Referral   Treatment   Social Inclusion

Inform/   Clinical
Consultancy   Focus   Innovate   Partnership

Figure 2.1 Working in a multi-agency context. Adapted from Huet and Springham (2010).

With this diagram they are describing the idea of offering art therapy within what will hopefully be a collaborative system of mental health care to allow for the greatest possible social inclusion. In the diagram they suggest the journey of a person using art therapy. A prospective user of art therapy might begin in orthodox services and have a period of more 'traditional' art therapy before moving into community groups and more 'adapted' forms of art therapeutic work. That might be enough. Or the person may feel they need to return for more interventions at a later stage: hence the idea in the illustration of a two-way bridge.

This idea adds another dimension to brief art therapy; it illustrates the responsibility of the art therapist to know about a range of care pathways and about what sorts of well managed groups exist in the communities near where they work. There are examples of such community groups in many cities. In Sheffield for example, there is a Service User led group known as CAST (Creative Arts Support Team; www.castsheffield.org) operates a wealth of community-based art groups that help sustain people who either use or who have used services. In Sheffield there is also a newly established *Art House*. Other examples in Britain include well-contained groups provided by MIND and an art-based movement with a journal *Reflections*, which fosters networks of people in services who use the arts as a form of sustenance and empowerment.

Vaclav Havel, the Czech playwright and between 1993–2003 president of Czech Republic, suggested that:

> Hope is definitely not the same thing as optimism. It is not the conviction that something will turn out well, but the certainty that something makes sense regardless of how it turns out . . . It is also this hope, above all, which gives us the strength to live and continually to try new things . . .
>
> (Havel, 1986/1990)

This kind of hope is the grist of brief art therapy: as a time-limited approach.

References

Aked, J. and Thompson, T. (2011) *Five Ways to Wellbeing: New Applications, New Ways of Thinking*. London: New Economics Foundation.

Aldridge, F. (1998) 'Images of Trauma in Brief Family Art Therapy,' in D. Sandle (Ed.) *Development and Diversity*. London: Free Association, 133–41.

Atlas, J.A., Smith, P. and Sessoms, L. (1992) 'Art and Poetry in Brief Therapy with Hospitalized Adolescents,' *The Arts and Psychotherapy* 19: 279–83.

Aveline, M. (2001) 'Very Brief Dynamic Psychotherapy,' in *Advances in Psychiatric Treatment* 7: 373–80.

BAAT (British Association of Art Therapists). www.baat.org

Beck, A.T. (1976) *Cognitive Therapy and Emotional Disorders*. New York: International Universities Press.

Betensky, M.G. (1995) *'What Do You See?' Phenomenology of Therapeutic Art Expression*. London and Philadelphia: Jessica Kingsley.

Brighton Therapy Works. www.brightontherapyworks.co.uk/ accessed 20.8.13

Cane, F. (1951) *The Artist Within Each of Us*. New York: Pantheon, republished in 1983 Washington, DC: Baker-Webster.

Chodorow, J. and Miller, C. (2004) *The Transcendent Function: Jung's Model of Psychological Growth Through Dialogue with the Unconscious*. New York: State University of New York Press.

Crawford, M. et al. (2012) 'Group art therapy as an adjunctive treatment for people with schizophrenia: multicentre pragmatic randomised trial', *BMJ* 2012:344:e846.

Ellis, A. (1993) *Better, Deeper and More Enduring Brief Therapy: The REBT Behavioural Therapy Approach*. New York: Brunner Mozel.

Feltham, C. and Dryden, W. (1992) *Brief Counselling: A Practical Guide for Beginning Practitioners*. Buckingham and Philadelphia: Open University.

Francis, R. (2013) *The Mid Staffordshire NHS Foundation Trust Public Inquiry*. London: The Stationary Office.

Francisković,T., Tovilović, Z., Suković, Z., Stevanović, A., Ajduković, D., Kraljević, R., Bogić, M. and Priebe, S. (2008) 'Health Care and Community-Based Interventions for War-Traumatized People in Croatia: Community-Based Study of Service Use and Mental Health,' *Croatian Medical Journal* 49(4): 483–90.

Havel, V. (1986/1990) *Disturbing the Peace: A Conversation with Karel Hvížďala*. Translated from the Czech which was published in 1986. New York: Knopf Random House.

Hill, A. (1948) *Art versus Illness: A Story of Art Therapy*. London: George Allen and Unwin.

Holmes, J. and Lindley, R. (1989) *The Values of Psychotherapy*, Oxford: Oxford University Press.

Huet, V. and Springham, N. (2010) 'Recession Survival Planning,' Annual General Meeting of the British Association of Art Therapists: Edinburgh.

Hughes, R. (2007) 'An Enquiry into an Integration of Cognitive Analytic Therapy with Art Therapy,' *International Journal of Art therapy formerly Inscape* 12(1): 28–38.

Kalmanowitz, D. and Lloyd B. (1997) *The Portable Studio: Art Therapy and Political Conflict: Initiatives in Former Yugoslavia and South Africa*. London: Health Education Authority.

Kalmanowitz, D. and Lloyd, B. (1999) 'Fragments of Art at Work: Art Therapy in the Former Yugoslavia,' *The Arts in Psychotherapy* 26(1): 15–25.

Kalmanowitz, D. and Lloyd, B. (2005) *Art Therapy and Political Violence: With Art, Without Illusion*. London: Routledge.

Kalmanowitz, D., Lloyd, B., Beagley, S., Miller, F., Kälin, A. and Murphy, J. (2002) 'Inhabiting the Uninhabitable: The Use of Art Making with Teachers in South West Kosovo,' *The Arts in Psychotherapy* (special issue) 29(1): 41–52.

Loth-Rozum, A. and Malchiodi, C. (2003) 'Cognitive Behavioural Approaches,' in C. Malchiodi (Ed.) *Handbook of Art Therapy*. New York: Guilford Press, 72–81.

Luzzatto, P. (1997) 'Short Term Art Therapy on the Acute Psychiatric Ward: The Open Session as a Psychodynamic Development of the Studio-Based Approach,' *Inscape* 2(1): 2–10.

Malan, D. (1963) *A Study of Brief Psychotherapy*. London: Tavistock.

Mann, J. (1973) *Time Limited Psychotherapy*. Cambridge MA: Howard University.

Marmot, M. (2010) *Fair Society, Healthy Lives: The Marmot Review*. Strategic Review of Health Inequalities in England: University College London (UCL).

McClelland, S. (1992) 'Brief Art Therapy in Acute States: A Process-Orientated Approach,' in *Art Therapy: A Handbook*. Buckingham and Philadelphia: Open University Press.

Northover, D. (2011) 'Brief Dynamic Art Psychotherapy,' in C. Wood (Ed.) *Navigating Art Therapy: A Therapist's Companion*. London: Routledge, 40–1.

Öster, I., Magnusson, E., Thyme, K.E., Lindh, J. and Åstrom, S. (2007) 'Art Therapy for Women with Breast Cancer: The Therapeutic Consequences of Boundary Strengthening,' *The Arts in Psychotherapy* 34: 277–88.

Papadopoulos, R. (2007) 'Refugees, Trauma and Adversity-Activated Development,' *European Journal of Psychotherapy and Counselling* 9(3, September): 301–12.

Papadopoulos, R. (2011) 'The Umwelt and Networks of Archetypal Images: A Jungian Approach to Therapeutic Encounters in Humanitarian Contexts,' *Psychotherapy and Politics International* 9(3): 212–31.

Papadopoulos, R. and Hilderbrand, J. (1997) 'Is Home Where the Heart Is? Narratives of Oppositional Discourses in Refugee Families,' in R. Papadopoulos and J. Byng-Hall (Eds.) *Multiple Discourses: Narrative in Systemic Family Psychotherapy*. London: Ducksworth, 206–36.

Rawson, P. (2002) *Short Term Psychodynamic Psychotherapy: An Analysis of the Key Principles*. London and New York: Karnac.

Richardson, L. (2011) 'Brief and Short Term Art Psychotherapy,' in C. Wood (Ed.) *Navigating Art Therapy: A Therapist's Companion*. London: Routledge, 38–9.

Richardson, P., Jones, K., Evans, C., Stevens, P., and Rowe, A. (2007) 'Exploratory RCT of art therapy as an adjunctive treatment in schizophrenia', *Journal of Mental Health* 16(4) 483–91.

Riley, S. (1999). 'Brief Therapy: An Adolescent Intervention,' *Art Therapy: The Journal of the American Art Therapy Association* 16(2): 112–20.

Riley, S. and Malchiodi, C. (2003) 'Solution-Focused and Narrative Approaches,' in C. Malchiodi (Ed.) *Handbook of Art Therapy*. New York: The Guilford Press, 82–92.

Rubin, J. A. (2001) *Approaches to Art Therapy: Theory and Technique: Second Edition*. New York: Brunner Routledge.

Ryle, A. and Kerr, I. (2002) *Introducing Cognitive Analytic Therapy: Principles and Practice*. Chichester: John Wiley.

Schaverien, J. (1991) *The Revealing Image*. London: Routledge.

Shazer, S. (1988) *Clues: Investigating Solutions in Brief Therapy*. New York: Norton.

Shepherd, G., Boardman, J. and Slade, M. (2008) *Making Recovery a Reality*. London: Sainsbury Centre for Mental Health.

Springham, N. (1992) 'Short Term Group Processes in Art Therapy for People with Substance Misuse Problems,' *Inscape* (Spring): 8–16.

Springham, N. (2010) Brief Approaches to Art Therapy. BAAT Short Course.

Stanley, P. and Miller, M. (1993) 'Short Term Art Therapy with an Adolescent Male,' *The Arts in Psychotherapy* (20): 397–402.

Stern, D. N. (2004) *The Present Moment in Psychotherapy and Everyday Life.* London: Norton.

Svensk, A. C., Öster, I., Thyme, K. E., Magnusson, E., Sjödin, M., Eisemann, M., Åstrom, S. and Lindh, J. (2009) 'Art Therapy Improves Experienced Quality of Life Among Women Undergoing Treatment for Breast Cancer: A Randomized Control Study,' *European Journal of Cancer Care* (18): 69–77.

Thyme, K. E., Sundin, E. C., Stahlberg, G., Lindstrom, B., Eklof, H. and Wiberg, B. (2007) 'The Outcome of Short Term Psychodynamic Art Therapy Compared to Short Term Psychodynamic Verbal Therapy for Depressed Women,' *Psychodynamic Psychotherapy* (21): 251–64.

Wilding, J. (2006) *Don't Shoot the Clowns: Taking a Circus to the Children of Iraq.* Oxford: New Internationalist Publications.

Wilkinson, R. G. and Pickett, K. E. (2006) 'Income inequality and population health: A review and explanation of the evidence', *Social Science & Medicine*, 62(7), 1768–1784.

Wilkinson, R. and Pickett, K. (2009) *The Spirit Level: Why more equal societies almost always do better.* London: Allen Lane.

Wilson, C. (2008) 'A Time Limited Model of Art Therapy in General Practice,' *Inscape* 7(1): 16–27.

Wolff, P. (1959) 'Observations of New Born Infants,' *Psychosomatic Medicine* (21): 110–18.

Wood, C. (2007) 'Agency and Attention: Purposes of Supervision,' in J. Schaverien and C. Case (Eds.) *Supervision of Art Psychotherapy: A Theoretical and Practical Handbook.* London: Routledge: 185–99.

Wood, C. (2011) *Navigating Art Therapy: A Therapist's Companion.* London: Routledge.

Wood, C. (2013) 'In the Wake of Matisse: What about Art Therapy and Psychosis?' proposed for publication in *International Journal of Art Therapy: Formerly Inscape BAAT.*

Wood, M. (1990) 'Art Therapy in One Session,' *Inscape* (Winter).

Yalom, I. (1975) *The Theory and Practice of Group Psychotherapy.* Reprinted 1985 Basic Books: New York.

Chapter 3

The integration of art psychotherapy and Cognitive Analytic Therapy in practice

Rose Hughes

Dr Anthony Ryle talking of the development of cognitive analytic therapy:

> The next stage of the development of CAT involved the more systematic incorporation of ideas from the object relations theories, notably as presented by Ogden . . . In this, the idea of *reciprocal role procedures (RRPs)* was emphasised. As in all procedures, the prediction of the outcome of one's acts is an important aspect of the sequence; in *role* procedures these are, above all, the responses of others. Reciprocal role procedures are seen to develop on the basis of early relationships. The infant is seen as learning to respond and elicit the caretaker's role behaviours, but also as becoming able to enact this other role (for example, to dolls, to others, to the self). Hence each relationship is the basis on which two (reciprocal) roles are learned. The *repertoire of reciprocal roles* so acquired is the basis of relating to others (one role played, the other elicited) and also of self management, insofar as patterns of relationships with caretakers determine how the self is cared for and controlled. The repertoire of childhood will be open to subsequent elaborations, but an individual's array acquires certain stability early on, due to the way in which others are chosen or induced or seen to offer reciprocations apparently confirming the repertoire.
>
> (Ryle, 1995 p. 3)

Time-limited therapy is both helpful to recipients and viable as a service model in public, private and voluntary sectors due to its effective use of resources, both the organisation's and the individual's; client and therapist. Lengths of time-limited treatment may vary from between one session to one year. However, CAT is usually provided in treatments lengths of eight, 16, 24 and 30 sessions. The session number is discussed in the therapy, early in treatment and is based upon the number of sessions it is anticipated will assist the individual to recognise efficiently and effectively their difficulties and possible progress and change that can be worked with during and after therapy ends. The CAT therapists craft is to *reformulate* with the client the difficulties that beset them and to create a plan for therapy that supports processing cognitively and emotionally. This is both an openly discussed and held in mind process, as space to feel is created qualitatively in the therapeutic relationship and the containment it offers. Client strength and vulnerability is an important consideration in agreeing a suitable time frame.

ACAT is the professional body working with a number of universities in the UK and abroad who ratify a number of different levels of training. A CAT practitioner is a health professional or therapist with another accredited training who embarks on an intensive two-year CAT training of theory, practice and a course of personal therapy in the CAT model. A CAT psychotherapist completes advanced four-year training that qualifies them to UKCP registration. There are also more tailored short courses such as CAT introductory courses, CAT skills courses and specialist courses for working with specific client groups (such as the elderly, BPD, learning disabilities, eating disorders or organisational contexts to name but a few.) The Association of Cognitive Analytic Therapists (ACAT) has up-to-date information for courses in the UK and good international links to CAT contacts and courses in other countries.

How long therapy sessions will last is planned and specific to each therapeutic pair (therapist and client), though some types of difficulty are generally understood to require a longer time than others. Duration of a course of CAT is intended to be enough to process whilst also limit the perpetuation of and effect of problematic reciprocal roles and problematic and traumatic mind states. The therapist aims not to collude with these roles by building a working alliance that is aware of identifying and reciprocating roles in the counter-transference. Transference themes are akin to 'reciprocal roles' and are named from early into the therapeutic relationship and throughout the course of therapy in a sensitive and collaborative way, alongside exploration of their expression in the person's life.

Time-limited structure of CAT, with its agreed treatment length, supports developmental processes in the client whereby clear knowledge of the ending date from the outset contributes to a therapeutic alliance that is interpersonal, reflective and active and so less regressive and dependency evoking. It is through a sense and an understanding of time and the inevitability of death that human beings learn to contextualise themselves in the world. Once we grasp this, we are able to feel normal and tolerate and work through productive depression. Emmy Gut writes about this in her book *Productive and Unproductive Depression* (1989) whereby depression, if productive, can lead to improved understanding and coping. Productive depression she likens to normal grief and anger and as such are part of the reality of life's processes and the pains of life, which in turn makes for the potential for joy. For night and day follow and to understand one, we must understand and know both. Perception of time's finite nature is therefore both a painful reminder of life's limitations, but also a frame that identifies us as adult and not infant. Time-limited therapy is therefore implicitly non-regressive, its effect is to limit regression through collaborative constructive goal setting, and the therapist's role is a more equal and explicit working alliance and provides attuned containment as for example with mutually constructed and agreed focus and aims for therapy whilst maintaining the container into which feeling and thinking can freely emerge. James Mann, M.D. in his book *Time-Limited Psychotherapy* quotes J. Frank on the dynamics of the long therapeutic relationship when he wrote that it is the ambiguity of the situation that encourages participation and willingness to be influenced. Mann points out that the paradigm here is; 'I know what is wrong with you, but you have to find out for yourself in order to be helped' (Mann, 1973 p. 14).

Both are critical of the end point as indeterminate and how therapist permissiveness increases this ambiguity and so further deprives the client of a target for therapy. Frank (cited by Mann, 1973 p. 14) maintains that there is: 'some evidence that the speed of the patient's improvement may be influenced by his understanding of how long treatment will last' and that 'there is some experimental evidence that patients respond more promptly when they know in advance that therapy is time-limited.'

Time for all of us is an emerging sense from the formlessness of time in early infancy, even prebirth. The gradual awareness of bodily time comes through need for food and digestion and human comforting and the like. Time gradually gathers more external referents as children learn to demarcate the day into, for example, the time frame of school and family life. Fisher and Fisher made a study of parental figures and how they inform our personal relationship with a sense of time. For example they found that a parent of the same sex or in cases where both parents were highly dominant the more the child's time sense was an over-evaluating one (Fisher and Fisher, 1953).

Over-evaluating time is the new zeitgeist as 'global' (Western) recession is felt to be one of under-production and cost inefficiencies. The political mantra of the day in social provision of public services demands 'More for Less' and this extends to the provision of therapy. This places pressure upon public organisations facing huge year on year government spending cuts in this period and the social nature of care is under attack by dint of loss of staff and reductions in services in more and more areas of treatment. Health workers have to redesign their working lives to try and compensate for the shift in budgets and its human aim being guided by a new, top-down public service ideology of financial profit.

For those of us who work as art psychotherapists a lot of our traditions were born in the cultural and economic factors of the previous century, the early 1900s. Our asylums were often a place of removal for those who could not keep up with the time frames of the Victorian industrial age and the task of these asylums, huge institutions, were as much about keeping people out of society as they were about diagnosis and treatment. This was also a time of increase in production due to Britain's lead in industrialisation. We are in a new epoch of time perception informed in no small part by the digital age and its incredible speed, leading to processes that human beings are encouraged to emulate in their ways of functioning. It is clear that humanity is being required once more to meet the economic strategies of universal competition for markets and profit. Unlike during the late Victorian era and onwards where asylums removed the vulnerable from the pace and hardship of that age we are required to return them to the mainstream

(Victorians became shorter in height during this period and infant mortality was phenomenally high, due to societal and economic focus on industry and the consequent demands on and neglect of working people).

It is therefore not surprising that the gentle expressive space to be creative and to discover our internal worlds that art psychotherapy has largely always stood for is jealously guarded by us and yet, I observe that time-limited art psychotherapy incorporating CAT can dance to a rhythm that is both sensitive and empowering. It combines the discoveries and transcendence of arts creative reverie with increased explicit knowledge of relational skills to live and feel better.

In the early days of therapy and psychoanalysis in the West, clients were inpatients in the large asylums or else wealthy individuals who were seen by psychiatrists (such as C. G. Jung and Dr Freud et al.) As professionals we have straddled these domains of privileged care and state care, drawing our theory from the educated elite of the early 1900s onwards. In the NHS many are suffering diminutions in their pay grades and nil salary growth and this sets a lowering of standards of employment copied by other voluntary and private employers. These reflect the oppressive factors that paradoxically enable us as a professional group to 'be with' those in our communities whose mental health suffer, as life gets harder. If we keep our nerve, this time offers opportunity for new creativity in our work and the expertise to treat effectively within time frames. Time-limited therapy means that we have scope to treat more people and not revert back to the social divisions in health care of the past by blinkering ourselves to the needs of mental health communities and providing plumb treatments for a few. In a sense the social dichotomy of the Victorian era is at another stage and we have a choice to progress whilst holding onto the best of the past or to be an efficiency saving for the NHS, as other mental health professionals take up the mantle in other ways of 'More for Less'.

My aim for this chapter is to outline the essential features of CAT for arts psychotherapists, arts therapists (music and drama) and related practices. I will illustrate how integrated into art psychotherapy is a helpful time-limited intervention by describing the cases of two men attending art psychotherapy within an NHS Community Mental Health Service in the southeast of England. One of the men came for therapy at the transition into adult life and the other at the transition of retirement. It is my hope that others will develop their skills base to include CAT in art psychotherapy.

Admin@acat.me.uk and www.acat.me.uk are the email and web addresses for the Association of Cognitive Analytic Therapy (ACAT) who provide information about CAT courses and supervision in your area.

Dr Anthony Ryle founded CAT, developing the first recognisable features of CAT at Guys Hospital in London in 1983 and to which he and others have added and developed the model since that time. CAT has a misguided reputation in some quarters as a manualised model of therapy, which in fact, were it so, would undermine the central tenets of CAT. CAT is more accurately described as a *relational* model of therapy. Another misconception is that CAT is analytic in dissecting cognitions, which overlooks the core of CAT as a psychoanalytically informed model. However, Ryle and colleagues are discriminating and there are aspects of some psychoanalytic perspectives of child development that are seen as unempirical and false. Inexplicit intentions of too inert an analytic stance within the therapeutic relationship may not facilitate but hamper and are part of the main tools of the regressive therapy approach. Focus in therapy allows reflection and time frames to hold the work and empower the client. Empathy and attunement build rapport especially with complex personality disordered individuals.

CAT utilises key concepts of Vygotsky,

> Vygotsky (1896–1934) . . . studied law, linguistics, aesthetics and psychology at Moscow university and simultaneously, at an alternative staffed by teachers who had lost their jobs on political grounds . . . His approach in to psychology represented a decisive and deliberate shift of attention from the concerns of the Pavlovian tradition to the study of higher mental functions, often assumed then as now to be inaccessible to scientific study. His interest was fuelled by his identification with the idealism and intellectual ferment of post-revolutionary Russia and by his non-dogmatic Marxism. Marx saw man's idea's as being the product of his historical activity; in transforming nature, social man had evolved tools, language and concepts which served in their turn to transform man . . . Vygotsky's aim was to develop a Marxist psychology, seeking to trace the historical and cultural origins of individual psychology . . . In an oft quoted remark, he said *'what a child does with an adult today, she will do on her own tomorrow.'*
>
> (Ryle, 1991a pp. 309–311)

Added to this social learning theory Bakhtin explores how the 'meanings' human beings form do not emerge independent of others but in the space between, in the narratives forming toward meaning. Bakhtin called this the dialogical self (Leiman, 1992).

Mikhail Bakhtin (1891–1975) was an original scholar, his work on signs, discourse and language has begun to attract increasing interest within Western semiotics, linguistics and psychology (Morson and Emerson, 1986; Wertsch, 1985). Mikael Leiman describes Bakhtin's view as a synthetic analysis, similar but not the same as the views of Vygotsky and Winnicott. Bakhtin/Voloshinov found the birth place of language in dialogue, the concrete, living activity between socially organised persons and that we should never lose sight of its supreme position in living communication (Leiman, 1992).

Bakhtin/Voloshinov said:

> Consciousness cannot be derived directly from nature . . . [It] takes shape and being in the material of signs created by an organised group in the process of its social intercourse. The individual consciousness is nurtured on signs;

it derives its growth from them it reflects their logic and laws ... By its very existential nature, the subjective psyche is to be localised somewhere between the organism and the outside world, on the borderline separating these two spheres of reality. It is here that an encounter between the organism and the outside world takes place, but the encounter is not a physical one: the organism and the outside world meet here in the sign.

(Leiman, 1992 p. 219)

This is not to demean the reveries of the individual's internal world, but to clearly and firmly note that that which causes distress is most often the machinations of actual experiences of and with others. This is the heart of a relational model in my view; an open heart, non-collusion and co-authorship.

The succinct explanation of CAT in this chapter will not lead the reader, I trust, to limit their exploration of CAT, which is a rich, flexible and evidenced-based model of treatment.

As I mentioned CAT roots are in object relations, not drive theory, but the post-Freudian developments in object relations, and in particular the British school of object relations. These were derived from the child observations in a scientific manner of the mid- to late 1900s rather than transposing the archetypical figures of Greek myth. Though in ancient mythology we find archetypes of relational themes embodied in characters. To make entire sense of the human state of mental strife, with only passing and reduced reference to lived relations and no mention at all of the majority who avail themselves of modern NHS services, working-class people are mitigated against in my view by this integrative use of art psychotherapy with CAT. In art psychotherapy we have a long history of incorporating the symbolic, which is similar to Bakhtin's sign, it is a unconscious and conscious use of metaphors and symbolism and can draw for its material on the creative unconscious (Jung) and free association (Freud) as well as the free expression in art psychotherapy art work. It facilitates an emerging understanding of self and other.

CAT integrates understanding of transference, counter-transference, projective identification, displacement and condensation for example as relational strategies to manage ourselves and others and embedded within these are the spectres of formative experiences of the world and ways of coping. These strategies can be problematic for the person. CAT therefore names these dynamics in everyday descriptions to speak the language more readily understood to assist the individual to grasp how they are processing and relating in the world and how others are relating to them. CAT also seeks out the healthy and adaptive patterns and roles as well as normal emotional processes, such a grief and joy. CAT therefore has an affinity to C. G. Jung's discovery of the collective unconscious, peopled by characters of both personal and collective significance, relational themes that are universal that grow out of our experiences in communities and in relation to living with nature, with societies and with personalities and their character traits. Jung worked to understand the creative potential of internal object relations in the presences' that emerged in dreams and fantasy. It is therefore easy to see the Jungian link to CAT that also draws out internalised characters to harness creatively and to liberate (Jung, 1986).

First, the interested reader needs to have information about some of the theories made into tools for CAT. I will do this by explaining the structures we might use in a standard CAT treatment. This is not to say that all CAT must be standard, but like all tools, serve a purpose and the therapy pair work out together which are best for the therapeutic aims desired and agreed.

CAT therapy structure

The therapy treatment process is divided into three phases known as

1   Reformulation
2   Recognition
3   Revision and ending

There is usually a 'follow-up' session after three months and other follow up sessions later if there is an identified need and benefit.

Reformulation

This is so called because it not only formulates the presenting problem, but reformulates in a letter known as the 'Reformulation Letter' given at the end of the first third of therapy sessions (fourth, sixth or tenth etc., depending on the treatment length and the readiness of the client). By reformulating, the process is one of jointly unpacking the client's history as they present it and as we draw out details we keep in mind the transference and counter-transference as further information about the person's sense of themselves both consciously and unconsciously, through words, tone, manner, gestures, body tension or ease as well as the themes that emerge. CAT helps the client and therapist to observe and recognise repetitions. In a sense this is one of the main indicators of something problematic. Repetition may link trauma at the heart of things. There will be themes within the precipitating environment, such as lack of parental protection, care or control for example. So, that we observe that there are types of feelings about one's self and experiences of others that tend us towards certain constellations, in CAT terms; Reciprocal Roles and Mind States. In the Reformulation Letter these patterns will be explained and they will have been discussed in the sessions prior to the giving and receiving of the letter. The Reformulation Letter may incorporate simple or more complex diagrams of relational procedures as best suits the therapist and client. CAT procedures are thought about in relation to self and self to others, hence 'relational'. This will become clearer to the reader in the cases described later.

Reciprocal roles

The Ryle quote at the head of this chapter describes reciprocal roles procedures (RRPs). These roles are often learned from caregivers and so may be simply mapped thus:

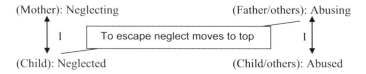

(Mother): Neglecting   (Father/others): Abusing

I   To escape neglect moves to top   I

(Child): Neglected   (Child/others): Abused

More qualitative words used by the client will be added to flesh out the sense of self and other within these roles and arrows moving between roles in a diagram indicate how the client may move into top roles too or how new roles have not sufficiently helped them to transform these patterns, so that their own elaborations have ultimately compounded the pattern's painful narrative.

The Reformulation Letter identifies the possible scope of the therapy work and clearly identifies mutually agreed 'Target Problems' and 'Aims'. This focus is important to time-limited therapy to provide coherency for the client and thereby recruit them in the task ahead. Agreement, may sound obvious, however it is not necessarily a clear focus in other models of therapy. I learned in training experience how therapy cannot progress if there is not a shared focus. In that case a woman whose betrayed mother had committed suicide spent much energy in the pursuit of her own adulterous success. It is perhaps not difficult to see the trauma to her childhood family she wished to conquer by changing the outcome in her own life repetition. This intention, through this path, was not so easy to spot for me at that time. Giving up her quest was antithetical to her sense of triumph, loveableness and ability to live, where her mother had felt unable to go on. Fortunately I was using art psychotherapy within this CAT treatment and a new possible exit from the dilemma she was in emerged in the images. In gentle landscapes she could connect with and feel joy in the solitude and thrill of the landscapes she knew and experienced. She was able to reclaim the joys of her own mothering to her young children, and find an adaptive and creative space amidst an unresolved response to the early trauma.

Psychotherapy file

This questionnaire is used with clients to help open up discussion of their experiences of themselves and others from their formative experiences onwards. It also helps to explain patterns of relating that are typically problematic for people. These are named as *traps*, *snags* and *dilemmas*, and for each a simple diagram can illustrate these problematic procedures and incorporate the language and unique experiences of the individual. These can be drawn on paper in the session side-by-side with the client. This assists the modelling and support of thinking through problems that have often been overwhelming, confusing and therefore unmanageageble. The psychotherapy file is in my experience, very helpful to many people but particularly for those with borderline personality difficulties (BPD) and those who have suffered much privation, whereby this joint task helps with the construction of a focused and containing attachment. Such tools enable a time-limited therapy process to help in situations previously considered unamenable to therapy. This is something to celebrate! The psychotherapy file also gives focus to confusing states of mind and helps the client and therapist work together to describe and name these and to think about how they are experienced and why.

A **Trap** is a circular pattern with a healthy aim, but derived from a negative core belief about one's self that ends up undermining the healthy aim.

A **Snag** is when a damaging core belief is such that the client approaches life by avoiding healthy and fulfilling aims, such as a deprived person might avoid attachment.

A **Dilemma** is when a person believes they have limited options in dealing with themselves, others or life and so become stuck in self-defeating strategies. We might think of this as a fight or flight, with vacillation between, or stuck in one pole of the dilemma as we encounter in those with border-line personality difficulties for example.

Ryle (1991b p. 2) wrote of his developing the CAT model that he observed:

> A useful description of a neurotic is that he is someone who continues to act in ways that work badly for him, but is unable to revise his ideas or behaviour in the light of adverse outcomes. Psychotherapy is designed to overcome these blocks on re-learning. The most helpful description of a neurotic problem is one which both describes it accurately and which embodies in the description an understanding of his inability to learn and identifies how it is maintained.

A **Psychotherapy File** is available at the end of this chapter and maybe photocopied for use.

Recognition

This is sometimes called the activity phase of CAT. It is the middle third of treatment. Recognition is beyond the reformulation phase and the giving of the Reformulation Letter as it is a time to become more familiar with the issues identified in the reformulation phase, letter and diagrams. It is during this phase that diagrams can be a helpful prompt to self-monitoring and new alternatives maybe added to the diagram to indicate progress, movement and to hold onto hope where change is anticipated as needing longer duration beyond the end of the regular therapy sessions. Follow-up sessions are arranged to support the process integration with a sustainable sense of the therapist's interest and care and support to review progress and any difficulties post-therapy. It is in this phase where creative media can be used to facilitate further identification and recognition of experience, to assist in development of self-observation and to enable a felt quality of being with and understood by another, in this context the therapist, so sorely missing in many of the lives of clients we meet. Increased sense of presence is greatly enhanced by combining art psychotherapies and CAT. Creative therapies can open up portals to parts of self that have been overlooked and which hold potential for therapeutic gain. For example an actively suicidal young middle aged man I worked with struggled to adapt to new ways of facing pain and so perpetuated his feelings of hopelessness. Then one day I invited him to bring his guitar to the session as he had spoken of himself enjoying playing. In that session he played with gentleness and confidence and when he described the creative process of making his music the words created a beautiful narrative for how to relate better to his internal world. He, like many artists do, put their solutions to life's questions into their art and it is reflected and introjected. For this man, it was the absence of the other in an attuned and helpful way during his formative years that made these introjections difficult to digest. However, his creativity led us to answers that as his therapist I could mirror and amplify in the Winnicottian sense. My role to embody the positive transference held in the music and to reflect it back in terms that described what he was saying creatively, thus holding up his unique understandings, values and solutions. This was his own creative potential amidst profound hurt and depression for this man abandoned by parental neglect, medical neglect following a road accident and sexual abuse. Without the narratives of the CAT process this consciousness raising may well have been less substantiated for him.

The 'recognition phase' may include homework tasks, such as trying out something new interpersonally or daring to withdraw repetition in a self-limiting or destructive approach to life that is not helpful or self-monitoring internal narratives as a scientist to the self, or it may be a creative project, such as a drawing, a collage, a photo, a poem or a piece of music. It is in these avenues that 'Recognition' moves into the domain of 'Revision'. It is the movement between understanding, action and numinosity.

Rating sheets

Rating sheets are a useful evidence-based CAT tool that can be used in session or between sessions to help clients attend to self-observation of their reciprocal roles, mind states, 'target problems' and aims. The rating sheets accumulate into two simple flow charts over the course of the weekly therapy sessions. In the top flow chart the client self observes the problem in therapy and between sessions, i.e. when, why particular identified enactments or mind states are occurring. A cross or dot is made on the rating sheet in the box for that particular therapy week. A mark towards the top of the box represents greater recognition and a dot or cross drawn lower indicates less recognition of the target problem procedure. Similarly in the lower of the two charts, which forms a record of the client's sense of revising their relationship to their difficulties in some way. These ratings can support self-reflection, containment and interpersonal and self-to-self awareness. Finally the dots (or crosses) are joined by a line to produce the flow graph in the areas denoting 'Recognition and Revision'. This straightforward, evidenced-based tool can help the client to become active participant in their therapy process and supports self-esteem and autonomy.

Rating sheets like most of the CAT repertoire of tools are optional, the therapist and the client may discuss which tools they feel will be useful. However, where clients have dynamic reasons to avoid collaboration in these ways, as maybe encountered in BPD for instance, this may usefully be explained in the Reformulation Letter, which therefore negotiates with defences and resistance in sensitive and explicit terms. CATs' relational style in the therapy room aims to make discussion of complex realities digestible and the respectful adult to adult stance supports this process.

A Rating sheet is available at the end of this chapter for photocopying.

Diagrams

Over the years since CAT began, CAT diagrams developed so that pairs of reciprocal roles are linked up procedurally to other pairs of roles in the individuals interpersonal and self-to-self narratives. For example:

Sequential diagrammatic reformulation (dynamic from 1 to 4)

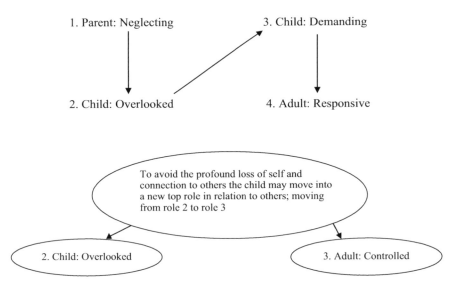

To avoid unbearable pain the child may move from role 2 to role 3 (fig UN2 UN3). Roles have their place at the time of their inception but may need reviewing in the longer term. The earlier coping roles may be partially successful but evoke other negative outcomes (with others or within themselves.) The CAT therapist or the use of CAT skills by an art psychotherapist within art psychotherapy can assist the client to explore new options or modify previous roles.

These diagrams are called sequential diagrammatic reformulations or abbreviated to SDR or Map. The visual descriptions can be simple or complex depending on the use for which they are aimed. Some clients find SDRs particularly helpful. For others, diagrams of 'mind states' have more felt resonance and utility for the individual. Mind states are listed at the end of the Psychotherapy file. These are the felt, qualitative experience of self and other that emerge out of the reciprocal roles one experiences. These can help self-knowledge and sense of being understood if clients' own words are also used. A Mind States Diagram can be drawn up in the session on a piece of paper in response to a description or enactment in the room. For example, I recall working with a young middle aged woman who found herself largely isolated and embroiled in neglecting emotional relationships with men. These relationships promised security swiftly followed by humiliation and abandonment. In the room with her I experienced myself as spoken at, as if all the rage, hurt, frustration and anger was a blasting force hitting me, meant for me and not the material to be contained and explored by us together. It took some courage (at least it felt so to me) to name my experience of her in the room and I used simple 'mind state' diagrams to illustrate the different feelings she was projecting. In this way, the relationship dynamic discussed was also about our relationship in the room. This discussion caused something to shift. She was raised by a prostitute mother, who took clients into bed with my client, as a young child, sleeping close by. There were further traumatic and destabilising memories of being passed between her divorced parents at motorway services. In both situations the prevailing sense was of her being overlooked, like dead baggage. It was not difficult to see where the difficulties arose, but she was inside it. CAT tools enabled her to understand her mind and her responses. This bright and feisty woman had not learned how the caring roles and feeling states she held inside her and those of others where part of attuning relationally and further to this, that she could manage this for herself. It was a revelation she felt keenly when she told me that she had not realised clearly that other people have different mind states to hers. In other words, she had lived in an abusive, depriving and frightening world feeling variably overlooked and intruded upon. She was learning how to be treated as a sensitive human being not an object and in turn to treat others more humanely.

A 'Mind States Diagram' represents through key words different ways the client feels in various circumstances, often historically linked. The states depicted in the diagram are then linked together with lines drawn between them that prompt or follow another state, so that contextual understanding of confusing or dissociated feelings can be established. This helps the client to recognise the dynamics of their internal world and to experience another person (the therapist) witnessing and attuning to the experiences they have struggled with, often alone and for many years. Words may be drawn along the lines connecting the states to describe how and why the client moves from one state to another. For example, Mind States Diagram: The alcoholic's daughter:

This person had been raised as an only child of alcoholic parents and as such had not learned healthy coping strategies, thereby mirroring the deficits in her

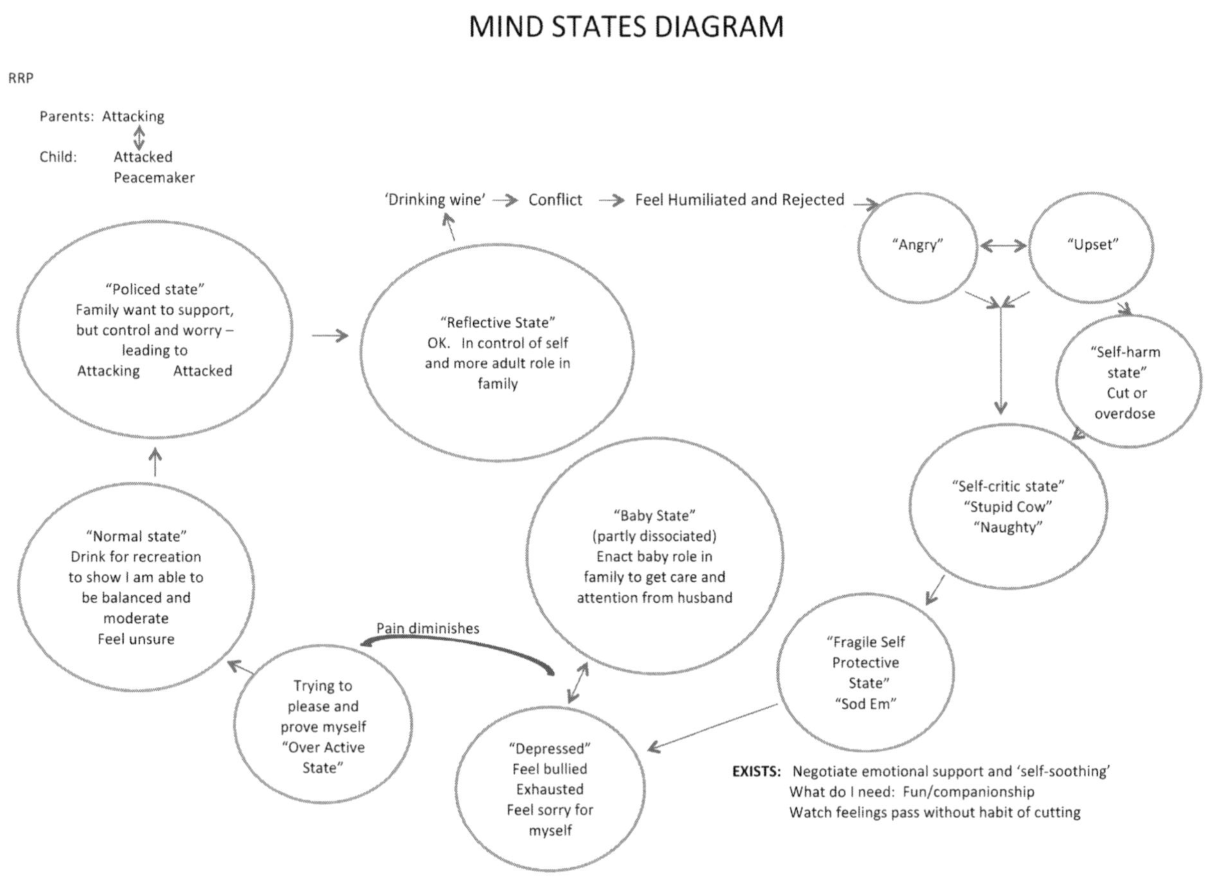

MIND STATES DIAGRAM

RRP

Parents: Attacking

Child: Attacked ↕ Attacked Peacemaker

'Drinking wine' → Conflict → Feel Humiliated and Rejected

"Upset"

"Self-harm state" Cut or overdose

"Angry"

"Self-critic state" "Stupid Cow" "Naughty"

"Fragile Self Protective State" "Sod Em"

"Reflective State" OK. In control of self and more adult role in family

"Baby State" (partly dissociated) Enact baby role in family to get care and attention from husband

"Depressed" Feel bullied Exhausted Feel sorry for myself

Pain diminishes

"Policed state" Family want to support, but control and worry – leading to Attacking Attacked

Trying to please and prove myself "Over Active State"

"Normal state" Drink for recreation to show I am able to be balanced and moderate Feel unsure

EXISTS: Negotiate emotional support and 'self-soothing' What do I need: Fun/companionship Watch feelings pass without habit of cutting

Figure 3.1 Mind States Diagram

parents' negotiations with life. Our work was to help make sense of her feelings and to understand how they emerged and to think together around new ways of being with herself and with others. Some shame in her struggle was enacted against her by some of her children and her husband took a judgmental role, which hampered her esteem, increased resistance and alienation and pathologised her tentatively normal social use of alcohol. She began to negotiate better, avoiding shaming from others, and we began to think of adaptive and fulfilling new strategies for herself outside of her domestic role and in potential new outlets and relationships in the future.

Revision

This is the final third of a CAT treatment. By this stage the client will have jointly worked on, and explored, their Reformulation Letter with its Target Problems and Aims, amidst the flow of an essentially none-directive method. In this phase the themes associated with endings and losses are often experienced and held in mind whilst the process of loss is visited. 'Working through' emotional processes like grief may contain feelings such as loss, confusion, denial, anger and acceptance. Time-limited therapy brings these processes sooner and provides scaffolding to support their revisitation in the future. In CAT clients are encouraged to internalise the time-limited frame throughout treatment, such as reminders of the session's number and the number remaining. This is a subtle exchange in the therapy room as well as incorporating at this last stage plans for ways to continue with work on themselves after therapy ends, reviewing what has come to light during therapy, what is improved and what is outstanding. The future may involve new strategies such as ways of being within themselves and interpersonally that are better understood.

Goodbye letter

These are letters written by the client for the therapist and from the therapist to the client. They are a way for each to describe the journey of therapy in any way they wish to summarise and review it. Usually these letters also comment on the feelings in the room during therapy, the focus of the work and where the client is now in their recovery journey and their feelings about endings. Clients who need further therapy with their therapist will have discussed this and not end in this way, but for some ending it is a relaunch, better equipped and held with new understandings of the reciprocal roles and mind states they have often chronically endured and repeated in ways that they are now able to recognise and modify to a greater or lesser degree. The art in this integrated approach is more fluid than a standard CAT structure. As with any art psychotherapy session this integration involves providing art materials, an art table, art folders for safe and confidential storage and invitation to make art. The balance of art to CAT depends very much on what works for the individual. For some clients art is the main route of self-expression and exploration with a few concise descriptions of their reciprocal roles, mind states and target problems/core pain brought to sessions. For some the art table is visited at moments when an image presents itself in the mind or when the space for reverie is more illuminating and cathartic than words. The verbal and the artistic expression act as a means of clarifying what is important to the individual and offer ways of exploring identity and feelings. CAT tools can speed up insight building and art can give ownership of the internal world in a powerfully self-potentiating way. Non-directive art psychotherapy facilitates the depth and breadth of feelings and internalised object relations. Images may also speak by omission of deprivation, neglect, as well as revealing places where hope has been held. CAT and CAT letters enable the process of being in, being with and agent to become explicit. The containing time-limited treatment frame, creating a safe and user friendly means for clients to better manage themselves, their internal worlds and their relationship with others. There is time to kindly be with pain, loss and suffering and in a non-regressive way, empower in both small and large steps mindfully and respectfully. You will see an example of a goodbye letter in the case vignettes that follow.

Case vignette: The young man 'John'

John was 21 years old when I first assessed and saw him for a combined art psychotherapy and CAT treatment. He presented in a confident manner of someone older than his years and with a relaxed and suave persona I'd observed in public school educated males in the past. He had a keen intellect and thought long and hard about social issues. In addition to this he had a keen sense of social responsibility such that he was involved in the youth branch of a political party. He had left home for some time and shared a flat with another young man. He worked for a struggling charity and had a steady girlfriend.

When John spoke he held an engaging and articulate narrative from an ethical and compassionate centre. However, as we progressed he was able to lower this well-adapted self and talk of some very painful life experiences that remained upsetting for him. He struggled to articulate and attune in expression due to the necessity of the defensive structure to his personality he had developed. However, by using painting and drawing within the session he was able to communicate feelings and sense of himself that he was grappling and so discussion moved from the external focus to his personal experiences and personal life challenges. He was additionally distressed and confused over a recent diagnosis from a training psychiatrist of bipolar affective disorder.

John was the youngest of three siblings. He had lived with both parents until aged ten when his parents separated. His mother had met another man. Father lived locally and was in regular contact. There was something of the outsider state communicated in his descriptions of his own life and his father's life since the family break up. John spoke of mum's second marriage in the period that followed and of a holiday very soon after this wedding, where mum took the three children camping and a previous post-break up boyfriend came along. During this trip John was exploring the camp site late one night when he became aware of his mother having sex with this man. John had not been consciously aware of the reason for his mother bringing this ex-boyfriend along and in his artwork he was able to hold on to and depict how truly shocking and confusing this discovery was for him. Also, there was a sense for him of his being in the wrong place at the wrong time by becoming aware of this illicit relationship and wanting to hide and lose himself into the darkness. It was as if he felt hurt, guilty and confused at a number of levels. The painting he produced in therapy that day was in contrast to the illustrative linear style of previous sessions. It was a dark scene with powerful use of colour painted in a loose expressive style. This brought to mind the theory of Rita Simon art psychotherapist in her book *The Symbolism of Style*, in which she describes the Archaic Massive style in which she points to its large scale and vibrant colours that give it an effect of convexity and weight. She wrote that this style is '. . . rooted in subjective experience, reaching beyond the limits of representation to the emotional reality felt by the painter for his subject' (Simon, 1992 p. 88).

The use of paint John came to in this and some other works were of a recognisable 'massive' style that indicated an emotional attunement through and by the paints' rich, free and evocative colour. This felt a moment of embodiment through the art to core pain and past the intellectual defence.

Robert Bosnak describes embodiment in his book *Embodiment: Creative Imagination in Medicine, Art and Travel*: 'Emotions are fully embodied states existing throughout the physical body. Adding this to the mix of stories told by neuroscience, dreaming [and art] may be seen as a simultaneous spatial experience of multiple embodied emotions' (Bosnak, 2007 p. 38).

It was as if this spontaneous creative reverie enabled him to lower the suave sophisticated persona to feel safe in the presence of another, with his distress owned and shared.

John had begun to not only bring distress as a concealed anxiety state, but to move into a transitional process of being with feelings without the isolation of his overwhelming early experiences. He spoke of a repetition of this sense of betrayal, confusion and duplicity with his previous girlfriend who he dated at school during his A-level studies and examinations. She went away on a school field trip and during this time had sex with another young man. Upon her return the events came to light and she embarked on normalisation of this betrayal. She wanted John to stay with her and to accept as reasonable that she should express her sexual desires with others if she felt inclined. John, as a thinking man, struggled with this question long and hard and as much as he could articulate a liberal rationale for it, he began to find he couldn't concentrate on his work and became increasingly anxious and depressed, which he endeavoured to manage by concealment to keep face. The outcome was that

Figure 3.2 The Trauma (also see colour plate section)

he failed his exams and ended the relationship with the girl. He came to the attention of mental health services when although having found himself a job, he was struggling to rationalise his unhappiness as a means to overcome it. In the combined therapy sessions he began to move into a different domain, by recognising that his suffering was not about his failure to adapt, but his trying to adapt himself to the unacceptable. It was as if an empathic internal narrative towards him had only a fragile voice, perhaps not surprisingly so given the misattunement of his mother to his needs as a boy and young man. The school girlfriend had reinforced his distress with her similar permissive behaviours. Though I came to hold for John the voice of a more traditional morality, this voice could not be found for himself as he had spent much of his childhood within his mother's value system. This had led his feelings to be buried and his intellect sought to fit. In therapy the art and the alliance allowed for a new attunement and facilitated new understandings and acceptance of his feelings and how feelings can inform values in a healing way.

We also explored his bipolar diagnosis by considering the features of bipolar disorder and it was clear that what may possibly have appeared as a manic phase, seemed to us to be the ruminations of an intellectually inclined young man, struggling with traumatic life events and unmanageable distress. This new perspective released some of his anxiety and I encouraged him to ask for a review of his diagnosis as there seemed never to have been any episode of psychotic mania.

As a thoughtful and intellectual person, John tried very hard to be what he was told was acceptable and accommodate. However, his world of feelings was unable to adapt or accept duplicity in attachments and he became increasingly depressed and anxious. To try and compensate he stayed up late trying to study and maintained investment in his intellect as a route to esteem and identity. However, this was too difficult and he failed his final A-level exams and left school without retakes.

A third into John's agreed number of therapy sessions at the end of the reformulation phase, I gave John the following CAT Reformulation Letter, drawn up from our discussions over the preceding sessions. John was invited to suggest any changes he would like made to this letter. This letter (Figure 3.3) assisted in the integration of formative experiences and gave name to his 'target problems' and aims for the work in the remaining two-thirds of therapy, i.e. the recognition and revision phases and beyond.

Dear John

Here is the letter I said I would write for you. It is based on our discussions and the therapy work from your sessions since starting in April. The purpose of this letter is to describe the narratives you have spoken of from early life and through the years until now. From this to identify central themes and the reciprocal roles and self states you have learnt either from others or as a means to cope with unmanageable feelings. Many roles are helpful but in therapy and in this letter we need to understand those which are not and from this, at the end of the letter I have identified 'target problems' for focus for the work ahead, based on our discussions. If you would like to change or add to this letter please let me know. It is important that it feels an accurate and useful description and that you agree with the focus for your continuing therapy.

When you first came to therapy there was some apparent confusion about the reason you were referred and soon this seemed to be linked in your mind to recent discussions with Dr – about bi-polar affective disorder. As you have experienced a lot of upset in the past it seemed initially that a diagnostic disorder could help make sense of your experiences. However as the sessions have progressed you have realised that locating your difficulties in your body and in an 'illness' was perhaps a description of symptoms but that the causes were based in your life experiences and very tangibly so. This seemed very important in that your anxiety and headaches could be made sense of and this offered new insight and new control over your sense of self and identity.

Figure 3.3 Letter to John

To go back to your beginnings, you told me how your parents broke up when you were a little boy and how you saw your father fortnightly and have an integral sense of his having been there for you and how many of your peers were in similar family situations. There was a sense that you learnt to be 'grown up' pretty quickly and that the trials and tribulations of your young life were managed by your recourse to philosophising and rationalising, drawing magnanimous conclusions most of the time. As sessions progressed more clearly unmanageable experiences emerged. You told me of some early difficulties with your English and how your grandfather helped you by giving you time and attention and how from a struggling young boy, you moved high in your school class. This movement between low esteem and accomplishment and valued success seemed to parallel the idea of extreme emotional self-states: worthless ↔ great.

As such your esteem has been an important theme it seems underlying the momentum and direction of your life. Realising that your mind is yours and not a freelance object so to speak has allowed you to think about your esteem freer of the constraints that equating stress with sickness inferred. We began to traverse some sad and shocking times for you. Your mother remarried and you had the misfortune to become a witness to some adult behaviours around sex and betrayal and you were required to conceal this knowledge to protect your mother, despite the disingenuous depths of that time. In a sense you could not process the witnessing and the double silencing of the collusion. By this it seemed you coped by trying to distance your feelings and by finding some long-term integrity in these acts. Currently you are seeing your mother's second marriage end in divorce and you have separated yourself from any underlying feelings that belong to this long experience of secrets and separation and have perhaps had to belie your own male identifications. This dynamic was sharply replayed with your first girlfriend who cheated on you and then normalised her behaviour so that you were expected to rebuff the possible sadness, humiliation and disappointment that this deceit represented. Your studies were badly affected and you felt depressed and unable to function.

With the passage of time you strove to reclaim your esteem in your strengths intellectually and through your work in music and politics and you have established an independent life for yourself as well as having a long term relationship. In your CAT sessions it has felt like an onion with new layers emerging with the passing of the weeks and your developing self observation of thoughts and feelings. Painting in the session has really added a depth to your expression and has taken understanding and meaning directly from you, moving away from the laid back 'clever' persona and showing the raw stuff of your self, an aspect that was either not allowed, buried or feared, becoming increasingly a real new resource, centring you in a richer dance of complexity and clarity.

Recently you have spoken of your dislike of the surrealist art movement and how its representation of the far fetched, the imaginal, can make you feel sick. This seems to show how you are informed by your physical senses about your feelings. It was, you felt not that abstraction distresses, but it seemed something of

Figure 3.3 (Continued)

the instability of the everyday world that upsets you. By developing understanding of these feelings, sensations and thoughts I believe you will be able to better integrate your sense of self and be equipped more for the trials and tribulations that may happen along the way, no longer feeling identified with 'illness', but owning and honouring the sensitivities and the robustness you own. It is good to know that along side this work in therapy you are also moving forward toward the further education and career you want and that your father is giving you practical support and encouragement.

We have explored a CAT trap and dilemma and you have felt how your headache is a result of not addressing in the moment with others hurt and anger. We have seen how your anxiety is a feeling which covers and works with other strategies to avoid painful and unmanageable feelings.

Can I suggest that the 'target problem' for the remaining therapy is:

I don't know how to routinely allow myself to connect to and understand my feelings and am left anxious.

The procedure leading to this could be summarised as:

TPP (target problem procedure)

Having had to manage painful struggles with my early learning style and family dynamics of break up, loss, and disappointment I have tried to bypass my emotions whilst inadvertently leading to increasing the fear and unacceptability that I have assumed they signify. Thus increasing their overload and my anxious avoidance.

John, does this sound like the area you would like to continue to explore?

I look forward to our continued work together.

Yours sincerely

Figure 3.3 (Continued)

It was later in therapy that John spoke of his sense of place with his elder siblings. It was a surprise to me in view of his suave persona to learn that in fact at home he felt treated like the fool, the fall guy. He was bullied in this insidious day-to-day manner. During therapy he felt able to challenge this behaviour with his siblings and felt less adrift in his capacity to hold on to, to name and to be securely in touch with his experiences. In the following image and others similar he was able to explore themes he had not shared or made so explicit. He did so in a representational style, clarifying for himself and for the viewer his more integrated self as consisting of different mind states.

Later he began to explore ways to go into further education and found that his work experience gave him accreditation to think again of the career he wished to pursue. This was a fraught time as so much depended on this step for his progress in life. His father assured him of help with course fees and following an assessment and interview process he was accepted by a prestigious university to study law.

Figure 3.4 The Pressure and the Pain (also see colour plate section)

Figure 3.5 The Customs Desk

The customs desk (see Figure 3.5) was produced towards the end of therapy and is in a sense about ending, departure and transition. For John it was an acknowledgement of societal constraints and rights of passage and control. But, he was not diminished and progressed through the barrier in the months ahead. We exchanged 'goodbye letters'.

Dear Rose

I started our sessions in a time of turmoil, more than anything I was confused and frustrated resulting in deep unhappiness. I viewed my situation as an unknown, a hole that I had attempted to fill with formal diagnoses of chronic mental health problems simply to gain some level of understanding. Such a situation was the obvious development of my problem and was indicative of the problem itself. I was suffering in a way that affected every aspect of my life, where I was simply trying to manage rather than get better. I had grown used to the idea that my problem was beyond my control, it is often too hard to think and accept that it might be anything different. The pain and difficulty of overcoming an issue that is manifested in your own personality and outlook on life is often too big to handle, especially when you have to use your personality and outlook to recognise the problem and change. The part of you that you rely on to solve the problem is the part with the problem. Taking the step to realise that you may yourself be the cause can almost seem insulting initially, and is a hit to your self-esteem. That is why it was so critical to separate the concept of myself and who I am from the way in which certain aspects of myself creates harm for myself.

Once I became able to examine myself and importantly my reactions to given situations critically and as objectively as possible I was able to perceive and separate the negative processes from the positive ones, and also recognise that the negative processes that I understood were often grounded in a positive attribute. I have learnt that as a person I am sensitive, the ground bedrock of my personality is a sensitive one, however that in itself cannot cause me the problems that I had. Because in addition to my sensitivity I had seemed to experience many varying traumatic instances at pretty much every stage of my life, which culminated in a trauma that was beyond my ability to cope with. This then created a problem where my body and mind was simply in shock and was hiding from current and potential future trauma. To use analogy, I had a soft sensitive fundamental bedrock in my personality, and in growing up and developing the following layers and structures of myself, my life and my personality were damaged and made inconsistent and unstable. This means that when trauma and pressure occurs now, my later personal developments are not able to sustain the pressure, which in turn transports and in a way extends and reverberates the issue down to my sensitive bedrock and below into my raw being. I have then developed an awareness of this potential, which causes worry and pain by simply waiting for something to come

---

Figure 3.6 Goodbye letters

and hurt me. I think in a sense it also makes me juvenile and childlike in my ability to deal with emotional pain, if the 'structure' of my latterly developed psyche is unable to handle the world and my adult problems, then it means I am relying on my formative childhood methods, my fundamentally sensitive formative self, that can only hide and ignore pain, waiting for a maternal or paternal figure to solve the situation, but this fundamentally sensitive juvenile self is having to deal with adult issues. In this sense I am helpless like a baby, but with no one to scream and cry to, no one to come running and make everything better, and a baby that is only too well aware of the real nature and severity of the issues that I cannot face.

I talk in the present tense because I feel that I am at a point now where I can recognise this issue, but I am still predominantly suffering with this issue. The initial issue for which I first saw you, where I did not know what was wrong and was suffering blindly has certainly come to an end. I can now consciously change certain aspects of myself and my reactions and engineer different outcomes that is certainly helping me now, but I feel that I have a long steady path before I can secure myself and feel truly comfortable and able to deal with life's normal and often unremarkable problems.

I have learnt to recognise that I create and suffer as a result of demands that do not exist, I create impossible standards that I can never live up to and then feel bad as a result. I am a worrier who is all too empathetic and conscious of the world and people around me and their issues and problems. I found that I am so ready to forgive other people and comprehend mitigating and explanatory situations, yet never allow myself the same forgiveness. I rely on living up to people's expectations of me and I think I let the value of my self-esteem rest in the perceived views of others. All of these things I am aware of and now changing with every new situation, recognising and altering my behaviour. I am working to stop bottling up my feelings and problems, and embrace expressing myself, even if it is contrary to others views and makes conflict. I am learning to handle conflict and see it is as a potentially positive process.

This therapy has been a hugely significant turning point in my life, and it is one that I am all too aware I could not have achieved in my own. It has taken the hard work, time, patience and help of countless people, many friends, family but also many health care professionals to bring me to this point. I would like to thank you for all the work, time and mental effort that you have put in. Had I not seen you I would not be in the overly positive situation that I am now. When I first came to you I had been signed off work because I was just unable to cope and in a horrific place, in the short time that we have seen each other I have achieved things that I could not have previously imagined. Just yesterday I had my first day at university, and it was you and our therapy that gave me the confidence and positivity to apply to university, and now I am undertaking a qualifying law degree at a prestigious university, an eventuality that just six months ago seemed totally impossible.

I feel that with your help I have located my problem and have begun changing myself in a positive way to overcome my issues. Issues which are in my past, issues that I no longer recognise or associate with myself, but issues with

Figure 3.6 (Continued)

a reverberation that still lives with me. I feel that it will take me a long time to completely recover, but I feel that you have given me the tools and abilities to make that happen, and in a sense I am fixed and all better, by realising that I was never broken or chronically ill in the first place. 'I' as a person am whole, positive and talented, and these negative characteristics are nothing more than external setbacks rooted in the past.

I would like to thank you again, and I look forward to our follow up meeting, where I am sure I will have developed and recovered yet more.

Figure 3.6 (Continued)

At our CAT 'follow-up' session John reported doing very well on his course and having got top marks in one assignment. He was still in a steady relationship with his girlfriend and had overcome assertiveness difficulties with his flat mate over domestic matters. In my view he was on track and well. As a clever and thoughtful man, he had begun the important journey of trusting his feelings as guardians to his soul and his well-being and may perhaps need support at times of difficulty to further integrate these self to self and interpersonal themes. In CAT we do not feel that the individual is immune to life's travails and that a good enough relaunch is part of the non-regressive nature of a time-limited art psychotherapy treatment with CAT.

Case vignette: The retired man 'David'

In this example, life at a different stage was causing distress and impasse. David was in his mid-60s when he was referred by his mental health care coordinator for art psychotherapy. David had a history of suicidal ideation and had overdosed on tablets in the past. He sometimes kept a stash of tablets as an exit plan. David was very unhappy and depressed.

David had overcome incredible odds in childhood and had managed himself well for many years. He was caught between life and death, where death seemed to offer sanctuary more than his sense of hope for life. I observed the horror and the courage that had been present throughout his childhood. He was regular witness during childhood to his mother being severely beaten by his father. She was regularly hospitalised as a consequence and David and his siblings were routinely taken into care when this happened. He was the eldest child and felt responsible for his mother and the younger children.

David experienced being taken into care as abduction, recalling how a black car would arrive outside the family home and he and his siblings were snatched up and bundled into the waiting car. He spoke of how futile this clumsy gesture of rescue was as he was invariably returned home the next day or soon after to exactly the same environment. As the son of the family, large and strong and looking like his father, David was worried about his own badness as if he was indivisible from his father in some way. But, he had managed to turn bad to good. However, his sense of becoming the capable survivor was deeply buried at the onset of therapy. He was revisiting psychologically the depressive modelling of his parent's marriage. David was finally rescued as he saw it when mother nearly died violently at father's hands and the local neighbourhood 'bobby' (policeman) impressed more forcefully upon father that his behaviour would have consequences. Father left the family. David's telling of this turning point introduced another force, where official sources had previously made only compromised attempts to relieve suffering, David's sense was that this policeman and his local constabulary had come to the end of the usual options available at that time and raised the bar for David's father such that the message was clear and categorical. He was out of their lives. The rescuer eventually arrived for this poor family. David made use of the positive, but it had been lean times on many levels.

David's mother was not able to manage the situation and resorted to suicidal gestures and acts throughout her adult life. David recalled witnessing an attempted suicide by hanging when he was around three years old. David felt responsible for the welfare of his mother and this constant threat of loss and abandonment combined with compassion for his mother led to a devotion to her throughout her life. It was as if to stay alive he had to keep his primary carer alive, his mother. He did not express any anger about her and in later life she had more stability until her last physical illness led her to the conclusion she had always held of suicide. She died quietly at home. As David was so unblinkered to the cruelties of violence and poverty he was also strongly wedded to his preservation of his mother as his one good object. She held both her own and his depression as his care for her eased his anxiety around fear of loss and of anxiety about his own lovableness. Through love he was able to sublimate the gross cruelty and neglect he suffered from both parents.

David moved out of the city to the suburbs with the slum clearances of his youth and although the family without dad was even poorer he was ingenious. He would pilfer milk from doorsteps on occasion and collected scrap from the local scrap yard to build himself his first bicycle. By these and other acts of assertion he made life better and nurtured hope. The 'spider and the fly' image in wire seemed to encapsulate the hopelessness of his early life and the repetition of futile and hopeless entrapment that seemed to define depressive narratives. The bicycle however, was about his liberty, his adventurous spirit and mobility. The availability of wire in the therapy room enabled a real time embodied connection with this emotion linked to physical activity and manipulation of material to change and create a good object. David hadn't sculpted before but he enjoyed art and had a joyous memory of Victorian architecture, like temples he said, in the ground underneath the city that formed the water system. As with the bicycle and the kind facilitating gestures of some early encounters, David had found

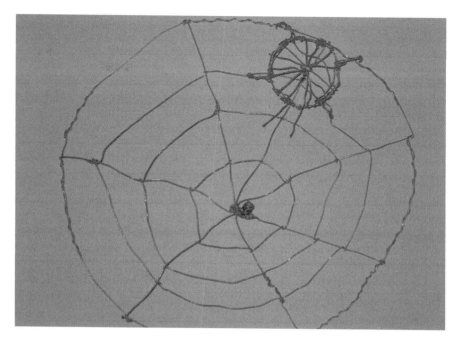

Figure 3.7a Spider and the Fly

Figure 3.7b The Bicycle – made of modelling wire

something transcendent in these hidden recesses left behind by his cities' fore-fathers. In his work in this industry he had found he was a good team manager recognising strength and weaknesses in the individuals he managed and working kindly and effectively with large teams of men. It felt as if all his negotiations with the world to survive had led to a compassionate and strong leader role. This revelation and those in the images combined to validate previously uncelebrated strengths, enabling him to begin to rebuild esteem at this later stage of life.

He suffered with a painful back and took strong medication that diminished his desire. His wife, he described as angry and frustrated with her unexciting life, blaming and taunting him. He came to therapy with ideas of suicide following in his mother's pattern. He had a dilemma in CAT terms of polarised reactions that embedded hopelessness. Like his inescapable experience of his violent father and his suicidal mother he felt not only trapped and limited by his own body, but by the vitriol and depression of his wife. In his CAT Reformulation Letter, the connections to the past and present were named, drawing upon his stories, but clarifying the patterns of relating and where he was currently stuck. He found this normalised way of articulating difficulties in the session to be real and he could recognise when he was 'shooting himself in the foot' as we coined it. Later we spoke in particular ways of how to manage his distress at his wife's unhappiness and his own sense of entrapment within this.

Reformulation Letter

Dear David

Here is the letter I mentioned at the beginning of your therapy. Its purpose is to pull together the experiences, thoughts and feelings that you have described and to consider how some of your difficulties in life have come about. From these descriptions we have identified aims for the work ahead and 'target problems' to focus on. It is, therefore, really important that this letter not only feels accurate to you, but also focuses on areas of change that you would like to make. Please let me know of any changes you need me to make to this letter so that it becomes a useful tool as well as a meaningful description and analysis.

David, you were born into a working class family in the – area of London. Your father was an extremely violent bully and your early life was tainted by the numerous beatings he gave your mother. You recall a pattern of violence, police being called, ambulances taking mum to hospital and you described feeling 'kidnapped' by social workers in black cars, taking you into care for numerous brief stays.

You too were beaten by your father as you tried to protect your mother and sisters. You have described how you lived with a heightened level of

---

Figure 3.8 Letter to David

on-going anxiety and slept with your clothes and boots on, ready to defend or be carted off.

You have spoken of the bleakness of your childhood situation and the mixed feelings about being taken into care. On the one hand the children's homes and foster homes could be pleasant places with care and comfort you did not receive at home, but the manner in which you were taken leaves an impression of additional trauma, as adults simply picked you up and dragged you away and the foster homes were sometimes unpleasant places as you were locked out all day and your sister was made to wash her bedding when she wet the bed. The pattern also created no lasting sense of being rescued and safe, and this seems to have contributed to your sometimes cynical relationship to potential, to hope and to a good life. This was such a sad and psychologically destructive pattern and your mother's inability, for whatever reason, to protect you from her depression is deeply distressing. You did not deserve this and you have internalised the dilemma of feeling hopeless or suicidal, both beliefs undermining you. You loved your mother, despite her maternal failings and recall the ways that she did cope, through her work, to keep you fed and clothed. We have discussed how difficult it is for you to recognise any anger at the home life and trauma you experienced.

Your mother was suicidal many times and when the police finally ejected your father from the family home life began to feel less oppressive. By late childhood/ early teenage years, you settled in ----------- as people moved out from the city. Though the violence ended, times were harder financially and you 'ducked and dived' to help the family. You had few possessions, but your ingenuity led you to build things from scrap left at the local dump. Your first bicycle was one such creation. Despite this unorthodox route, you grew to be a well organised man and with solid family values.

You met and courted your wife in your late teens/early twenties. She was your first love and together you provided a secure and caring home for your children. You put phenomenal energy into being the provider that your father had never been. But, you have shared with me how ashamed you feel about slapping your wife's face on occasion in the early years. When telling me you note how much you look like your father and implied the degree to which you identified with his horribly violent traits at this time. Your wife stood up to you and you stopped.

There has been another active dilemma between two powerful parental identifications, your dangerous and selfish father and your suicidally depressed mother, abandoning her parental care and traumatising you and your sisters, though you loved her dearly and empathised with her depression.

You recalled her suicide attempts, witnessed by you from as early as about three years old. Your mother, therefore, threatened in this way to abandon the baby David, and it is not surprising that your infant adorational love for your mother led you to spend the rest of your life trying to keep her safe. Young children try to rescue parents to keep themselves safe and bonded. This was a terrible scenario, but you took your part; you cared as much as you could and

Figure 3.8 (Continued)

provided for your wife and family. Your mother ended her life after a distressing illness a few years ago and you have retired early from your successful career as a manager. You had good people skills and seem to have drawn upon the streetwise, problem solving and hopeful self of your practical side.

However, in retirement some of the difficulties in your relationship with your wife are now clearly visible. It seems that she can feel disappointed by the absence of more closeness to you. This feeling was probably always there as you worked every day and though provided for and loved your family, you also at some level avoided family life. It may well be that work and life outside the home felt safer for you than home life, as your only model of family life was from your childhood family; a place to escape from and 'survive'.

As your parents could not resolve difficulties and had only violence and self harm as strategies to deal with distress, you and your wife seem to not know how to develop your care for each other than in the safety of basic provision of food and shelter. You describe feeling limited in what you can offer in terms of quality of life, and perhaps as we have discussed, a part of this lies in some passive aggression for all the insults and insensitivity you sometimes feel is directed at you. You describe feeling so sad that you are unable to be closer to her and sad that the relationship can be so bitter and un-nurturing at times. In the weeks ahead we can revisit the dilemma you have explored in therapy of self defeat and the relationship diagram.

Over the weeks of therapy, this seems to be the understanding that we have been edging towards.

The aim of the work ahead may be: To find ways of harnessing more of the creative and ingenious parts of you to help you and your wife have a happier life.

The target problem: I do not know how to stop myself from self and other depriving behaviours.

Target problem procedure: Growing up in a deprived and abusive family I have learnt to survive by working hard and keeping those I love safe. However, this has been at the expense of caring relating and quality of emotional understanding. In addition, I have struggled with the dilemma of either being too bullish or self-sabotaging – both narratives of hopelessness and defeat.

It is a credit to you that you have come for therapy, that you have sought sanctuary to think, process and heal. Unlike the children's homes, this is not a quick fix, but requires all your adult skill to make genuine and lasting changes in your relationship to yourself, your relationship with your wife and life – abundance and generosity seem to be the watch words to support and underpin this change.

I look forward to our continued work together and hold in mind the quality and love that your grandparents showed to you. You have begun the work of opening up about yourself and your life and unpacking and reworking past and present relationships, both to yourself and with others.

I would envisage that following on from your one-to-one art psychotherapy and Cognitive Analytic Therapy, that you be assessed in the future for my colleague's art psychotherapy group.

Yours sincerely

Figure 3.8 (Continued)

An image David drew and others similar represented a way forward that he found encouraging. He showed himself on a rambling holiday he'd never had (see Figure 3.9). With him is a dog for companionship and he sits by a campfire on a beach with his knapsack containing everything he might need settled on the ground nearby. For him with his back problems he was unable to take such a trip. However, within it were psychological longings that could be thought about and reached for in other ways. For example, he could be alone sometimes without a catastrophe either to himself or his wife and the simple discussion of how to civilly make space when he felt crushed and overwhelmed was something he had not given thought to as a man grown out of a trapped and hurt child. Where to leave mother alone ran the risk of her taking her life was a constant pressure throughout his life. Gerhardt (2004 p. 24) wrote:

> The expectation of other people and how they will behave are inscribed in the brain outside of conscious awareness in the period of infancy, and they underpin our behaviour in relationships through life.

Stern described these internalised experiences as 'Representations of Interactions that have been generalised (RIGs)', which he later restated as 'Ways of being with' (Stern, 2004 p. xv).

Figure 3.9 The Ramble by the Sea (also see colour plate section)

As he used the art and the CAT processes he began to feel better and as the end of our time-limited therapy approached he was connected to his generative self once more. However, we recognised that supportive and creative outlets would be important to assist him to keep up the momentum. He joined a group and then another, before settling for a co-facilitator role in a small community based arts project. At subsequent follow up he described feeling much better and at peace. He may possibly join an art psychotherapy group with CAT for a small group who have benefited already from a combination of these two models in individual treatment.

Carl Jung described clearly how art can assist with trauma when he wrote:

> Even with ordinary therapeutic measures you can get a patient's mind at a sufficiently safe distance from the unconscious, for instance by introducing him to draw or paint a picture of his psychic situation. Painting is rather more effective, since by means of the colours his feelings are drawn into the picture too. In this way the apparently incomprehensible chaos and unmanageable chaos of his total situation is visualised and objectified. It can be observed at a distance by his conscious mind, analysed and interpreted. The effect of this method is evidently due to the fact that the original chaotic or frightening impression is replaced by the picture which, as it were, covers it up. The tremendum is spellbound by it, made harmless and familiar. And whenever the patient is reminded of his original experience by its menacing emotional effects, the picture he has made of it interposes itself between him and the experience and keeps terror at bay.
>
> (Jung cited by Edwards, 2010 p. 81)

Here is my goodbye letter to David:

Dear David

We have arrived at the end of our time-limited art psychotherapy and cognitive analytic therapy sessions and in the CAT tradition I am writing you this letter to pull together the process of your therapy work from my perspective and to name some of the themes that you may wish to continue to work on when you join the art psychotherapy group.

When you first came to therapy you described your childhood experiences of your family and in particular your parents and their difficulties; your father's rage and violence and your mother's periodic feelings of hopelessness and self violence. You highlighted your vigilance in trying to stay safe and help the family out. This was a raw deal for a child and has had its consequences for you that we have gradually named in the course of our work together.

It is as if you have internalised as part of your sense of identity aspects of both parents and this has presented you with difficulties as your parents were

---

Figure 3.10 Goodbye letter to David

unable to solve their difficulties and did not provide you with a template for resolution. Your parents' eventual separation saw an end to your father's violence in the family, but the material hardship was made worse for the remainder of your childhood. Your mother was able to empower herself on her own and provided for the family by working long hours. However, this was hard for her and her depression and feelings of hopelessness returned periodically. In turn you were not to see if your father ever managed his violence and so the spectre of male violence became something in your self, as boys identify with fathers and during our sessions we have seen how you have managed outward violence and your wife made very clear boundaries around acceptable treatment. However, we have seen that you have so buried aggression that you are left only with a deep sense of disempowerment at times, the futility and pain your mother felt and acted on has been copied by you. We named a dilemma you struggle with something like:

Self-sabotage dilemma

Defeatest thoughts   Modesty
(depriving/hopelessness)   (unexpansive and unentitled)

In a way it is like your parental drama carried forward for you to successfully resolve in your life and succeed in so many ways you most surely have. You have used the art-making to bring to life in the room the powerful creative skills and resources you have. The bike and the spiders web holding in their symbolism limiting and expansive messages. The use of 3D materials brought to life in memory and in sense of self the highly competent you, including amongst other things, your capacity to overcome. Your first bike, made from parts found at the dump, reveals the foundation of your early use of creativity and flexibility to make life better. Psychologically, this creative making of things also seems to symbolise your flexibility in thinking, your drive to reach out to extend your experience and your understanding.

The challenge in recent years has been your back problems and retirement. With this has come limitation and your wife has in a way enacted the rage in the limits and the challenge that these have brought into your lives. This was perhaps inevitable as you have so buried your voice as a form of protest at life, as a form of externalising and releasing emotion. Like tears, anger and frustration need not be harmful but honest responses to life. What you describe has happened is that you have felt so blamed, humiliated and shamed by your wife's behaviour that you feel your only recourse is to remain silent and you describe how you can feel suicidal when made to feel so useless. At these times you forget how much you have provided over the years and how retirement can be a creative chapter in life, free of many of the earlier demands and childhood hardships. Recently we discussed possible ways of being when your wife is in a distressed and annihilatory mood state and you were keen to try new ways of protecting your self from the protracted complaints by defining a boundary, not as an act of passive aggression, but as an act of respectful self

Figure 3.10 (Continued)

preservation. Your passive response to the complaints has defended you from identifying with your father's violence, but the strategic voice that dances cleverly with life has been sabotaged. It has been great to hear your stories of your long career and the various paths you took and how you enjoyed the variety of life. In addition you excelled in your people management skills in the work place.

What lies in therapy work ahead would seem to me to be about reclaiming your interpersonal skills within the group and also how to transfer new insight and themes into your intimate relationships within the family. The group will offer you other voices to both enrich and challenge and this will give you a safe place to move out of your defeating dilemma and overcome and process the difficulties of life. The group works on a 'recovery model' and so along with the psycho-therapeutic there will be chance to think about the future in real terms and the art-making will be a medium to express, explore, reveal and connect you and the group members.

The 'target problem' for our work together has been to work on resolving self to self and self to other self sabotage and depriving behaviours. I believe you are really on to yourself in this area of difficulty now and beginning to develop some distance from the self sabotage without shifting into self annihila-tory thinking. The work ahead would seem to me to be to build on this and to be open about this rather than polite and compliant . . . the group will want to know you!

I am sorry if I have disappointed you by giving time-limited therapy, but I have great belief that you are ready for the richness that is group art psychotherapy. I will miss seeing you on a Thursday morning and I hope that you will achieve your goals relationally and creatively.

Yours sincerely
Rose

Figure 3.10 (Continued)

David reported improvement nearly two years later when we met to discuss the group option. Here is the diagram that helped him to recognise how his past played out and like Jung's words, he was enabled to engage with this and as such new distance was created.

Both of these clients were given 24 sessions of CAT with follow-up appoint-ments three months after the end of therapy and again some months later.

The integration of art psychotherapy and CAT combine to help better facili-tate access to conscious and unconscious, feelings, thoughts and memories. Art psychotherapy harnessing the non-verbalised and in the case of traumatic life events, the unspeakable. Whilst CAT helps to move this consciousness raising and emotional processing to a reflective and functional level by is descriptions of 'reciprocal roles' and 'mind states' and helps to map out, plan and test new ways of approaching self to self and self to self difficulties.

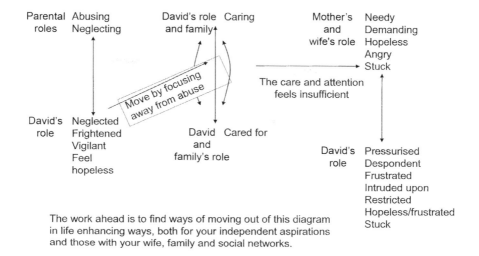

The work ahead is to find ways of moving out of this diagram in life enhancing ways, both for your independent aspirations and those with your wife, family and social networks.

Figure 3.11 Reciprocal role diagram

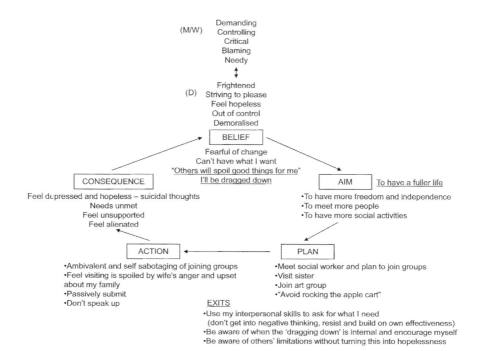

Figure 3.12 David's depressed thinking trap

This integration avoids too much intellectually based cognitive processing and too much floating in the rich and immeasurable psychic ocean. It assists people to manage that which has been largely dissociated by contextualising in empathic terms the harm that has so often beset clients in their lives and which has been perpetuated by them and by others. Hayward and McCurrie refered to Anthony Ryle's work on the development of self-observation (in CAT known as the observing eye) when they wrote:

> Ryle's . . . distinct procedural levels in his work with people who had presented with or had been diagnosed with Borderline Personality Disorder. Reciprocal Roles are at level 1 which develop from patterns of repeated patterns linked to caregivers. Level 2 procedures he labelled metaprocedures which provided a link between the immediate interpersonal action- level 1- and the process of self- reflection which are level 3.
>
> (Ryle cited by Hayward and McCurrie, 2008 p. 42)

Anthony Ryle also developed the Personality Structure Questionnaire (PSQ), which has eight questions with options between polarised states. One circle is shaded on each line. The numbers above the shaded choices are added together. Ryle found people in the borderline personality zone scored about 27 upwards. There is a PSQ available at the end of this chapter for copying.

To conclude, it has to be said that to discuss the integration of two models of therapy both of which require intensive training is not easy to condense into one chapter. But I trust I have provided the reader a sense of the therapeutic value of this integration that may inspire those with particular interest to pursue further. I have found that it can help in complex cases and that it enables our small art psychotherapy team to provide a broader service to the local community helping us meet the demand for treatment available to those who need it, due to its time-limited structure and clear descriptions. It enables us to plan waiting times more objectively as part of a package of various art psychotherapy options and with our developing post-therapy networks, we are able to do 'more for less'. This is achieved in the hope that one day we can expand our service. We are holding on to the best, adapting and articulating whilst not being annihilated by the economic and ideological limits of this epoch. To manage this intensive work it is important that art psychotherapists and cognitive analytic therapists are given resources and contextual support for their work and careers. Finally this time-limited structure may one day provide a culture in the public sector whereby; in addition, longer-term therapy can once more be a viable provision for those for whom it is recognised as essential. Such as some cases of psychosis, learning disability, endured chronic physical illnesses and other forms of psychological struggle and suffering.

THE PSYCHOTHERAPY FILE

An aid to understanding ourselves better

In our life what has happened to us, and the sense we made of this, colours the way we see ourselves and others. How we see things if for us how things are, and how we go about our lives seems 'obvious and right'. Sometimes, however, our familiar ways of understanding and acting can be the source of our problems. In order to solve our difficulties we may need to learn to recognise how what we do makes things worse. We can then work out new ways of thinking and acting to change things for the better.

These pages are intended to suggest ways of thinking about what you do; recognising your particular patterns is the first step in learning to gain more control and happiness in your life. You should discuss this questionnaire with your counsellor or therapist.

KEEPING A DIARY OF MOODS AND BEHAVIOUR

Symptoms, bad moods, unwanted thoughts or behaviours that come and go can be better understood and controlled if you learn to notice when they happen and what starts them off.

If you have a particular symptom or problem of this sort, start keeping a diary. The diary should be focussed on a particular mood, symptom or behaviour, and should be kept every day if possible. Try to record this sequence:

1. How you were feeling about yourself and others and the world before the problem came on.
2. Any external event, or any thought or image in your mind that was going on when the trouble started, or what seemed to start it off.
3. Once the trouble started, what were the thoughts, images or feelings your experienced.

By noticing and writing down in this way what you do and think at these times, you will learn to recognise and eventually have more control over how you act and think at the time. It is often the case that bad feelings like resentment, depression or physical symptoms are the result of ways of thinking and acting that are unhelpful. Diary keeping in this way gives you the chance to learn better ways of dealing with things.

It is helpful to keep a daily record for 1-2 weeks, then to discuss what you have recorded with your therapist or counsellor.

Figure 3.13 The Psychotherapy File

PATTERNS THAT DO NOT WORK, BUT ARE HARD TO BREAK

There are certain ways of thinking and acting that do not achieve what we want, but which are hard to change. Read through the lists on the following pages and mark how far you think they apply to you.

Applies strongly ++
Applies +
Does not apply 0

1. TRAPS

Traps are things we cannot escape from. Certain kinds of thinking and acting result in a 'vicious circle' when, however hard we try, things seem to get worse instead of better. Trying to deal with feeling bad about ourselves, we think and act in ways that tend to confirm our badness.
Examples of Traps

1. Fear of hurting others Trap

Feeling fearful of hurting others* we keep our feelings inside, or put our own needs aside. This tends to allow other people to ignore us or abuse us in various ways, which then leads to our feeling, or being, childishly angry. When we see ourselves behaving like this, it confirms our belief that we should not be aggressive and reinforces our avoidance of standing up for our rights.

People often get trapped in this way because they mix up aggression and assertion. Mostly, being assertive – asking for our rights – is perfectly acceptable. People who do not respect our rights as human beings must either be stood up to or avoided.

2. Depressed thinking Trap

Feeling depressed, we are sure we will manage a task or social situation badly. Being depressed we are probably not as effective as we can be, and the depression leads us to exaggerate how badly we handled things. This makes us feel more depressed about ourselves.

Figure 3.13 (Continued)

3. Trying to please Trap

Feeling uncertain about ourselves and anxious not to upset others, we try to please people by doing what they seem to want. As a result:

1. We end up being taken advantage of by others which makes us angry, depressed or guilty, from which our uncertainty about ourselves is confirmed, or
2. Sometimes we feel out of control because of the need to please, and start hiding away, putting things off, letting people down, which makes other people angry with us and increases our uncertainty.

4. Avoidance Trap

We feel ineffective and anxious about certain situations, such as crowded streets, open spaces, social gatherings. We try to go back into these situations, but feel even more anxiety. Avoiding them makes us feel better, so we stop trying. However, by constantly avoiding situations our lives are limited and we come to feel increasingly ineffective and anxious.

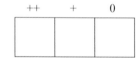

5. Social isolation Trap

Feeling under-confident about ourselves and anxious not to upset others, we worry that others will find us boring or stupid, so we do not look at people or respond to friendliness. People then see us as unfriendly, so we become more isolated from which we are convinced we are boring and stupid and become more under-confident.

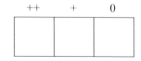

6. Low self-esteem Trap

Feeling worthless we feel that we cannot get what we want because (1) we will be punished, (2) that others will reject or abandon us, or (3) as if anything good we get is bound to go away or turn sour, (4) sometimes it feels as if we must punish ourselves for being weak. From this we feel that everything is hopeless so we give up trying to do anything; this confirms and increases our sense of worthlessness.

Figure 3.13 (Continued)

2. DILEMMAS (False choices and narrow options)

We often act as we do, even when we are not completely happy with it, because the only other ways we can imagine, seem as bad or even worse. Sometimes we assume connections that are not necessarily the case – as in 'If I do "x" then "y" will follow'. These false choices can be described as either/ or or if/then dilemmas. We often don't realise that we see things like this, but we act as if these were the only possible choices. Do you act as if any of the following false choices rule your life? Recognising them is the first step to changing them.

Choices about myself: I act AS IF:

++ + 0

1. Either I keep feelings bottled up or I risk being rejected, hurting others or making a mess.

2. Either I feel I spoil myself and feel greedy or I deny myself things and punish myself and feel miserable.

3. If I try to be perfect, I feel depressed and angry; if I don't try to be perfect, I feel guilty, angry and dissatisfied.

4. If I must then I won't; it is as if when faced with a task I must either (1) gloomily submit or (2) passively resist. Other people's wishes, or even my own feel too demanding, so I put things off or avoid them.

5. If I must not then I will; it is as if the only proof of my existence is my resistance. Other people's rules, or even my own feel too restricting, so I break rules and do things which are harmful to me.

Figure 3.13 (Continued)

	++	+	0

6. Either I keep things (feelings, plans) in perfect order, or I fear a terrible mess.

7. If I get what I want I feel childish and guilty; if I don't get what I want, I feel frustrated, angry and depressed.

8. Either I keep things (feelings, plans) in perfect order, or I fear a terrible mess.

Choices about how we relate to others: I behave with others AS IF:

	++	+	0

1. Either I'm involved with someone and likely to get hurt or I don't get involved and stay in charge, but remain lonely.

2. Either I stick up for myself and nobody likes me, or give in and get put on by others and feel cross and hurt.

3. Either I'm a brute or a martyr (secretly blaming the other).

4. With others either I'm safely wrapped up in bliss or in combat.

5. If in combat then I'm either a bully or a victim.

Figure 3.13 (Continued)

	++	+	0

6. Either I look down on other people, or I feel they look down on me.

7. Either I'm sustained by the admiration of others whom I admire or I feel exposed.

8. If exposed then I feel either contemptuous of others or I feel contemptible.

9. Either I'm involved with others and feel engulfed, taken over or smothered, or I stay safe and uninvolved but feel lonely and isolated.

10. When I'm involved with someone whom I care about then either I have to give in or they have to give in.

11. When I'm involved with someone on whom I depend then either I have to give in or they have to give in.

12. As a woman either I have to do what others want or I stand up for my rights and get rejected.

13. As a man either I can't have any feelings or I am an emotional mess.

Figure 3.13 (Continued)

3. SNAGS

Snags are what is happening when we say 'I want to have a better life, or I want to change my behaviour but . . .'. Sometimes this comes from how we or our families thought about us when we were young; such as 'she was always the good child', or 'in our family we never . . .'. Sometimes the snags come from the important people in our lives not wanting us to change, or not able to cope with what our changing means to them. Often the resistance is more indirect, as when a parent, husband or wife becomes ill or depressed when we begin to get better.

In other cases we seem to 'arrange' to avoid pleasure or success, or if they come, we have to pay in some way, by depression, or by spoiling things. Often this is because, as children, we came to feel guilty if things went well for us, or felt that we were envied for good luck or success. Sometimes we have come to feel responsible, unreasonably, for things that went wrong in the family, although we may not be aware that this is so. It is helpful to learn to recognise how this sort of pattern is stopping you getting on with your life, for only then can you learn to accept your right to a better life and begin to claim it.

You may get quite depressed when you begin to realise how often you stop your life being happier and more fulfilled. It is important to remember that it's not being stupid or bad, but rather that:

a)   *We do these things because this is the way we learned to manage best when we were younger,*

b)   *We don't have to keep on doing them now we are learning to recognise them,*

c)   *By changing our behaviour, we can learn to control not only our own behaviour, but we also change the way other people behave to us.*

d)   *Although it may seem that others resist the changes we want for ourselves (for example, our parents or our partners), we often under-estimate them; if we are firm about our right to change, those who care for us will usually accept the change.*

Do you recognise that you feel limited in your life:

1.   For fear of the response of others: for example I must sabotage success (1) as if it deprives others, (2) as if others may envy me or (3) as if there are not enough good things to go around.

Figure 3.13 (Continued)

		++	+	0

2. By something inside yourself: for example I must sabotage good things as if I don't deserve them

++	+	0

4. DIFFICULT AND UNSTABLE STATES OF MIND:

Some people find it difficult to keep control over their behaviour and experience because things feel very difficult and different at times. Indicate which, if any of the following, apply to you:

	++	+	0

1. How I feel about myself and others can be unstable; I can switch from one state of mind to a completely different one.

2. Some states may be accompanied by intense, extreme and uncontrollable emotions.

3. Other states by emotional blankness, feeling unreal or feeling middles.

4. Some states are accompanied by feeling intensely guilty or angry with myself, wanting to hurt myself.

5. Or by feeling that others can't be trusted, are going to let me down, or hurt me.

6. Or by being unreasonably angry or hurtful to others.

7. Sometimes the only way to cope with some confusing feelings is to blank them off and feel emotionally distant from others.

Figure 3.13 (Continued)

5. DIFFERENT STATES

Everybody experiences changes in how they feel about themselves and the world. But for some people these changes are extreme, sometimes sudden and confusing. In such cases there are often a number of states which recur, and learning to recognise them and shift between them can be very helpful. Below are a number of descriptions of such states. Identify those which you experience by ringing the number. You can delete or add words to the descriptions and there is space to add any not listed.

1. Zombie. Cut off from feelings, cut off from others, disconnected.
2. Feeling bad by soldiering on, coping.
3. Out of control rage.
4. Extra special. Looking down on others.
5. In control of self, of life, of other people.
6. Cheated by life, by others. Untrusting.
7. Provoking, teasing, seducing, winding up others.
8. Clinging, fearing abandonment.
9. Frenetically active. Too busy to think or feel.
10. Agitated, confused, anxious.
11. Feeling perfectly cared for, blissfully close to another.
12. Misunderstood, rejected, abandoned.
13. Contemptuously dismissive of myself.
14. Vulnerable, needy, passively helpful, waiting for rescue.
15. Envious, wanting to harm others, put them down, pull them down.
16. Protective, respecting of myself, of others.
17. Hurting myself, hurting others.
18. Resentfully submitting to demands.
19. Hurt, humiliated by others.
20. Secure in myself, able to be close to others.
21. Intensely critical of self, of others.
22. Frightened of others.
23.
24.
25.

The Psychotherapy File was developed by Dr Anthony Ryle, Emeritus Consultant Psychotherapist and Senior Research Fellow, Department of Psychiatry & Psychotherapy, Kings College, Guys Hospital, London SE1 9RT

Figure 3.13 (Continued)

RATING SHEET

TP: Description of TARGET PROBLEM:

TPP: Description of TARGET PROBLEM PROCEDURE or RECIPROCAL ROLE:

	S4	S5	S6	S7	S8	S9	S10	S11	S12	S13	S14	S15	S16	F-up
RECOGNITION Rate how far you were able to recognise the TPP/ Role this week														
REVISION Rate how far you were able to stop or change the TPP/Role this week														

Description of AIM, EXIT OR GOAL FOR THIS TP: TARGET PROBLEM:

Figure 3.14 The Rating Sheet

The aim of this questionnaire is to obtain an account of certain aspects of your personality. People vary greatly in all sorts of ways: the aim of this form is to find out how far you feel yourself to be constant and 'all of a piece' or variable and made up of a number of distinct 'sub-personalities' or liable to experience yourself as shifting between two or more quite distinct and sharply differentiated states of mind.

Most of us experience ourselves as somewhere between these contrasted ways. A state of mind is recognised by a typical mood, a particular sense of oneself and of others and by how for one is in touch with, and in control of, feelings. Such states are definite, recognizable ways of being; one is either clearly in a given state or ne is not. They often affect one quite suddenly; they may be of brief duration or they last for days. Sometimes, but not always, changes of state happen because of change in circumstances or an event of some kind.

Please indicate which description applies to you most closely by shading the appropriate circle.
Please complete ALL questions.

Shade circles like this: ● **Not** like this ⊗ or ⊘
Shade one circle per question only

THANK YOU FOR YOUR HELP. ALL INFORMATION WILL BE TREATED AS CONFIDENTIAL

	1 Very True	2 True	3 May or may not be True	4 True	5 Very True	
My sense of self is always the same	○	○	○	○	○	How I act or feel is constantly changing
The various people in my life see me in much the same way	○	○	○	○	○	The various people in my life have different views of me as if I were not the same person
I have a stable and unchanging sense of myself	○	○	○	○	○	I am different at some times that I wonder who I really am
I have no sense of opposed sides to my nature	○	○	○	○	○	I feel I am split between two (or more) ways of being, sharply differentiated from each other

Figure 3.15 The Personality Structure Questionnaire

My mood and sense of self seldom change suddenly	o	o	o	o	o	My mood can change abruptly in ways which make me feel unreal or out of control
My mood changes are always understandable	o	o	o	o	o	I am often confused by my mood changes which seem either unprovoked or quite out of scale with what provoked them
I never lose control	o	o	o	o	o	I get into states in which I lose control and do harm to myself and/or others
I never regret what I have said or done	o	o	o	o	o	I get into states in which I do and say things which I later regret

Figure 3.15 (Continued)

Previous publications

Art Therapy as Psychotherapy With the Mental Handicapped; Destruction and Repair and the Primary Therapeutic Experience. *Inscape* (Spring) 1986.

The Application of Object Relations Theories to Art Therapy With Three Women With Mental Handicaps. Transitional Phenomena and the Potential Space in Art Therapy With Mentally Handicapped People. *Inscape; Journal of the British Association of Art Therapists* 1988.

Chapter 7. Rape! The violation of integrity and will. In Mair Rees (Ed.), *Drawing on Difference: Art Therapy With People Who Have Learning Difficulties*. Routledge, 1998.

An Enquiry Into an Integration of Cognitive Analytic Therapy With Art Therapy. *International Journal of Art Therapy; Inscape* 12 (1, June) 2007.

Plugging In and Letting Go: The Use of Art in CAT. *Reformulation; Theory and Practice in Cognitive Analytic Therapy* (Summer) 2008.

Dear Reformulation. *Reformulation; Theory and Practice in Cognitive Analytic Therapy* (36, Summer) 2011. (An article about my father's death.)

Comment on James Turner's article on Verbal and Pictorial Metaphor in CAT. *Ethics and CAT* (37, Winter) 2011.

Integrating Art Psychotherapy and Cognitive Analytic Therapy (CAT). *Ethics and CAT* (40, Summer) 2013.

Bibliography

Bosnak, R. (2007) *Embodiment: Creative Imagination in Medicine, Art and Travel.* Hove, Sussex: Routledge.

Edwards, M. (2010) *A Jungian Circumambulation of Art and Therapy: Ornithology for the Birds.* Exeter, UK: Insider Art (Publishing) Ltd.

Fisher, S. and Fisher, R. L. (1953) Unconscious Conception of Parental Figures as a Factor Influencing Perception of Time. *Journal of Personality* 21, 496.

Gerhardt, S. (2004) *Why Love Matters*. New York, USA: Routledge.

Gut, E. (1989) *Productive and Unproductive Depression: Success or Failure of a Vital Process*. London, UK: Tavistock/Routledge.

Hayward, M. and McCurrie, C. (2008) Metaprocedures in Normal Development and in Therapy. *Reformulation* 30 (Summer), 42–45. Dorchester.

Jung, C. G. (1986) *Four Archetypes: Mother. Rebirth. Spirit. Trickster*. London and New York: Ark Publications.

Leiman, M. (1992) The Concept of Sign in the Work of Vygotsky, Winnicott and Bakhtin: Further Integration of Object Relations Theory and Activity Theory. *British Journal of Medical Psychology* 65, 209–221.

Mann, J. (1973) *Frank and Frank in: Time-Limited Psychotherapy*. Cambridge, Massachusetts and London, England: Harvard University Press.

Ryle, A. (1991a) Object Relations Theory and Activity Theory: A Proposed Link by Way of the Procedural Sequence Model. *British Journal of Medical Psychology* 64, 307–306.

Ryle, A. (1991b) *Cognitive Analytic Therapy: Active Participation in Change. A New Integration in Brief Psychotherapy*. Chichester, England: John Wiley and Sons.

Ryle, A. (1995) *Cognitive Analytic Therapy: Developments in Theory and Practice*. Chichester, England: John Wiley and Sons.

Simon, R. M. (1992) *The Symbolism of Style: Art as Therapy*. London, England: Tavistock/Routledge.

Stern, D. (2004) *The Interpersonal World of the Infant*. (2nd Edition). London: XU Karnac Books.

Grateful thanks for consent from Dr Anthony Ryle to reproduce the CAT questionnaires in this chapter.

Chapter 4

Portrait of self and other

Developing a mentalization-focused approach to art therapy within a personality disorder service

David Thorne

Darkness has all come together, making an egg.
Darkness in which there is now nothing
A blot has knocked me down. It clogs me.
A globe of blot, a drop of unbeing.
Nothingness came close and breathed on me- a frost
A shawl of annihilation has curled me up like a new foetus.
(Ted Hughes 'Cave Birds, an alchemical Cave Drama'
beginning of poem – A flayed crow in the hall of
judgement. 1978 – permission granted)

The crux can be the 'nothingness that is neither repression nor simply the mark of the affect but condenses into a black hole – like invisible, crushing, cosmic antimatter' (Kristeva 1989; 87), or the tumultuous vacillation between fullness and emptiness that Bollas speaks of, 'the primary object is less an introjectable possibility . . . than a recurring effect within the self. Like the wind in the trees it is a movement within the self' (Bollas 1996; 5).

Failures of attachment can mean that the good object is not, or is only partially introjected. The trauma or neglect resounds, careering around the self, sending echoes down the line through disruptive acts, and through the transference relationship.

Chronic feelings of emptiness and *unstable sense of self* are two of the nine DSM-IV-TR diagnostic criteria for borderline personality disorder. The initial event marked by trauma or absence meant that the self did not gather around a good object interjected. Without a consistent anchorage of experiencing by a stable sense of self then we may expect; *impulsive self harming acts, affective instability* and *inappropriate anger*. These affective disturbances are three more of the criteria.

With a disturbance in relationship with self, there may well be a disturbance in relationship with other. A *pattern of unstable and intense interpersonal relationships*, and *frantic efforts to avoid real or imaged abandonment*, and *transient, stress related paranoid ideation*, mark three relational criteria points.

The last of the nine DSM IV TR criteria, of which only five have to be present for a diagnosis to be given, are *suicidal and self-harming behaviour*.

The equivalent category in the ICD-10 is Emotionally Unstable Personality Disorder, borderline type (F60.31) characterised by instability in emotions, self-image and relationships.

The image I have of the borderline state, is that at heart there is something so difficult to grasp hold of, be it a nothingness, or an emptiness or wind, like a tornado that rips apart creating emotional storms, then seems to die down, to nothingness. There can be little to hold onto, and in some cases, a sense that no history can be made. Where some people with this diagnosis are very vivid and immediate with their affect storms, others show a public face of rigid control and containment, like a leadened box, distortions betraying an inner turmoil.

When work is done to try and understand this turmoil, often opposite and conflicting traits/positions/elements are found. Where Winnicott 1971 termed 'the false self' Mentalization theory talks of the 'alien self'. This is where the representations of attachment figures are internalised (swallowed whole as it were), rather than an internalisation of a modified version of the child's own state through mirroring (part pre-digested), 'This creates what we term an alien experience within the self; ideas of feelings are experienced which do not seem to belong to the self' (Fonagy 2001;1).

I sometimes feel battered and bruised. Powerful projective experiences of my patients' pain and distress are sometimes hard to weather. Helen Greenwood conveys the strength of counter-transference in 'Captivity and Terror in the Therapeutic Relationship' (Greenwood 2000). She also notes her observation in vignettes that emotional closeness can cause a counter-action, a pushing away, so that the course of therapy oscillates. The therapist can feel useless and unwanted at times, and then essential at other times. Supervision is valued to help mentalize the counter transference.

The ability to mentalize allows us to; know our own thoughts and feelings; make reasoned judgements of the thoughts and feelings of others; it is the basis by which we regulate affect; and gain and maintain a sense of self, and gain the seat of our perspective, opinions and authority.

Mentalization was a term used in analytical circles linked to concepts of 'metabolization', 'representation', 'symbolization', or 'symbol formation' and 'secondary mental processes', and 'alpha function' (Choi-Kain and Gunderson 2008; 1127–1135). The term was originally used to signify the process by which infant somatic experiences become encoded into images, ideas and then words, allowing felt experience to be recognised, linked and modulated. The body creates the image in mind. The process of representing experience (the image) allows us to get a handle on what we are feeling, rather than being swept along by affect. Fonagy expanded the concept to 'the capacity to conceive of conscious and unconscious mental states in oneself and others' (Fonagy 1991; 72; 639–656).

The ability to mentalize is instigated within an infant by a caregiver able to adequately relate meaningfully to what they are able to imagine the child is experiencing. The caregiver's responsiveness through gesture and expression helps represent the experiences of the child, allowing it meaning and marking affect as communicative.

Where the caregiver cannot or will not imagine the child's mental experiences, the child's inner experience is not marked or represented, and the weaving of inner and outer expectations that Winnicott (1971) described happening in potential space, fails. This interconnecting of inner and outer is important in gaining the sense that; *my inner experiences can make sense in the outside world*, and the sense that; *I can make sense of the world, and my needs and desires hold possibility to be met in the world, and make sense.*

Deficits in the ability to mentalize are a feature of all mental disorders. The work of Peter Fonagy and Anthony Batemen amongst others, has laid down an approach for Borderline Personality Disorder, in the form of Mentalization Based Therapy (MBT).

The MBT therapists starts with validation of the others predicament, but explores with the patient the interweaving opposite poles, i.e. a focus on self with reflections on the other, cognitive meaning with feeling sense, and certainty with a not knowing curiosity, etc.

Training courses in MBT have been developed in the Anna Freud Centre, and at University College London (UCL). At present the British Association of Art Therapists (BAAT) offer intensive training for Art Therapists, and the International Centre for Arts Psychotherapies (London, UK) offers training under their Research Based Practice series.

The present political and economic climate of sweeping changes favours therapeutic intervention approaches with succinct models that multi-professional staff teams can adopt. The whole staff team subscribing to one therapeutic approach benefits the borderline/emotionally unstable service user in providing a consistent and comprehensive approach. MBT is well suited for a whole team approach.

It is also a climate of reduced budgets and competition for resources. The course of economic contraction is often attributed to NICE guidelines (National institute of Health and Clinical Excellence). What is cut are interventions not supported by an evidence base, what are promoted are interventions that can make sense to budget holders and directors of services. In this regard MBT has done its homework. The work at the Halliwick Centre (Barnet, Enfield and Haringey Mental Health NHS Trust) has coherently connected diagnostic factors for BPD, to a team approach that focused specific change (i.e. the ability to mentalize), and has evidenced the clinical effectiveness (Bateman, Fonagy 2009).

Art therapy has not fared so well. NICE 2009 5.2.4 states; 'There is very little research on the effectiveness of arts therapies for people with borderline personality disorder. No recommendations could be made.'

To help survive, the profession needs to align and pull resources. For this purpose, time-limited art psychotherapy interventions that are measurable and effective, can be repeated by other clinicians, supported by practice research universities and critically reviewed by peers, are our best hope.

The research there is in this area is in the form of case studies (Lamont et al. 2009) and small sample pilot projects (Franks and Whitaker 2007, Springham et al. 2012) and patient preference surveys that found art therapy a treatment of preference by service users (BAAT 2008, Karterud, Pederson 2004, Burgess, Butler [unpublished] conference).

Karterud and Umes (2004) found a correlation between patient rating art therapy highest in treatment preference in a day hospital setting, with positive therapeutic outcomes.

Karterud and Pederson (2004) and Springham et al. (2012), sought service user views on what are the effective components of art therapy. For detail discussion see the special edition of the *International Journal of Art Therapy*, November 2012.

Models of art therapy within a MBT intensive out patient programme (IOPP)

The Personality Disorder Service in which I am employed, runs on the IOPP model. The standard IOPP model is 18 months of individual and group psychotherapy with an MBT approach. This comes after a 12-week introductory psycho-educational programme referred to as MBTi. Both the IOPP and MBTi programmes have been evidenced by randomised control trials (Bateman, Fonagy 2009; 166; 1355–1364).

To develop my own approach I reviewed three models; Johns, Karterud (2004), Franks, Whittaker (2007) and Springham et al. (2012).

I looked at;

- structure (length of treatment, time of sessions, arrangements of the time),
- the role of the therapist,
- the expectation on participants,
- what the therapist thinks is important,
- what the participants think is important,
- then any concluding thoughts.

In Siri Johns and Sigmund Karterud's paper Guidelines for 'Art Group Therapy as Part of a Day Treatment Program for Patients with Personality Disorders' (2004), art therapy is offered as an 18-week treatment programme as part of a co-ordinated approach in a day hospital. Size of group is six to eight with a rolling membership, a new member each third week. Session time is 1.5 hours twice a week. Participants are encouraged to draw or paint their mental images – 40 minutes painting time then discussion. There is an initial structured task where people are asked to draw two concentric circles to fill with patterns, colours or whatever comes to mind. There is also a concluding review of work where the therapist focuses on 'what has changed'.

The role of the therapist is in maintaining the frame of the group and bringing feelings and conflicts to come to the surface, and also to help individuals contain emotions as they arise in the making time, until they can share them verbally in discussion.

In discussion time patients talk of their intention before others are invited to comment. Stated as central to the Therapeutic approach is empathy, and a caution against interpretation, and being aware of patients understanding to regulate the depth and complexity of the discussion.

The stated task of the therapist is to encourage the exploration of imagery, actively challenge if there is avoidance in the group and focus in transference material.

Participants are expected to draw mental images, and discuss their work and give perspectives on the work of others, and to take on core functions of the group in initiating newer members into the norms of the group.

The paper cites as important; the instillation of hope through witnessing resolutions within the group especially conveyed at leavers reviews; the universality of common images, and experiences; and corrective emotional experiences, and the trust that develops through group cohesion around creative activity.

The paper follows a survey that found art group therapy is rated highest in the therapeutic programme by patients (Karterud, Pederson 2004). Participants felt what was important was that the group was; calm and non-competitive; had time for self-focus in image making; encouragement to find expression for images; receiving responses from group and art therapist; witnessing others; and comparing and contrasting own mind with the minds of others.

M. Franks and R. Whitaker published 'The Image, Mentalisation and Group Art Psychotherapy' in the *International Journal of Art Therapy*, 21 June 2007.

Their MBT model is for group art psychotherapy alongside individual therapy in a joint therapy programme. Their pilot was with five patients for nine months. The once-a-week session was 105 minutes, divided between an initial 'business' gathering, then individual art making, then verbal interaction.

Their term 'Joint Therapy Programme' describes establishing links between Group Art Therapists and Individual Therapists through feedback meetings.

Much of the description of sessions indicates the therapist's observation in response to participants work and verbalisations.

In their conclusion they value art therapy and image making as allowing experiments in hypothesis of self. I understood this as referring to the ambiguous nature of what is proffered within art making affording the space to assert and retract notions of selfhood without the definite statement of talking therapy.

They restated Karterud and Pederson's 2004 finding that the art therapy group is 'a safe method of exploring the mind in the presence of mentalising self objects'.

The pilot showed significant improvement for two measures, CORE-OM (34-item outcome measure for psychological distress) and BSI (Brief Symptom Inventory, a 53-item enquiry in depressive symptoms).

'How can art therapy contribute to mentalization in borderline personality disorder?' Springham, Findlay, Woods, and Harris (2012) describe a model that includes a 6-week psycho-educational introduction programme then 18-month group and individual therapy. Art therapy was offered in addition to group and individual therapy. The sessions were two hours long including 30-minute painting time.

A pilot for time-limited art psychotherapy had places for six people of which four completed the programme.

There was a structure to the discussion of artwork, in that the maker speaks of the work, then others are invited to comment and explore.

The art therapist sometimes makes work, or 'potters' during making time so that they are ready to respond. The therapist is there to keep the group safe and to task, and be available. Complex or abstract interpretations are to be avoided, as this can confuse, anger or send this client group into pretend mode (intellectual understanding decouples from felt sense). The therapist takes an active stance in promoting the process of self and group mentalizing.

One of the participants responses were analysed after the pilot. From analysis of responses eight themes were distilled:

- art replaces the words service users can't find;
- joint attention in art therapy is enhanced by homogenous group composition;
- the therapist models the application of inquiry, rather than pre-determined knowledge to exploration of artworks;
- service user to service user comments on artworks support capacity to accept multi-perspectives;
- continuous movement between art making and sharing artworks develops emotional regulation;
- the unresponsive therapist is iatrogenic (*anti-therapeutic, harmful* – my definition) in BPD treatment;
- the art therapist's 'watchful, not watching' stance during art making supports immersion in art making;
- and art therapy can be used as self-help.

There was a range of outcome measures used for this pilot including the Borderline Personality Disorder Severity Index (BPDSI), the Distress Tolerance Scale (DTS, a 15-item self-report questionnaire), employment status and hospital admissions. Scores indicated positive increase in distress tolerance, lower service use and at least two service users no longer meeting criteria for BPD diagnosis.

Time-limited art therapy within the personality disorder service

The model I work with is an art therapy group alongside a talking exploratory group and individual sessions. There have been two exceptions; of someone having art therapy and individual therapy only for a shortened six-month period, as it was felt there was not a need for the full 18-month programme; and also of someone having individual and art therapy as it was felt they needed extra time and work before joining the 18-month programme.

There are eight places in the art therapy group, once a week with each session being 75 minutes long.

I have found a navigable awkwardness within the staff team that stems from art therapy not being prescribed as standard, and was not part of the evidenced practice, and so is sometimes annexed in the thinking within team supervision. Art therapy input is offered as an exception rather than rule, and some work is still needed in developing a service-wide understanding of a referral rationale.

I have also been looking at other uses of art therapy within the IOPP model.

The NICE guideline CG78 states;

> Do not use brief psychological interventions (of less than 3 months duration) specifically for borderline personality disorder or for the individual symptoms of the disorder, outside a service that has the [following] characteristics: an explicit and integrated theoretical approach used by both the treatment team and the therapist, which is shared with the service user structured care in accordance with this guideline provision for therapist supervision.

Providing that time-limited art therapy interventions are held in a cohesive therapeutic programme, I think focused 'pulses' of work (intensive periods of therapeutic work then with time to reflect and incorporate change) can be powerful and enriching of the overall therapeutic endeavour. For instance, I have conducted a three-month intervention specifically focusing on understanding an individual's pattern of eating disorder. The work identified the patient's predicament at each part of their cycle, how they were feeling behind the behaviour. This work concluded in an audio image recording. The understanding gained was shared within the whole team, and the work on the eating disorder was picked up through individual talking therapy.

With the aid of a trainee I also ran a pilot 12-week intervention using art therapy techniques. This exploratory workshop introduces both MBT and art therapy, and also useful as an extended art therapy assessment.

In this pilot project four randomly selected participants diagnosed with BPD participated in the 12 mentalization focused, directive art therapy sessions, compared to four people not receiving the 12-session art therapy intervention.

Both groups received a 12-week psycho-education programme (MBTi), and both groups were given outcome measure questionnaires to fill out before, during and after the programme.

The measures used were the SCL-90-R (Symptom Checklist with 90 items, revised), and BIS (Barrett Impulsivity Scale, 30 items measure different factors of impulsivity).

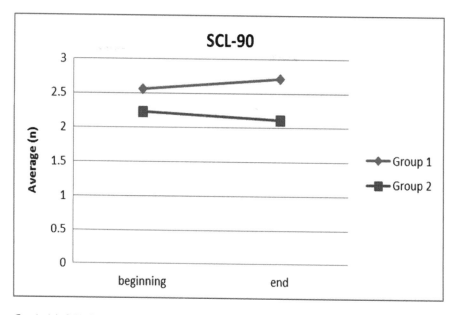

Graph 4.1 SCL-90 scores indicating little change between beginning and end of sessions

Both the group receiving the art therapy programme (Group 1) and the group receiving only the MBTi (Group 2) showed little change in symptomology on the SCL-90-R scale.

The was a decrease in 27 of the 30 items of the Barrett Impulsivity Scale for those receiving both the art therapy intervention and the MBTi (Group 1), compared to little over all change in the BIS scores for the group receiving MBTi only (Group 2).

Barrett Impulsivity Scale results for first-order factors shows a higher level of impulsivity for those randomly selected for the with art therapy group, that decreases generally with treatment. Those randomly selected without art therapy begin in MBTi at a lower impulsity rate, generally increases, or remains at the same level.

It is true that this pilot study is comparing a group who are getting something extra (the art therapy intervention) with those that are not, and so a favourable outcome may be expected. However the indication that the intervention shows a clear effect on impulsivity in the pilot is promising. More data needs collecting, and I invite others to use the programme to gather more evidence, making adjustments, and using different outcome measures and comparison groups as deemed fit or as available.

I offer the following template for this time-limited art therapy intervention, refined from the pilot project, which is repeatable and adaptable.

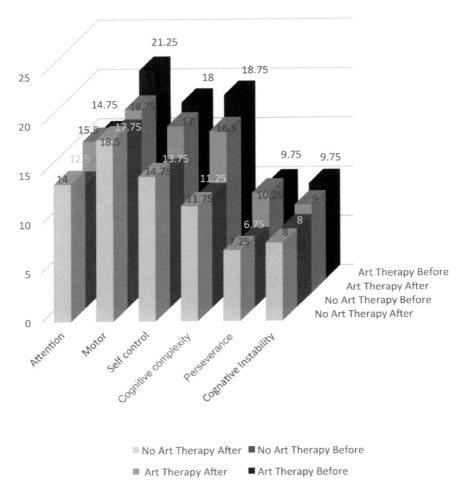

Graph 4.2 BIS scores indicating decrease in many areas of impulsivity for Art Therapy group as opposed to without Art Therapy

Art therapy focused MBT

Art therapists are well versed, and the profession has a developed theory base that already share commonalities with Mentalization Based Therapy (MBT). There is the not knowing stance, the venture of opening up exploration, and the skills of inviting and handling different perspectives. This is the case of most psychodynamically informed therapies including Cognitive Analytical Therapy.

Generally art therapy involves three phases of activity; that of art making, looking and discussion/reflection. Art therapists have skills in facilitating patients in these areas (Mottram 2001/02). Including the skills to maintain a negotiated responsive and safe space in which to facilitate art making, and actively enabling exploration of the work that either opens out or focuses down the attention depending of the service user's defences, needs and awareness.

The art therapy space should be one that promotes enquiry and exploration. The patient should be encouraged to use art materials to research into themselves, and use the group and/or therapist to gain different perspectives into their work, as well as give their perspectives when called for by others. The art therapist needs to support each participant with their exploration while also being transparent that they are also a thinking, feeling present person.

As is usual with many art therapy approaches, during the art making activity the therapist needs to be available but non-intrusive, engaged in their own art making, or 'pottering'.

In coming to discussion of the work, as with other models, it is important to give some structure to feedback. There can be an open negotiation of who talks of their work first, and this can be revisited each session with room to vocalise anything that may emerge from this process. Feelings of being in the spotlight, or guilt of taking up too much time, or being left until last, are all valuable conversations to note.

In both the 18-month IOPP art therapy group, and in shorter interventions I have used a structured form of discussing the work. In this I regularly remind people of the choices that;

- they can talk of their work first, and then invite others to give their views,
- or invite others to give their reflections first, and then comment;
- they can speak and not have anyone else comment,
- or not comment themselves but receive the views of others.
- The work can also be shown with no-one commenting on it.

Even when it is not verbally explored, the therapist can sensitively mark how this alerts us to what is contained in the work by saying something like 'it seems too painful/confusing/difficult to speak of at the moment, but thank you'. It can equally be recognised that person may not know, or be unable to explain in words what they have done, in which case it can be useful to get other's ideas on it by asking 'what do you see?'

It should also be held that feedback is not a judgement on the skill displayed (neither negative comments or praise), and is not telling someone what they have made. The therapist suggests comments are phrased as 'it reminds me of. . .', or 'I see a. . .', rather than 'it is a. . .', or 'you have done a. . .'.

When there is discussion the Therapist should be explicit in their own reflections, 'ie this aspect makes me think of. . .' or 'in my mind. . .' rather than adopting an authoritive voice. Plunging interpretations (Meares and Hobson 1977) are to be avoided with this client group, and generally within relational models of therapy.

The British Association of Art Therapist's personality disorder special interest group (PDSIG) have published clinical guidelines to help structure positive interventions (PDSIG 2012).

The following is the refined script for a 12-week introductory course. It is intended as a psycho-educational extended assessment for Mentalization Based Therapy and Art Therapy.

It is also worth bearing in mind the role of psycho-educational interventions are generally about clarifying perspectives on conditions and common problems, and finding a handful of memorable ideas and/or techniques that are useful in times of crisis.

You are invited to try the exercises as you read.

Portrait of self and other. MBT art therapy introductory workshop (MBTATi)

At the beginning of each session the art therapist is involved in maintaining the frame. I think this is best done with a degree of flexibility, certainly at the start of a course of sessions, when people may come in late due to anxieties, or travel problems where routines are not yet established. Rather than holding tight boundaries, and riding stormy dynamic effects, the door can be left open for the first 15 minutes or so. A general welcoming and enquiring chit-chat and checking in of how people are can take place for the first five to ten minutes. Of course there may be challenges to the most congenial of hosts, and boundaries need to be held reasonably. As the sessions move on then the Therapist can gauge how much expectancy on attending on time can be held by individuals. At some point in the initial conversation the exercise is introduced. The therapist should be well versed in the theory and practice of MBT in order to tether what is raised by the group to an appropriate understanding, or sign posting how it may be worked on in the therapy programme. The focus of the session has to be maintained however.

The exercises are intended as frames for exploration of self, and self in relation to other. Some of the material for this exploration will inevitably be felt in the dynamics within the room. This material is more readily available for reflection with this client group, when already highlighted through psycho-educational work, or experiential exercises.

Time should be accounted for in the planning for management of outcome measures. If patient reporting questionnaires are used then participants should be asked to fill these out before beginning the programme. Using at least three points to measure is preferable – i.e. beginning, middle and end. For these 12 sessions it is then before session 1, at session 6, and at session 12.

Consider the timetable with any breaks factored in.

Having a co-facilitator is advisable, who may not be an art therapist. It would be a good opportunity to gain support and awareness of a colleague, and/or a rich experience for a student on placement.

Session 1: Meet and greet

This session is for housekeeping and orienteering. Attendance issues are most likely to emerge in this session.

The initial sessions should give an over view of the scheme, and of the service. People are told they are expected to attend each session, and to bring difficulties into the group. People are clearly told not to meet up and form any kind of relationship outside of sessions as it hampers treatment. The first outcome measure should be arranged.

People are introduced to fire procedures, to the wider environment, and to the room, and to where materials are. This may induce either a positive or negative reaction in people, depending on how ready they are to use art materials.

Short exercise: to write your name on a piece of paper, considering style of lettering and colours.

Making time is flexible depending how comfortable people are with it. The therapist is open in acknowledging the first people to finish, and their situation of waiting, with how much time others still working may need, and their situation of not wanting to feel rushed. A round of introductions through people's names can then unfold. This may develop to discuss people's expectations of the sessions, and information of what can be covered through the sessions.

The therapists should prepare beforehand, in being able to explain the diagnosis, and to define mentalization in your own words.

Session 2: Introduce the diagnostic criteria and circle drawing

The aim of this session is to begin. The first sessions are often anxiety provoking for participants as well as facilitators. There is an unknown quantity in who will attend, who else is in the group, what will others think of me and what will be expected of me.

Group activity: Each participant is given paper with a circle drawn on it (or a blank sheet and asked to make a circle with compass, or dish/plate provided).

This is like that described in Johns, Karterud (2004), except rather than two concentric circles it is one circle. See also Diane Silverman's chapter (1991). It is visually similar to Malcolm Learmonths 'Articulating Art Therapy' 'Draw anything you wish sheet' except the instructions here are;

'A circle simply divides an inside space and an outside space. We talk of a family circle, a circle of friends, going around in circles, and vicious circles. For this circle draw what is in your life, within the circle, and what is outside of your life in the area around the circle. Think about what is in your life that you are glad is there, and what you would prefer to be out of your life. Also think if there are things outside of the circle of your life that you want to be in your life. This can be

around the outside. There may be things outside of your circle you are also glad are not in your life.'

This exercise is a way that participants introduce themselves to each other. It allows the therapist to see how someone makes use of art material. There may be a range from diagrammatic, illustrative icons that label aspects of someone's life, as well as embodied work with expressive mark making and use of colour suggestive of an internal emotional world.

It is likely that someone may illustrate issues connected with their difficulties with personality disorder symptoms. Room should be given to acknowledge this and connect it to the treatment programme as a whole. If no one's work makes any reference to emotional difficulties, or feeling lost, hollow, chaotic inside or tortured relationship problems, then the therapist should vocalise wondering why this is – knowing what the treatment programme is here to help with. This should not be persecutory, or critical, but curious.

It can be stated that people with this diagnosis tend to get better with age, growing less intense, with more skills to deal with situations. Also findings are that MBT quickens the rate to recovery.

The exercise is reported as an example of mentalizing – *'In making the work you have taken time in thinking and feeling about yourselves and your own life. It may have changed your views hearing different perspectives given by others. You have also had thoughts and feelings about others work, and your views can be useful for others. This kind of mentalizing culture is what we hope to encourage.'*

At the end of the session, a reminder of the importance of arriving on time for next week, conventions of where the work is to be kept and any 'business' arising for outcome measure questionnaires should be dealt with.

Session 3: 'Coal, fire, smoke'

This session maintains group-as-a-whole working through short exercises and discussions.

The Art Therapist welcomes the participants, and some conversation may be had while the group settles.

Using just paper and charcoal, the therapist demonstrates how different types of mark-making produce different qualities, from the hard shiny blackness of coal, the chaotic quickness of fire and the slower, drawn out and soft fading quality of smoke.

People are asked to work in cycles of these three qualities, not necessarily making an illustration, but taking note of how they feel going from one quality to another.

'Coal is hard and black and angular before it is burnt. Fire is fleeting, ever changing. Smoke trails and fades away to nothing. Then back to coal. Go through each element a few times, noticing what each feels like and the transition between them.'

Figure 4.1 Coal smoke fire drawings

The exercise can be taken on face value, exploring the use of charcoal through drawing a coal fire. In discussion there is a simple link to be made between the picture and emotional states. For people who do not easily recognise their own emotions this speculation should not be forced, but it can be asked 'was there any difference in what it felt like to make hard black coal, to the wisps of smoke?'

When I have done this exercise with a group, usually one or more people speak of being drawn to one of the three states. Some have found a fourth state after smoke, of stillness.

A further area to discuss is that of the transition between emotional states, and how easy or difficult this might be. 'Was it easy to go from hard black coal to fire, what about to smoke trails? Was it easy to start again?'

Following this discussion, the therapist talks of hyper-activated emotional states such as blind rage, or panic, where it is difficult to mentalize. People may have examples of this, which should be gratefully received, and held with reference to fight/flight activation, and the work of the sympathetic and parasympathetic nervous systems (or simply that we literally go to a different mode). If the therapist is aware of it, a graph of the switch point within the continuum of emotional arousal

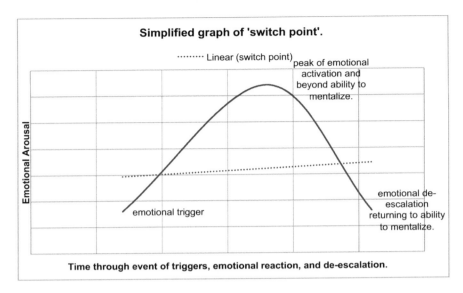

Graph 4.3 Simplified graph of the 'switch point' in trajectory of emotional arousal

that marks the shift from prefrontal functioning to the automatic flight and flight reaction can be drawn.

In this discussion people often say they cannot remember what happened after a certain point. They were 'out of their minds' on anger or fear, and it can be put that literally a different part of the brain had taken over.

At the time it would not be possible, but looking back at these hyper-activated times what was going on may well be very complex. The therapist can explore a little with any given example, or use a hypothetical situation to show under the rage, for example, there may have been feelings of humiliation, or rejection. It should be offered that given the complexity of emotions and feelings, therapy should allow time just to see what is happening for us.

Group activity: Using silhouettes on a neutral outline figure record by mark making what you currently feel in your body.

(A template for a neutral body outline can be made beforehand by using a figure drawing or anatomical book).

This is a short five- to ten-minute exercise, and discussion can be brief if nearing end of the session. It may be useful to pick up of the difference between body sensation feelings and emotion.

It can be striking what this exercise can reveals. Some people have little awareness of what is happening within their bodies. Pain is often more readily found than some more subtle sensations. Some link directly to emotions and feelings.

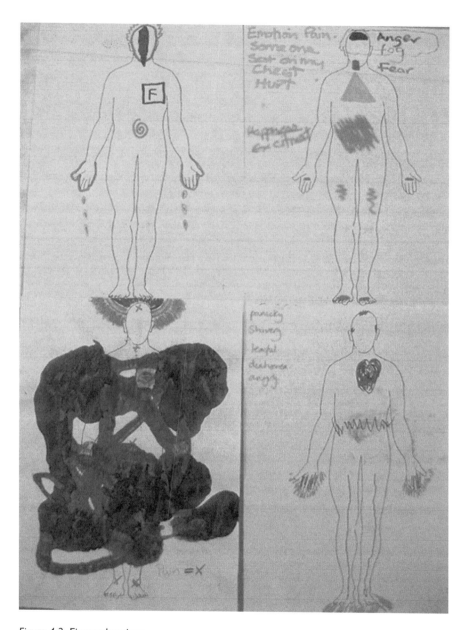

Figure 4.2 Figure drawings

Session 4: Expressive mark making

This session leads into more individual working.

The work of the last two session is made available and the therapist encourages a review.

Group exercise; (devised from Edwards 1988 Chapter 7).

Divide a sheet of paper into eight boxes, either by folding in half down the length, and the half again, and the half vertically and half again, or using a ruler. Label the first square 1) Curiosity and then proceed, 2) Fear, 3) Anger, 4) Lust, 5) Separation, 6) Love/caring, 7) Play/joy, 8) Something of your choosing.

Quickly, and without thinking too much, make a few marks in each box – that express these words. (15–20 minutes)

Discussion can note the similarities and differences of participants' marks.

The discussion may be rich and further exploration necessary to give space for each person to explain their difficulty or experience with each emotion. The discussion can be contained in referring to the principles of a mentalizing culture, whilst marking and valuing different perspectives, noting when people describe rigidity in thinking when highly emotional, then returning to the importance of curiosity.

If there is enough time people are asked to make their own work, in whatever way they choose, bearing in mind the marks they use.

By this stage it should be evident who is more, and who is less confident in using materials. People may obviously stay with the style of the exercises, or diverge wildly from them. Both should be validated, and each image explored as time allows.

Session 5: Analog drawing

Analog drawing was termed by Edwards (1988 Chapters 8–9–10).

'Think of a person you know and a problem they have. Holding this in the back of your mind make a gestural mark drawing. The person or problem does not have to be spoken, and the drawing is not an illustration.' (20 minutes)

When coming together, this time the maker is silent and others are encouraged to think about what sort of problem they see in the work. This may be one or two words of each person's reaction, or develop into more detailed storytelling. The maker is then asked if any of what has been said was anywhere near what they see. People are not asked to talk of the people or problems they have in mind, but this may happen anyway. It is worth noting any ideas of solutions that come out of the conversation, while stressing that we may not know if it is a good solution or not as we are not clear of what exactly the problem is. We can try and know, and that might help the other person understand their problem. Reference can be made to group therapy and how it can be useful if people are trying to mentalize about each other's problems.

Time allowing, people are then asked to make work on a problem of their own.

Unexplored work can be reviewed at a later date. It may become evident through this exercise, what problems participants have in mentalizing the other.

In any session with this client group, strong and challenging dynamics may well have emerged. It is well to remember, and can be said that everyone loses the ability to mentalize at times. Some of the problems may illustrate how problems in mentalizing of one person can affect the ability of another.

Remind people that the next session approaches the mid-point. The first half of the 12 sessions have been designed to think more of ourselves and own emotions, the second half looks at relationships.

As homework people are asked to note a situation that happens in the week where they have been able to avoid making a situation worse.

Session 6: Adaptable session

All sessions are potentially adaptable for any issues the therapist/facilitator envisages is needed for the particular group. This session is designed to be adaptable, coming at the mid-point and at a time a group identity may be forming. There also may be reactive aspects, and anxieties of ending.

This session is designed as a more open session where there is space to recap or clarify aspects that participants raise. The programme structure can ideally be designed so that there is a break after the sixth session. This provides space to think about the work, and also can be a relief and thinking space to contemplate if tensions are building within the group. The Middle outcome measures should be completed in this session.

Suggestion 1: Group work. 'Pass the paper'

A variety of pencils, pastels and pens are made available on a table all participants can sit around.

Each person begins with a sheet of paper, on which they clearly write their name. They are asked to make a single mark or expression on it. Each sheet is then passed on to the left. Participants are asked to add something to what is already there. This process of passing on continues until the paper is returned to the original place. The therapist joins in this exercise, and at each change reminds people to add something that moves the work closer to becoming something.

The work is then said to have gone through a journey of change before being returned to the original owner, as if the group has made a gift for each one of us. The work is then discussed and explored. This can be done by asking simply what people see, and though retracing the steps of its development.

It may or may not emerge that the work relates to the person it is returned to. Any link should not be forced, but held by the therapist with light intrigue.

Suggestion 2: Individual work, open claywork

Participants are handed lumps of clay and asked to play around with them, a more open and flowing conversation can then be steered into talking about the work, asking if anyone managed the homework, and recapping on previous ideas.

Suggestion 3: Discussion and possible role play

Discussion should be structured around people's experiences of the homework, recapping of the importance of what is helpful, rather than impressing how awful things can be (if this is the tone of the conversation) and out of people's scenarios it may be possible to do a role play. It is best to keep the scene simple, and get a clear direction of what is in one person's mind, and then use the group to think of what may be in the other's, as well as what they see as going wrong (misunderstandings, unfair expectations) and how things might be put right.

This session marks coming to the midpoint of the programme. If a break has been timetabled in it hopefully leaves people with a sense of the group in their memories.

A break can allow the group to realign itself, and a time to take stock.

There may be tensions and questions of what comes next. Resistances and volatile dynamics may be present. Remind people it is an introduction.

The mid-way outcome measure should be performed.

Session 7: 'Personify an emotion/body sensation'

The group is allowed to gather in conversation of how people have been. The therapist introduces the questions;

> 'How do we recognise emotions in ourselves?'
> 'How do we recognise emotions in others?'
> 'How can emotions be regulated (changed, de-esculated)?'
> 'How can others help us regulate our emotions?'

These should be discussed, but presented in a way of 'just getting us to start thinking about these things again' before the exercise is presented.

The exercise is similar to the body psychotherapy work described by Reynolds (2009).

'Choose at random either a part of your body, or an object in the room to think about. Write down on a piece of paper 5 or 6 descriptive words that come into your mind when thinking or looking at this bit of your body, or object. For instance, if I were thinking of my foot I might write, supporting, aching, constrained, tired, squeezed, if I were thinking of the light I might write, bright, dazzling, illuminating, electric, hot. You may well come up with very different words, but the idea is to have some sense of the thing.'

Once people's lists are made then the therapist says *'Look at these words and imagine, if they were describing a person, what this person would look like.'* A basic upside down egg shape is drawn on a flip chart, with the general spacial proportion indicators given for a head looking forwards (i.e. bottom of eyes about half way, ears in line with eyes to base of nose etc.). Participants are asked to draw a face using the aid of the diagram, and using their list of words as a character description. Facial expressions are to be considered, and people are encouraged to change the basic structure by rubbing out or over-working.

Although the idea of creating a face can produce lots of anxiety for some I have found it is achievable, and actually people express enjoying the aspect of 'learning to draw'. The idea of personifying a body part would not be advisable for someone who is psychotic. The psychosis associated with the diagnosis of Borderline Personality disorder is of a different order of that associated with Schizophrenia. It is of the lack of 'as if' of the psychic equivalence mode. As this exercise involves a good deal of 'as if', confusion is the most likely adverse reaction, which a responsive therapist should be able to work through.

Time is given to explore the work, with a reminder of the feedback structure, i.e. keeping to the artwork, respecting how the maker wants to explore it by introduction or asking the group first, and reminding people to speak in terms of 'it reminds me of . . .' or 'it makes me think of . . .', open to different perspectives rather than a definitive meaning.

Session 8: Two faces in relation to each other

Group activity: The group are reminded of the exercise of session seven, but this time are asked; 'pick either two parts of the body, or two random objects in the room. Take one at a time and write a list of their attributes – about 5 or 6 descriptive words.'

The art therapist then shows or draws two faces in profile, like the faces in profile/vase illusion, but asymmetrical and each profile taking on different expressions and characters.

People are invited to comment on the art therapist's drawing, inviting them to develop stories about these two characters. The therapist enquires what people are basing their impressions on, i.e. what about the actual marks is giving them their ideas.

People are then asked to; *'make your own faces, begin with basic profiles, and then using your list of words change the faces to build up characters.'* (30 minutes)

In the discussion of the work careful exploration on how one face relates to another is undertaken. What would this one say to that one, would they speak at all? The maker and then the group can help create this dialogue.

The discussion around these dialogue pictures may well become about the opposing sides of themselves, which are at odds. If people are volunteering this insight into themselves the therapist should value this material to work with, spend some time clarifying the different positions, and if the person is tolerant of their example being viewed, ask the group for different ideas of how the inter-relating may be better.

This exercise is a little like Greenberg's 'two chair exercise' (Greenberg et al. 1993, and Whelton and Greenberg 2005), where a person is encouraged to consider how different parts of themselves react to any given situation, or each other. The drawing exercise however, can remain as a story, or a curiosity. Often with

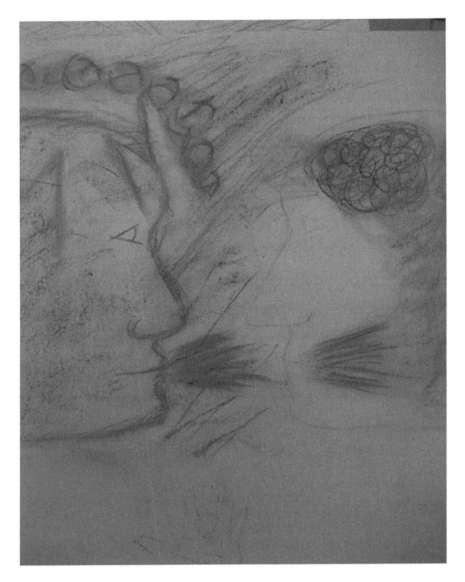

Figure 4.3 Dialogue drawing (also see colour plate section)

this exercise the opposites of the critical self and the criticised self, or the angry and the anxious self will emerge.

People are asked to bring in an object for the next session. This may be an object special to them, or an object where there is a story to tell.

Figure 3.2 The Trauma

Figure 3.4 The Pressure and the Pain

Figure 3.9 The Ramble by the Sea

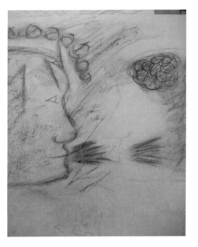

Figure 5.1 Playing between surface and depth

Figure 4.3 Dialogue drawing

Figure 5.2 Navigating the accessible

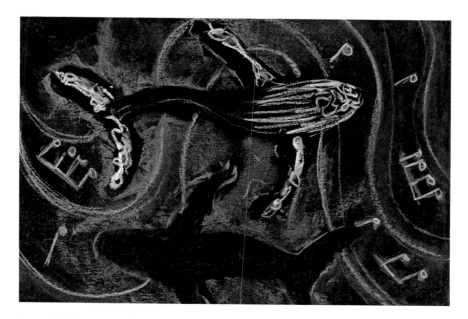

Figure 5.3 Sharing together in the deep

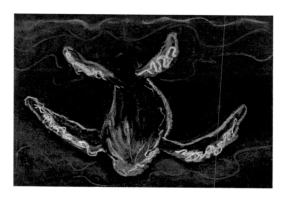

Figure 5.4 Immersed in the deep

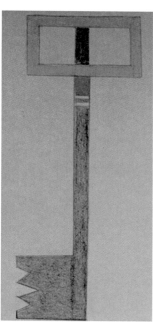

Figure 6.3 Author's diagrammatic representation of how Neil painted his keyblade

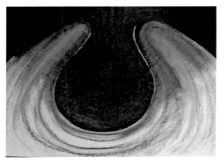 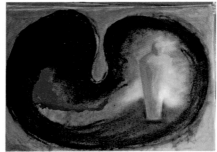

Figures 7.1–7.5 Depression paintings

Figure 9.2 Depression cycle

Figure 9.3 Connecting green and blue

Figure 10.1a My start in life

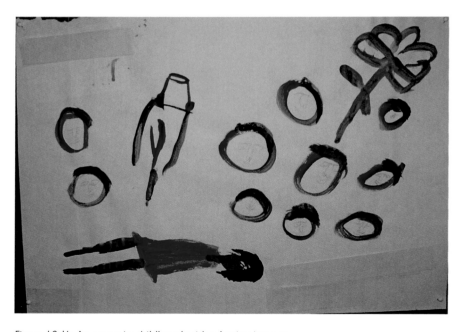

Figure 10.1b An event in childhood with a lasting impact

Figure 10.3a The future I would like

Figure 10.3b Review and a strength

Session 9: Story objects

This session is designed to be consolidating. It may be that the sessions have been very stimulating, and there is a need for space to take stock.

If people have brought in objects then time is given for them to tell their stories. It is likely that the stories relate to positive attachment figures, and/or personal achievements. It could also be that some or all have forgotten to bring in anything. People then are asked if a special object comes to mind. Within conversation, positive attachment, and achievement should be noted. It may be that this discussion takes up all the time, or there may be value in asking people to draw the story of their object before discussion. The story is the important thing in this session, and they should be valued in importance to each person's life. The therapist may be required to pay close attention to keeping the discussion on the objects, and their significance, and giving weight to what feels like genuine openness, and genuine struggles with openness. *Pretend mode* is a term in MBT to mark the decoupling of thought and feeling, inner and outward concerns, that can occur. This is normally felt and understood quite quickly, as the story, and the tone in which it is spoken, not quite ringing true. It takes some skill to get someone in pretend mode to apprehend what others may find curious about the story.

Session 10: 'How the world looks at me'

There is a recap and a review of work. People are asked to think if there are common patterns of relationship they find themselves in. They are asked to consider if relationships always seem to end the same way, or if they often have a similar relationship with authority, or if they recognise a 'default mode' in the way they feel, i.e. always let down, or always judged wrong. If someone volunteers their stance they are thanked for helping the whole group to think about these ingrained presumptions. The discussion should be maintained at a group level where possible, rather than going deeply into an individual's case, and people can be encouraged to put their energies into the artwork.

Group exercise: people are asked to draw, or make in clay, a face. People are asked to consider the face they are drawing, or making in clay, is looking at them. It is to be the face they feel others commonly look at them with, or how they feel the world looks at them.

Within group discussion time is taken to understand the interaction between the maker and their artwork. Explore how the 'look' of the face leaves one feeling. People may speculate at the historic root of their presumption, and how it effects them in the present.

The discussion can be rich in exploration. Does the expression of how the world sees me, lead me to act in a way that it induces the feelings in others? If the sense is of not being believed or taken seriously, how does this lead me to react? Do I stand questioning others, especially nearest and dearest, so that eventually they feel I do not believe them? If I see the world looking at me harshly, do I become aggressively defensive? What reaction does this stance induce? If I feel everyone loves me, what happens if there is evidence to the contrary? Is there a hidden assumption that does not get enacted but which then undermines all honest attempts at feedback?

The work may provide a model of what may go wrong in relationships if clear examples are found available to be worked with. It also can be linked with what may go wrong in therapy, with emphasis that this work may be very useful as a reminder to both patient and therapist of what may go wrong unless they are vigilant.

Figure 4.4 'How the world looks at me' artwork; this example is of a sneering, disbelieving expression

Session 11: Review

The purpose of the last two sessions is to review and to recap, and also to approach any needed topic of discussion that emerges as a priority from the group. This might include self-harm, anxiety, depressive thinking, eating disorders, drug and alcohol use. Obviously an in-depth exploration of any of these areas cannot be performed in the time left. But it may be identified and met as a priority for this group, and some thinking given to how these issues might be worked upon. What should be aimed at is at least one example of how the thoughts and understanding from the exercises, can be linked up. Ideally this should be from the material people have offered about themselves, so that it is possible to form a working formulation with them within these sessions. For example, a person who has illustrated feeling very judged by others, feels very self-critical themselves at times, as well as a resentful sense of injustice at others. This leads them to assumptions that people are not to be trusted, and are out to hurt you, with an internal depressive thinking predisposition to think 'I am useless, I will always fail,' which makes it incredibly hard to have any hope or faith in contact with others, and with therapy. Others may take that stance as mistrust, aloofness, feeling sorry for self, etc. These misinterpretations, in turn, re-enforce the original sense of being judged and seem to verify the depressive thinking, whereas it is based on miscommunication.

Equally someone who adopts a more aggressive stance rather than depressive, may express expectation of being attacked by others, possibly from a bad authority. They themselves may feel a split between caring, or not giving a damn what others feel, leading others to react to them judgementally as bad, or dangerous to know. Attempts should be made to draw the internal experience and the external reaction in order to illustrate what MBT is involved with.

The beginning of the session is purposely left open in the design, in case work from the last session needs more time for discussion. People may want making time for their own ideas stimulated from the work so far. Alternatively people may need consolidation time in the form of a review and open discussion. For this I have had people's folders of work available on a table and hold an open discussion. If anyone has missed sessions the missed exercises can be discussed and even taken up if fitting. Verbal feedback of what people think work well, and not so well is collected and marked. Any points of theory can be restated. Some organisations have developed leaflets on mentalization, emotional regulation, anxiety and depression. These can be useful at this point.

People are told there will be a review, and a chance to feedback what people have found useful and not so useful next session.

People may be anxious to know what happens next. The frame of the review will depend on the host organisation, but this as far as possible should be talked through. The next session will be a continuation of this session.

Twelfth (final) session: Summary and conclusion

The group is open to work on unfinished work, or make suggestions for an exercise. The group themselves may have an idea for how they would like to work together, be it possibly from a choice given by the therapist (see session 6). Attempts of drawing together internal experience and external reaction should continue. It is key as an introduction to further therapy, to mark the idea of not knowing, rather than fixed assumptions (of what others think of me, or what I always do). State the importance of being open, flexible and curious.

The conversation is directed to gaining feedback about what people have found useful, or difficult/unhelpful.

A final feedback questionnaire, and outcome questionnaires given/collected.

Final thoughts

This programme of work may seem a far cry from what has come to be known as art therapy. Certainly when I left my training full of the anxieties that I might be asked to explain what art therapy is, I knew what it was not was art teaching, and it was not the psychological test that people might expect. At that time I would have seen this programme as the antithesis of art therapy. However, it does not have to be 'either this way or that way'. Room has to be made for research and different ways of working.

It also comes with the challenge of building into practice something time-limited, researchable and focused. I hope it is something that can be repeated, and refined, and even enjoyed.

Areas of focus in this 12-week introductory programme are;

- Body sensation awareness.
- Encapsulating life awareness and problems.
- Exercising expressive mark making to represent emotion.
- Practising giving the inanimate an expressive persona.
- Outwardly representing internal relating.
- Depicting basic affective assumptions.
- Retaining own mind while relating to perspectives of others (discussion).
- Exploring tensions between self and other relating (group work).

As I have said, the initial outcomes are positive. If you are considering implementing this within you own practice and wish for further information, resources and advice, please contact me on david.thorne@beh-mht.nhs.uk or through the BAAT directory.

References

BAAT Survey (2007–8) www.baat.org/art_therapy.html
Bateman, A., and Fonagy, P. (2004) *Psychotherapy for Borderline Personality Disorder – Mentalization based treatment*. Oxford: Oxford University Press.

Bateman, A., and Fonagy, P. (2009) 'Randomized Controlled Trial of Outpatient Mentalization-Based Treatment Versus Structured Clinical Management for Borderline Personality Disorder', *American Journal of Psychiatry* 166: 1355–1364.

Bollas, C. (1996) 'Borderline Desire', *International Forum of Psychoanalysis* 5: 5–9 Para 10.

Choi-Kain, L., and Gunderson, J. (2008) 'Mentalization; Ontogeny, Assessment, and Application in the Treatment of Borderline Personality Disorder', *American Journal of Psychiatry* 165: 1127–1135.

Edwards, B. (1988) *Drawing on the Artist Within.* Harper Collins.

Franks, M. and Whitaker, R. (2007) 'The Image, Mentalisation and Group Art Psychotherapy', *International Journal of Art Therapy* 12(1): 3–16. Abingdon, Oxford: Routledge, Taylor and Francis Group.

Fonagy, P. (2001) 'The Psychoanalysis of Violence', *Dallas Society for Psychoanalytic Psychology.*

Gilbert, P. (2012) Attachment and the Arts Conference on 'Compassion and the Image'. His talk – Compassion and Fear of Affiliative Emotions.

Greenburg, L. S., Rice, L. N., and Elliott, R. (1993) *Facilitating Emotional Change: The moment-by-moment process.* New York: Guilford Press.

Greenwood, H. (2000) 'Captivity and Terror in the Therapuetic Relationship', *Inscape* 5(2) 56–61.

Hughes, T. (1978) *'Cave Birds, an alchemical Cave Drama' beginning of poem – A flayed crow in the hall of judgement.* New York: The Viking Press.

Johns, S., and Karterud, S. (2004) 'Guidelines for Art Group Therapy as Part of a Day Treatment for Patients with Personality Disorders', *Group Analysis* 37(3): 419–430.

Karterud, S., and Bateman, A. (2011) 'Manual for Mentalization-based Psycho-educational Group Therapy, MBT-i,. Locally available, as yet unpublished.

Karterud, S., and Pederson, G. (2004) 'Short Term Day Treatment for Patients with Personality Disorders: Benefits of the Therapeutic Components', *Therapeutic Communities* 25(1): 43–54.

Karterud, S., and Umes, O. (2004) 'Short Term Day Treatment Programmes for Patients with Personality Disorders', *Nordic Journal of Psychiatry* 243–249.

Kristeva, J. (1989) 'Black Sun: Depression and Melancholia' pg 87 2nd para. Columbia University Press 1989. Translated by Leon S. Rondiez, New York: Columbia.

Lamont, S., Bunero, S., and Sutton, D. (2009) 'Art Psychotherapy in a Consumer Diagnosed with Borderline Personality Disorder: A Case Study', *International Journal of Mental Health Nursing* 18(3, June): 164–172.

Learmonth, M. (2005–15) 'Articulating Art Therapy' Workshop Presentation. www.insiderart.org.uk

Meares, R. A., Hobson, R. F. (1977) 'The Persecutory Therapist', *British Journal of Medical Psychology* 50: 349–359. (As quoted in NICE guidelines 2009).

Mottram, P. (2001/02) 'Research into the Skills and Interventions Used by British Art Therapists in their Work with Clients Images', *International Arts Therapies Journal* 1–12.

National Institute for Health and Clinical Excellence (2009) Borderline Personality Disorder Treatment and Management. National Collaborating Centre for Mental Health. Royal College of Psychiatrists, British Psychological Society, RC Psych Publications. www.rcpsych.ac.uk/nice

PDSIG (2012) 'Professional Consensus Clinical Guidelines', *International Journal of Art Therapy* 17, 130–134 (3, November).

Reynolds, A. (2009) 'Chapter 3 Gestalt Body Psychotherapy', in *Contemporary Body Psychotherapy: The Chiron Approach.* Oxford: Routledge.

Silverman, D. (1991) 'Art Psychotherapy: An approach to borderline adults', chapter in Landgarten, Lubber (Eds.) *Adult Art Psychotherapy*. Bruno-Routledge.

Springham, N., Findlay, D., Woods, A., and Harris, J. (2012) 'How Can Art Therapy Contribute to Mentalization in Borderline Personality Disorder?' *International Journal of Art Therapy* 17(3, November): 115–129.

Whelton, W. J. & Greenberg, L. S. (2005). Emotion in self-criticism. *Personality and Individual Differences, 38,* 1583–1595.

Winnicott (1971) *Playing and Reality* London: Tavistock.

World Health Organisation (1992) *International Classification of Diseases* (10th ed.). Geneva.

Chapter 5

Brief solution focused therapy techniques in assessment, treatment and review of art psychotherapy

Michael Atkins

Introduction

In this chapter I will describe the process of my integration and appreciation of solution focused therapy in the practice of art psychotherapy. Brief Solution Focused Therapy (BSFT) was created in Milwaukee, Wisconsin, USA, in the 1980s by a group of family therapists led by husband and wife Steve de Shazer and Insoo Kim Berg. Whilst developing ideas about brief therapies they became particularly interested in what clients reported to have been helpful. Building on their pioneering work I will describe how I use solution focused interventions in my clinical practice as an art psychotherapist, outline key elements of the model, and give examples of their use in clinical sessions. I will expand the theme to include its use in other contexts relevant to art psychotherapists such as supervision and professionals meetings. I will consider some of the issues art psychotherapists face when adopting a new therapeutic model; and the process by which a new approach becomes part of a clinician's expertise.

Solution focused therapy, for instance, is deceptively simple to grasp. Without recourse to extensive theoretical knowledge a therapist can learn the basic skills over a two-day introductory course. Once the practitioner is familiar with the approach it is relatively easy to consolidate and deepen one's practice through reading and practice based observation. Saying this should not suggest it is quite so easy to practice effectively. Though a semi-structured approach, the techniques still require the foundation of a good working relationship between client and therapist. For art psychotherapists BSFT might seem utterly alien: to the theoretical and experiential knowledge the clinician already possesses and the scripted quality may feel awkward and incompatible with the therapist's personal style. I was no exception. I aim to describe how I became familiar with the approach, offer suggestions as to how others might do so, and similarly find it a useful approach in the time pressured resources of present services. I have found a solution focused approach an invaluable asset. It has given me a structured tool to use in assessment for treatment that has benefits even when art psychotherapy is not the preferred treatment outcome. Additionally it begins a process of evaluating treatment options in terms the client understands and finds meaningful. In turn BSFT's clarity can be used to describe therapeutic goals and reasonable expectations for outcomes to others, for example in a multidisciplinary team, or family meeting using language that is both client friendly and jargon free. It can helpfully describe *what* we do; while *how* we do it might reasonably use the language and theory associated with art psychotherapy.

I will talk about working with clients from the perspective of a Child and Adolescent Mental Health Service (CAMHS) art psychotherapist. Not only is this is my area of expertise but it is also a field where there are a wide number of factors impacting on clinical work. The age range of my clients ranges from around six years of age to 18. Clients referred to art psychotherapy in my service commonly have longstanding emotional problems associated with emotional, sexual, and physical abuse, domestic violence, and neglect as well as psychiatric disorders such as Attention Deficit Hyperactivity Disorder (ADHD), Anxiety, Depression, and mild Autistic Spectrum Disorder. Their presentation is commonly a complex one, with attachment issues, possible developmental and learning needs as well as stresses like bullying, all simultaneously impacting on the child or young person's presentation. Self-harming is not uncommon, nor is the (non-psychotic) hearing of voices or the taking of overdoses. Art psychotherapy referrals are often made to assist the broader multidisciplinary team gaining greater insight into a child or young person.

Younger children frequently attend with members of their family. These may be families of origin, adoptive, or foster families, while some young people are placed in residential units away from home. There are commonly other agencies involved, and negotiating safeguarding issues with the need for confidentiality is a regular challenge. Therefore the ability to communicate with and understand a range of individuals, of different ages, professional backgrounds, and with different expectations and experiences (not infrequently all present in the same meeting) is essential. Examples might be multiagency meetings, clinical review meetings, and professionals meetings. In my experience a solution focused approach offers a flexible, adaptable, and straightforward means of doing this successfully.

I became involved in solution focused therapy for quite pragmatic reasons. The Trust I work for introduced a target of seven weeks from receipt of referral to treatment. As solution focused therapy is seen as a treatment from the outset, our CAMHS introduced a solution focused clinic for all new appointments. This meant no triaging and no assessment with a hidden wait for treatment. Needless to say the reality is somewhat more complicated than it might appear. There is inevitably a need to be alert to risk and risk management, and assessment is an integral part of a therapist's thinking whatever their approach. The new target also brought a degree of urgency and necessary reorganisation. I volunteered to be part of the new approach, which meant I would establish a generic caseload. I had some experience of general CAMHS case work from a previous post and additionally felt it would be a useful opportunity to work more closely with colleagues from a number of different disciplines.

As this was a new way of working for the majority of the staff involved we embarked in some BSFT introductory training, which concentrated on experiential learning. This was in-house training, led by a clinician experienced in working in the solution focused approach. A common technique was to role play in a small group of three; a 'therapist', a 'client', and an 'observer'. This kind of learning is particularly useful because it gives the 'therapist' confidence in the strange new types of questions, and the 'client' discovers that it feels surprisingly positive being asked these questions while being listened and responded to in the solution focused way. The group takes turns at each role. The 'observer' feeds back and asks further questions of both parties. The 'observer' also does this in a solution focused way. An ice breaking start to such training might be for the 'therapist' to ask, 'Tell me something you enjoyed about your journey to work today.' Note that there is an expectation that there is something positive to bring to mind. In addition we were supported with our clinical cases through observed practice using the family therapy 'screen' (a one-way mirrored window) and close support from the colleagues behind it. Initially this felt very exposing and quite uncomfortable. I remember finding it very off-putting to see my own reflection in the screen, and deliberately arranged seating so I could avoid this. It was an opportunity to reflect on how awkward therapy might feel for the clients, and how comfortable I usually felt in my art psychotherapy studio. There was a shared commitment to the model by all involved and, as we each took turns in being observed, it soon felt supportive rather than uncomfortable. During the training phase we regularly took a break, a feature of the model, and left the therapy room to discus with colleagues behind the screen. This helped us stay on task, and prepare feedback for the closing stage of the session whilst also building an open sense of collaborative working.

Our supervision was solution focused as well. This helped promote a modelling of the behaviour we hoped our clients would adopt. I found the emphasis on what had gone well rather than what had gone 'wrong' challenging. I began to see that I was very good at seeing faults (particularly in other people) and less practiced in noticing successes. Noticing positive changes is a good skill to develop especially in solution focused work. After a few months of clinical experience I attended two days training run by BRIEF, which was both enjoyable and rewarding. Significantly, as my experience grew and I became more confident in being solution focused, I increasingly enjoyed the work and the positive results reported by my clients.

The solution focused therapy approach does not usually provide a time-*limited* framework from the outset; but it does enable a time *sensitive* approach and is usually brief. As you will see the model tries to elicit an image of what the end might be like right from the beginning of therapy; and the model then encourages a regular checking of progress towards this client-identified goal. With this in place it is possible to identify the time for ending as it arises.

This brief description inevitably simplifies the process as it is likely to play out in practice, but I hope it gives the reader a suggestion of what to look out for and how it utilises time as a tool towards specific aims and with an explicit use of time's utility and containment. In my practice art psychotherapy usually lasts for between 4–30 sessions.

Before I explore the model in detail, I would like to explain the images that accompany the text. They arose when I was invited to talk about being an art psychotherapist who used a solution focused approach to a local solution focused therapy network group. This subject was something of a novelty for the audience, and I felt they would naturally expect images with my presentation. I thought about the models of working and these images emerged. The ocean readily appeared as an image of 'depth' and the Unconscious. I likened myself, in my art psychotherapy role, to the humpback whale seen in Figure 5.1, which, I believe, is a fairly sociable creature that cares for its young, enjoys playing, singing, and being curious. They travel great distances and dive into and are immersed in the 'depths'. In my solution focused role I saw myself sailing a small boat, seen in Figure 5.2 across the deep ocean (surface, not depth now), but still connected. The boat could move by my will (be directed), or go with the flow of sea and wind. The boat would take me to new uncharted islands that I would need to explore cautiously and with curiosity, as, for example, I would not know the local customs or language. I believe the curiosity of the humpback whale might make it intrigued by the little boat above it. I will return to these images as the chapter proceeds.

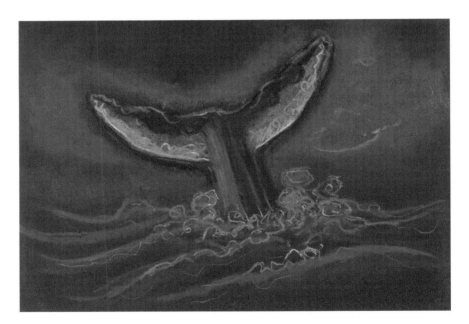

Figure 5.1 Playing between surface and depth (also see colour plate section)

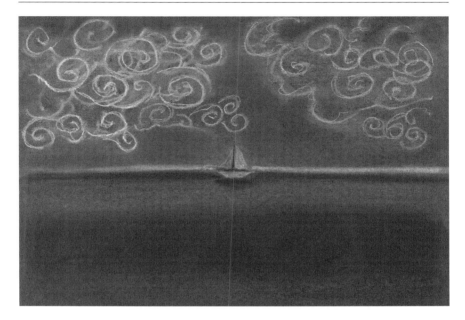

Figure 5.2 Navigating the accessible (also see colour plate section)

At the close of the chapter I will briefly discuss how the approach might inform supervision, professionals meetings, and provide evaluation material for outcome measures.

Key features

The key features of the solution focused approach that I find helpful are: problem free talk, best hopes, using scales, the miracle question, giving feedback, and a 'non-expert' position by the clinician. I will describe each of these in turn and consider how they contribute to actual clinical work followed by the model's use in reviewing and ending work with clients.

There are particular kinds of questions that are used regularly in solution focused work; questions that ask for more information: 'what else?' questions, questions about the *difference* something makes, questions about what someone might do *instead* of something else, questions exploring exceptions to the rule of the problem. We might imagine the arrival of a boat on an inhabited island. In therapeutic work, this might be first meetings with client and family. A solution focused approach orients itself around the *exceptions* to the rule of the problem; times when the problem is *not* in evidence, perhaps this is where the ship's compass would point.

I hope the descriptions and explanations along the way are sufficient to enable therapists and clinicians amongst the readership to try the method out; if like me, you can see the usefulness of the approach. In addition I hope it becomes evident how the approach lends itself to an efficient, time sensitive model of working, by frequent checking on progress towards clear goals. I would add that there are excellent books (listed in the bibliography) that explore the history and practice in much greater depth and detail than I am able to here and are well worth reading.

Problem free talk

When meeting a client and their family for the first time I will introduce myself, ask who they all are, ask if they mind if I take notes and then ask if they would each mind telling me a little bit about themselves. I say that they are new to me and I don't know a lot about them. I say I would like to know what they are good at and what they like doing. I like to take notes as we go along, as actual quotes are very useful. It helps the client feel heard by the therapist and the particular meaning of what they say is really important, as we will see. One thing that is very much part of the approach is 'checking things out' with the client, e.g. 'Is it ok if I take notes?' 'I hope it's OK to ask . . .', 'Would you mind if I checked what your mum thinks about that?'

> 'Hello, my name is Michael Atkins, I am an art psychotherapist. I think we are all here to talk about art therapy for John.'

I make a visual check for nods or looks of puzzlement.

> 'As we have never met before I would find it really helpful to learn a little about each of you; in particular things you are good at and things you enjoy.'

Often there are glances between family members.

> 'Who would like to go first?' Pause, 'John, who do you think should start?'

I try to engage with my named client and give him some choices and a voice, with children this really helps to establish the idea that their voice and views are important.

When hearing about things they like doing and things they are good at, I try to maintain a positive focus. Negative views or 'problems' are either gently left aside or noted to be returned to later on. I will be explicit about this and often write things down to one side of the paper. It is good to have a clear focus as it shows that you can manage your own objectives and *how* you do it shows the family something of your personality. The message might be 'problems aren't the only thing I am interested in; other things are important about you too'. However it is important not to impose the structure on a client; and clients do sometimes have a pressing need to start with what is troubling them. When this happens the important thing is to hear what they need to tell you. In practice one can return to find out more of their strengths at a later point.

The substance of problem free talk gives us lots of information that may be helpful later. I am keen to note examples of problem solving, overcoming frustration, determination, and humour. Each person gets a turn, and I stick to both parts of the question: some people don't feel they are good at anything they do, but have plenty of things they enjoy. Others are good at things they don't enjoy. All answers provide interesting opportunities to develop there and then or at a later date, at a review for instance. If someone gets really stuck I might ask what they think their best friend would say if I were to ask them. 'If Mark were here what do you think he'd say?'

Another key element to solution focused approach is asking 'What else?' and repeating this question. Initially it can seem awkward, as it can feel a bit intrusive and socially incongruent, but experience confirms it reaps rewards. If it is driven by genuine curiosity it comes across more naturally. 'What else do you like doing?', 'What else are you good at?' There is an assumption that there will be something, even if it is not immediately brought to mind.

Problem free talk is really good for breaking the ice and establishing a framework for therapy. Problem free talk might take up quite a lot of a session, and it is important not to forget the client is here for something important. Very often the problem free talk starts to drift towards the problems and it can be a useful cue to say, 'This seems to lead me to my next question for you all: what are your best hopes for coming here today?' Or 'Thanks for all those answers, I really appreciate how much effort you put in to thinking about the questions. However, I know you are here for a reason, which brings me to my next question to each of you: What are your best hopes for coming to art psychotherapy?'

Best hopes for art therapy (aims and goals)

What does the client and family want? This is another way of saying 'what brings you here?' or 'what ails?' However, it is deliberately asked in this way to make the client think about the future. The solution focused approach is future oriented: it is interested in what people want to be different and what it will look like *when* they get there. Once again, I will ask everyone their view, and tell them that they do not all have to agree and it is not my intention to try to make them. The referrer, the school, the social worker, grandparents, even the family dog may have a best hope and it is sometimes very valuable to ask the client what they think this is. Never more so than when the family's best hopes seem initially quite incompatible with art therapy.

> 'I think Dr Jones would want to know more about what sets John off being aggressive, or what makes him unhappy, as John doesn't seem to know: or won't tell us, anyway.'

I think this kind of preamble to establishing a contract is of great benefit. We gain a number of potentially different views about 'the problem' and the therapist can establish a position in relation to these views but not necessarily wedded to any of them. One can say what one is comfortable to agreeing to, which might be a bit vague to start with; spending time with John to develop a relationship and see what comes up, for example. Sometimes it happens that we discover at this stage a real mismatch between what the family was expecting and what the art psychotherapist feels is realistic. Better to find out now. The meeting can still be of benefit as we can ask more about what the family does want. There is a slight shift of role here, as the art therapist does exercise their expert position in terms of realistic goals for art psychotherapist. Just as the family can be considered the experts on their family, the art therapist occupies an expert role in relation to therapy.

I will usually suggest that it is good to have an idea what everyone at the BSFT assessment wants at the start and that we will check out progress towards these goals as we proceed. To help with this I routinely use another solution focus standard: a scale question. At first I will try to establish where we are right now.

Scales

I like to ask: 'How are things?' I say, 'I would like you to be really honest and not just say 'fine' as we may do in everyday life. Imagine all the numbers between 0 and 10. Zero would be things at their worst, whenever that was (implying it is now past) and 10 is things being fine or ok. Where are you at the moment?' I never cease to be surprised at how readily people answer this question sincerely with this kind of permission to rate their feelings and experience.

Scales let us know quickly how the family sees their situation; but it does not require us to know all about it, in the sense of taking a history. I would ask 'what makes it a 4?' and again ask '*what else* tells you that things are a 4?' Scales are also visual, and I often use a smiley face for 10 and a sad face for 1 when asking younger children. I find actively involving them brings them on board. Even quite small children get the idea.

Scales form an easy reference point to check in with clients and get a feel for change as therapy progresses. Scales also form a record of this progress becoming a useful evaluation tool. 'How are things today?' I may ask at the beginning of each session. 'Six', might be all I get in reply. 'Better than last time; what happened?' 'I've been arguing less with dad this week.' The questions might keep coming while the client is happy to answer. They might not want to talk, but I still have an idea where they are: the same, better, or worse than the previous time I asked. If they show a significant deterioration we might just have to jump in and find out more. One client chose to name a self-harming scale 'Dave' so I could check in with, 'How's "Dave" this week?' Her reply could be very brief and lead to no discussion at all, or could invite more questions. We had worked out quite an elaborate scoring for 0–10. Neither of us could quite remember it in detail, the ensuing muddle was a creative part of our working alliance. It humanised it.

A scale might help us think about a concern, rather than react to it. It can help us start to organise our thoughts. I tend to think out loud with clients, so muddling through a false start can be helpful in that the client knows I am at least trying to be useful. Scales are meaningful to the client, even if the therapist does not really know what the significance is; it may not matter at all to the outcome. If I really am struggling and the scale is not improving I may plead ignorance and ask the client to explain how they see things progressing, or otherwise.

If the scale shows things are getting worse we may ask different questions. For example,

'I'm sorry to hear "things" are getting worse, I wonder why that is?'
'Well, last Tuesday I fell out with Kelly on Facebook and she started a rumour at school.'
'I know Kelly is your best friend, so that must have upset you. How did it make you feel at the time?'
'Really bad, I thought about cutting, which I haven't done for weeks.'
'Yes, I know, you've done really well. You said you had "thought" about cutting; did you cut?'
'No.'
'I'm curious now; can I ask why not? What stopped you?'
'Well, dad would be disappointed.'
'Ok, so what did you do instead?'
'I went and ate a load of biscuits!'
'I guess that's better than cutting!'

In this exchange we can see curiosity, empathy, positive feedback, checking things out, attention to detail, and an interest in what someone did, not just how they felt.

Another example:

'I am really shocked that things have got so bad since last week. What made them drop from a 5 to a 2?'
'My girlfriend dumped me.'
'Oh no! That sounds really upsetting. How are you doing just now?'
'I am really thinking about hurting myself again, I just don't see the point anymore.'
'Yes, I guess I can see why.' (Pause).
'You know you said "things" were a 2, can I ask how come they didn't reach a 1 or 0?'
'I don't know. Mum knows, so she is watching me all the time, and my friend Ryan has been texting me a lot. I know it would hurt them if I did anything.'
'Yes.' (Pause)
'What else stops things being worse?'
'Last time, when I ended up in hospital, it was horrible and I don't want to go through that again.'

So, having discovered some protective factors we might ask.

'What needs to happen for "things" to move up a point?'
'I don't know.' (Pause). 'I don't know, maybe distracting myself and not being on my own at home all the time. That helped before. I spent more time playing football and being at Ryan's on his Xbox.'

Of course, if the risk being discussed requires a management plan that takes precedence. That is always an option in the back of the therapist's mind, but here the client is coming up with a plan on their own and the therapist might just need to encourage some detail in exactly how or who is going to do what. The focus is on action rather than inner experience. Once the plan is established it is possible to revisit the emotion. If the conversation emerged from an image I would be leaping back into my little sail boat magically transforming from the humpback whale self to become the solution focused captain of the ship. But the conversation might have been quite a different one, about the image itself, and then we might consider two humpback whales singing to one another, sharing communication from their mutually immersive experience as in Figure 5.3.

We have seen that asking about best hopes gives us information about where the client wants to be, which a solution focused approach calls the 'preferred future'. Additionally, the use of scales gives a sense of where they are in relation to that. If the best hopes and scales are not providing the detail and descriptions I am after then I may try another approach and ask what is known as the 'miracle question'.

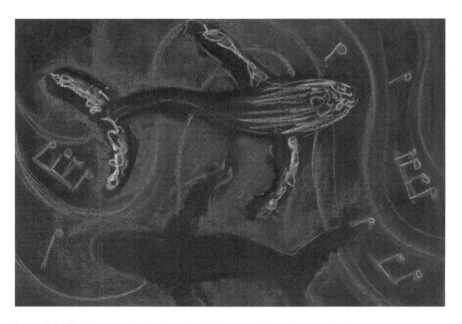

Figure 5.3 Sharing together in the deep (also see colour plate section)

Miracle question

This classic solution focused way of asking about the preferred future is established like this:

> 'Imagine that while you are all asleep tonight a miracle occurs and all the things you want to be different are fixed and just how you want them to be. As you were asleep when it happened you don't know until you wake up that anything has changed. What are the very first things you notice which tell you things are different?'

This can take a while, and may need prompts about observable behaviours or actions, rather than feelings as such. For instance someone may say they will feel happier. As we know, a solution focused approach needs detail about behaviour and action that is concrete and observable.

> 'When you are feeling "happier" what do other people notice about you that lets them know it too? What do you do?'
> 'I am smiling and sing when I'm in the shower.'

This gives a clear indication of what this person will be doing when they feel happier. Mum says,

> 'You were singing that Rihanna song in the shower last weekend; did that mean you were happy last Sunday?'
> 'Mmm, I guess I was.'

Therapist notes an exception and asks,

> 'What was going on last Sunday?'
> 'I was feeling good because I wasn't at school, and Beth was coming over.'

So now we have a clue about school and that Beth might be a good influence. As you can see the conversation could open up in lots of directions. Beth is a more positive one so I might follow that rather than school, at first anyway.

Preferred future

Another way to find out about the client's preferred future is to ask about the scale we established at the first meeting: 'things'. One could ask about this in a number of ways. If the score is a low one, that is 'things' are pretty bad, we might concentrate on how someone is staying at a '3'. What is stopping it from being worse? Alternatively we could ask, 'What needs to happen for you to move one point up the scale to a 4?' Again we need concrete and observable details. Another approach is to ask if the person can imagine what a '10' is like? Has this ever actually happened? If it has we can be increasingly confident that it is a realistic aim. I sometimes ask. 'Have you ever been at a 10? When was that and what was happening?' If they have, it is very likely that they have a wealth of detail about the experience, which will help. If not they still might be able to imagine it in detail.

It is also worth checking what would be 'good enough' on a scale as people sometimes see 10 as an unreachable ideal. If they would be happy with an 8 or 9 our distance to a satisfactory outcome just got shorter. Frequently on our 'things' scale I am surprised by how individuals interpret the idea of 'OK or fine'. Some will assume 10/10 is the goal but others see it as an ideal and are happy to accept a lower score, as 10/10 is unrealistic.

Imagination, art therapy, and solution focused therapy

Imagination is central to the solution focused approach. I think art psychotherapists might consider how our ability to help another person imagine is part of our expertise. Our skills at enabling playfulness and creativity can be of great benefit to the client, who may be struggling to articulate what they want. For a solution to be found it has to be imagined first and art allows imaginings to emerge and be held. Once it has been expressed families can be on the lookout for times when it happens. These times; when the 'problem' is not in charge, are 'exceptions' and are gold dust for solution focused work. We can ask for increasing detail about what happened on the occasions where something happened 'instead' of the problem. As art psychotherapists our creative skills can be put to good use in navigating the choppy waters, hidden reefs, rapids, and other challenges our client will present with. A solution focused approach is not a manualised one; I hope I have conveyed the potential benefits of the approach without insisting either we do it 'by the book' or that our existing therapeutic talents will not be of great value.

If the best hopes and art psychotherapy contract aims are compatible an initial contract is agreed. I usually offer four sessions then a review.

Feedback

Offering feedback is a feature of solution focused work. The art, I suggest, is for it to be truthful. If there are signs of warmth, empathy, shared concern within a family it is easy to say one had observed this. If there are examples of people managing difficulties successfully, finding their own solutions again it is quite easy, one only has to be able to remember the event described. When it gets harder one might need to reflect this also, in a positive way.

> 'I really think it was hard for you to come here today, and I really appreciate that you stayed with us and answered so many of my annoying questions.'
> 'I think you did really well not to leave the room when things got tough earlier.'

'I think you are all under a huge amount of stress and just coming here today shows you want things to be different.'

I offer feedback as I go along, especially with younger children as it is helpful to comment on positives when one sees them. I frequently sum up a review meeting with positive feedback. In my experience if the feedback fits it is well received. I am wary of offering reassurance, although there are times when one can do this confidently, for instance.

'I am glad you have told me these difficult things today, and yes, we are the right people to talk to about them.'

Non-expert position

When working in a solution focused way we assume we do not necessarily know what is wrong, or what will make it right. Instead we ask the client and are guided by them, as far as it is possible. A successful outcome is surely one in which the client is reporting they have achieved their best hopes at a level they are happy with. They may not be 10/10, but at their 'good enough' score on our 'things' scale. This does not mean we disengage our usual therapeutic practice with its experience and theoretical underpinning. This process is still working and informing our thinking. One illustration of this is when the client is giving us non-verbal clues of being unengaged, by sitting with their back to us or not lifting their head. We might experience an emotional response to this in ourselves such as annoyance or anger and recognise the possibility that this may also be how our client is feeling (transference/countertransference). Our response might be to say,

'I get the feeling I have messed up here and have annoyed you. I am sorry about that; I did not intend to frustrate you. I'm not really sure what I said that started things going wrong but I would really like to know, so I don't repeat the mistake.'

Solution focused therapists take responsibility for therapy not going well, to encourage reflection. I hope this example shows how our experience can inform and shape the way we use the solution focus approach. We are acknowledging something is wrong, being curious about it and taking responsibility for any mistakes. Successfully repairing such breaks in the therapeutic alliance are great opportunities to re-engage the client more fully.

Reviews

The review might begin the way the second solution focused session would start, with a bold question. 'What's been better since we last met?' If we do not ask we may not find out. It is surprising how often there is something, however small, that has been better. Once again there is an assumption about change, particularly positive change. The other starting point is to revisit a scale from the initial meeting and/or the client and family's best hopes. Ideally there will be some shift in the right direction for at least one of the people present. But it is equally possible to work with things going the other way.

While this may be frustrating or disappointing to all parties, using the solution focused approach one can explore the situation in a constructive way. In these situations we may find we are working from a more negative standpoint rather than a positive one. Things have not gone well, we need to ask about what contributed to this, but on hearing what is wrong we might ask what might have been a better alternative or what people might have done *instead* of what they actually did.

Case example: Art making as reflective space

'OK, so you got frustrated with me asking questions all the time, what could I have done instead that would have worked better for you?'

'Just left me to paint for a while before asking me stuff.'

'Alright, I'm glad you have told me that; I can easily do that. How will I know when it's ok to ask stuff?'

'I'll tell you.'

'Great! I like it that you'll tell me, it makes my task easier. Can I ask, what difference doing things this way will make to you?'

'I will get a chance to calm down after school and be less stressed.'

'I see, and what difference will *that* make?'

'I don't know, maybe some of the sad feelings will come instead of just the angry ones.'

Here we can see some checking out, some positive feedback, asking an 'instead' question, asking what difference something will make and asking this again like our 'what else?' question. The questions will only work successfully if there is a working alliance, there needs to be a relationship in which these conversations can take place.

I have seen the benefits of art making as a reflective process. With Gabrielle, a 16-year-old young woman experiencing low mood and regularly self-harming to manage her distress, I was impressed by how she could use even a short period of making or painting to get in touch with her emotions. After a conversation about how 'things' were, or about how she was managing her stress she would regularly turn to materials and become involved in activity. I soon learnt to simply be quiet and wait. Sometimes her efforts would be half-hearted and she would appear slightly distant; at odds with her work. Other times vigorously engaged, full of energy and commitment. Then she would speak. She might tell me how unhappy she was or how angry, or how let down and hopeless. Watching her it seemed she entered a reverie while rather aimlessly letting her hands be occupied, or she channelled her energies into something that revealed itself through the image. Either way, something new emerged through the process, which she then found no difficulty in articulating verbally. Interestingly the images often had more to say, if given the chance. They held other elements of her life, offered alternative perspectives or completely un-thought of possibilities. With Gabrielle, art making and a solution focused approach complemented each other.

Things, however, do not always go to plan. After all, the creative process necessitates times when creative projects fail and mistakes occur. I rely on it. Sooner or later something goes adrift, is forgotten, or otherwise presents the therapist as fallible, or therapy as place where difficult things happen too. So starting the session by asking about what has been better invites trouble! We do not express surprise or indeed disappointment if we are told that nothing has changed, but we will be delighted if something is reported to be better. It is an interesting way to start a conversation. When something is different we can ask, 'How did that come about?' or 'What made that happen?' or 'How did you do that?' Not forgetting: 'What else helped this take place?' or 'What else did you do to keep the peace?' or 'What else stopped you from shouting and throwing the remote?' Once we are on the right track we will find observable details that are significant to the client, but may surprise us. Being surprised reminds me that I really did not know what was right for this client.

Time-sensitive considerations

At the first review we have to agree one of three options: carry on as we are, stop altogether, or do something different. If no agreement is reached in the allotted time I will often suggest we simply meet the following week to continue talking it through. At the review we start to look in more detail at those original best hopes. Very often the process is one of refining the hopes from the general to more specific, and observable, goals. If the initial best hope had been for the client to be 'happier', I would now start to ask about what that would actually be like, what people would notice, and so on. The details help us be clearer about progress, and increase the chance of exceptions being noted by the family.

The review is a testing ground for how the family is getting along, and how the client is able to communicate within the family: do they feel heard? Do they even want to be? Can I share my knowledge of being with the client in a way that facilitates greater understanding and better communication? My experience with a client can often lead to a parent feeling validated in their experience: 'Oh, so you get that too!' I would usually prepare the client in advance by asking them what they are happy for me to share, or not. I try to be directed by them, safeguarding and confidentiality issues aside. Checking things out is a very empowering act. I will also bring this openly into the review if it seems helpful; by saying I have discussed with my client and have been asked not to talk about some things. The client gets to see I meant it, and the issue of things not being talked about is now in the room for consideration.

Reviews are planned at negotiated intervals with the understanding that any one of us (parent, carer, referrer, and therapist) could request one at any time, which is preferable to inappropriate conversations in the waiting area. Reviews also help to structure the goals and time frames for the remaining therapy sessions.

With regards to input from the therapist in reviews, it makes sense to switch between being an 'expert' art psychotherapist and being solution focused about the session. As a therapist one does have an opinion, so it is important to share that, and it may be that the therapist is the one who decides to end work, if, in their opinion there is nothing more to be gained. This is discussed openly and empathically with clear explanations.

I have found that it has helped me be clear with clients if I have gained good information from them about what they want to be different. After all, establishing what is realistic and achievable from the client's point of view has been on-going and it should now be possible to discuss this in straightforward terms. Their best hopes versus what they have actually experienced. Is it good enough? The therapist should have a realistic view of what therapy can achieve. To me this is being congruent. I will often say 'I don't know' if I can help at the beginning. Once a therapeutic alliance is established it will become more possible to know. Being realistic and clear is always of benefit in my view, even if it means saying one cannot help. The client may not like it but they can begin to address it. We can't fix everything, and maybe their original best hope was unrealistic and needed to be modified towards something more achievable. In this sense turning people down for therapy can be a good thing. The point I hope to stress is how useful the solution focused approach is to working with these challenges, either because therapy does continue with more appropriate goals or it does not but something helpful comes from the conversation.

Ending

Once the agreed goals from our best hopes are met, or the client is reaching a 'good enough' score on their scale of 'things' it is certainly time to consider if this is enough. Usually this is discussed in a review and if the decision to end is made there is normally an agreed winding down period of not more than four attended sessions. I prefer this to offering four weeks because if sessions are missed it spoils the planned end, and renegotiating confuses things somewhat. Alternatively, the scales may indicate that no progress is being made and art psychotherapy is not considered to be helping. That situation can be explored as we have seen.

It is not uncommon for art psychotherapy cases that began with individual work to increasingly involve other family members through reviews. This is most frequent with the younger age group; as the young person feels increasingly confident that their voice will be heard. It is a healthy development that the family is able to talk about their problems together, and for me, a sign that it may be time for a change in how therapeutic work is delivered. Using a solution focused approach it is possible to build on the established alliance with the client to work with the whole family together.

Observation about clinical practice

There are times when a psychodynamic approach is the right one and times when a solution focused approach makes sense. I mean times *within* a therapeutic session, not only specific times like reviews. When client and therapist are in conversation, then maybe that conversation is aided by this approach. It is sometimes suggested that solution focused work does not allow the client to express their emotions, frustrations, feeling stuck, and so on. To me it does seem a very talkative way of working, however feelings and emotions are very much part of this process. They are acknowledged and we can empathise, or 'acknowledge', to a very great depth. Solution focused therapy as a model does not dismiss, ignore, or try to hurry the client over difficult issues; but individual therapists might. Art psychotherapists know how to be patient, be silent, allow the client to work at their own pace. This is the realm of the humpback whale in my illustration Figure 5.4 swimming in deep water, immersed, and submerged. One of the things I value about the solution focus approach is that when I feel it is time to see if the client is ready to move on from an expression of feeling, it gives me some direction and structure to help me. Acknowledging another person's experience succeeds when they feel heard and validated.

When the client surfaces, we surface too; maybe for some whale play or singing. If they surface and we find ourselves talking in a way that suits a solution focused approach then it can be most useful way to work. For instance they may

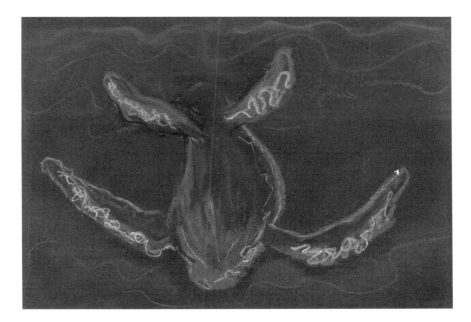

Figure 5.4 Immersed in the deep (also see colour plate section)

casually remark that school is a pain or they did well in a test; something low key, conversational. Having solution focused awareness seems to me to elicit useful information about the impact of the described event; we may be able to add pieces to the emerging jigsaw of knowledge about the client. It might be an example of an exception to a previous experience of others.

What I am hoping to impart is how useful this approach is when the opportunities arise for more organised verbal exchanges and conversations. This certainly means initial meetings and reviews but also at any time in the course of a session when something prompts a verbal exchange. This could be a reflection or comment, but if the exchange opens up more fully then it is argued that the solution focused approach gives structure and coherence to this exchange and in turn this can support time sensitive and often short- to medium-term therapy treatments (i.e. 8–24 sessions).

The ability of an art psychotherapist to work where verbal communication is minimal or the establishment of trust and containment are the priorities are not in question, nor does a solution focus approach undermine this. It offers a way of organising and working with material that is readily accessible. I propose that in dynamic work there are opportunities for verbal exchanges that emerge organically and it is these where the solution focused approach comes into its own.

Supervision, professionals meetings, evaluation

I hope the general principles of the solution focused approach have become clear to the reader. Once the underlying ideas are understood it is not difficult to adapt them to other situations. In supervision the supervisee might be asked for their best hopes for the session, or for bringing a particular case, event, or issue. The future focus can lead us directly to the heart of the matter. For example, a supervisee whose best hope about a case is to feel less stressed might lead to the question, what difference would being 'less stressed' mean to them? As the questions elicit more detailed responses we can home in on the concrete and observable. In the above example it may be a chance to separate specific concerns about risk from more general counter transference/transference matters arising from the supervisee's last session with the client. Asking about best hopes is another way of discovering what will make the session useful to the supervisee. However, as in client work, it never hurts to ask towards the end, 'Are we talking about the right kinds of things? Is there something I have not asked about which you were hoping to talk about? Anything we haven't touched on that you will think about after you leave?'

Similarly in professionals meetings, the idea of eliciting what everyone wants from the meeting and checking out whether the meeting is addressing this is a helpful one. Scales can be used here too, as a quick reference point and one which can be used to check progress at a future meeting.

'On a scale of 0–10, with 0 being complete failure and 10 being complete success; where do you each think we are in regard to your hopes for this client?'

The answers lead nicely into the next question,

'What would need to happen to move everyone up a point on this scale?'

Once again the search for concrete and observable evidence can really focus a meeting on to practicalities. If the meeting is a follow up we can check the scales and ask, 'How has that happened? What made a difference?' This kind of approach in meetings can quite naturally lead to specific action points. Checking things out helps everyone feel heard.

As we collect data from scales we are evaluating progress. If the client, supervisee, or professional group has confidence in how the information was gathered then they are likely to have confidence in what it tells them over time. When our involvement occurs over an extended period it is often helpful to be able to look back and reflect on where things were at the start. Scales are a good way of capturing this. As the information is provided by the client, and in terms the client themselves has validated, a scale can add weight to professional opinion about the value of work being undertaken.

A brief mention of Session Rating Scales (SRS) and Outcome Rating Scales (ORS) is relevant here. Developed in the early 1990s the SRS was a means for clinicians to better understand the therapeutic alliance as research showed that a good alliance was a good predictor of outcome. The tool is now widely used and has become increasingly respected. It is freely available from the internet. The similarity to BSFT use of scales is readily apparent though I draw the reader's attention to the care over the specific descriptions the client is asked to measure. In practice the tool allows a wealth of relevant material to come to light and be attended to. More structured and formal than the introduction of scales that arise through conversation with the client, they have a precision and broad applicability that might make them a good choice for any clinician evaluating their practice.

Conclusion

We have seen how a solution focused approach might inform the establishment of therapeutic work, monitor progress, and help clarify when it is time to conclude. Additionally we have seen how the model may be adapted to other situations, and noted that the use of scales can form a valuable evaluation tool. In practice the model serves to describe and explain progress to other professionals, family members, and managers. It supports our professional opinion in discussions about the value of work. It does not require extensive training to learn the approach, though it is as well to remember that support in adhering to it might be advantageous.

Donald Winnicott wrote in his 1962 paper 'The Aims of Psychoanalytic Treatment' that his clinic motto was 'How little need be done?' Winnicott appreciated that his clients needed only what was necessary to get them back on track, as it were, and get on with living their lives. I have found this motto helpful to me.

Winnicott's motto seems just as appropriate today where brief and time-limited therapies and the need to manage resources efficiently are inescapable. Interestingly one idea that informed Steve De Shazer in the early stages of developing Brief Solution Focused Therapy was that of Occam's Razor, which has a similar ambition to Winnicott's clinic motto; to make use of the simplest means that will suffice.

I have found a solution focused approach allows me to ask the client directly about 'how little need be done?' and then be guided by them in the delivery of therapy. This in turn means the outcome is more likely to fit well with the client's expectations and be less grossly affected by mine.

Previous publications

Using Digital Photography to Record Clients' Work. (2007). *International Journal of Art Therapy: Inscape.* 12 winter, pp. 79–89.
Navigating Art Therapy (2009), edited by C. Wood. East Sussex, Routledge, pp. 70, 89.
Art Therapy (2nd edn) (2014), edited by D. Edwards. London, Sage, pp. 119–120.

Bibliography

Duncan, B. L., Miller, S. D. et al. (2003) The Outcome Rating Scale: A Preliminary Study of the Reliability, Validity, and Feasibility of a Brief Visual Analog Measure. *Journal of Brief Therapy.* 2(2) Spring/Summer, pp. 91–100.
Duncan, B. L, Miller, S. D, et al. (2003) The Session Rating Scale: Preliminary Psychometric Properties of a 'Working' Alliance Measure. *Journal of Brief Therapy.* 3(1) Fall/Winter, pp. 3–12.
George, E., Iveson, C., & Ratner, H. (2007) *Briefer: A Solution Focused Manual.* Brief, London.
Kim Berg, I., & Steiner, T. (2003) *Children's Solution Work.* New York, Norton.
Macdonald, A. (2007) *Solution Focused Therapy: Theory, Research & Practice.* London, Sage.
Ratner, H., George, E., & Iveson, C. (2012) *Solution Focused Brief Therapy: 100 Key Points and Techniques.* East Sussex, Routledge.
De Shazer, S. (1994) *Words Were Originally Magic.* New York, Norton.
Winnicott, D. (1962) The Aims of Psycho-analytical Treatment. In: *The Facilitating Environment and the Maturational Processes.* London, Karnac, pp. 166–170.

Chapter 6

Time-limited work in an art psychotherapy group

Rosalyn Doyle

I am going to describe part of my experience of working in a time-limited way with clients in a group. I also work with individual clients in the same setting. Both group work and individual work has developed new care pathways to accommodate the needs of the setting and the needs of the clients. The art psychotherapy group was a time-limited bridge group that could receive new members from referrals or from an art psychotherapist at the same NHS mental health community service who considered the service user would benefit from moving onto the group from individual work. In addition, a new care pathway has been formed that service users could potentially follow at the end of their time in the group. This other group (An Expressive Art Group) was set up jointly with Mind Network and the art psychotherapy provision, which embraces flexible recovery approach to treatment.

I co-facilitated the bridge art psychotherapy group as an honorary art psychotherapist for approximately 18 months. I am a qualified art psychotherapist but have continued with my art and design lecturing job until I find work as an art psychotherapist. I have paid attention to my CPD hours and kept my HCPC membership current. When the opportunity came to co-facilitate an art psychotherapy group in an honorary position I welcomed the opportunity to continue my professional development as an art psychotherapist.

From November 2011 until March 2013 I co-facilitated the group with a salaried NHS art psychotherapist and the group was known as the bridge group, as the intention was to bridge the gap between service users who had, or were being, treated by mental health services and who would benefit from a period of time attending the weekly art psychotherapy group. In this way, the gap to be bridged was the pathway into the wider community. The benefits of group work are well documented particularly by Yalom (1995). On reflection about working with the group members, I believe each one was able to connect with at least one curative aspect of the group work. The value of discovering that at least an individual is not alone in their suffering cannot be underestimated. Yalom names this aspect, 'Universality'. Yalom writes that the group experience can also be a learning forum as clients can imitate behaviours by taking on the manners of someone else in the group who functions more adequately. Regarding group members giving direct advice for handling problems, Yalom says that this can make the advisor feel useful, in an altruistic sense.

I also benefitted from working in the group as I worked with art psychotherapist and co-facilitator Lisa Banks who set up the group in liaison with Rose Hughes. Lisa was also providing services users with individual art psychotherapy and as I have written, in time they could move on to the group if this felt of further benefit to them. At the moment, I am working with individual clients too, who when they have ended individual art psychotherapy, could quite possibly be assessed for joining the art psychotherapy group. As an honorary art psychotherapist, I am able to offer longer-term therapy where my colleagues are more keenly aware of the demands of incoming referrals and the waiting list. In Lisa's case, she was also able to offer art psychotherapy sessions in preparation for the group. This combination of various one-to-one therapy options followed by group therapy is a new care pathway for service users designed to facilitate recovery in the context of group practice.

There were a number of unexpected and useful overlaps connected to how I related to a group of people as an art psychotherapist and how I was regarded by the group. Historically, art psychotherapists have often evolved from teaching careers into art psychotherapists. Notably, Adrian Hill and Edward Adamson came from this background at a time when art therapy was in its beginning stages. Hill was an artist and also a lecturer at Westminster School of Art and Hornsey School of Art. When convalescing in 1938 from having had pulmonary tuberculosis he became interested in the effects that image-making (painting) had on himself and others who were recovering in hospital and he is said by Hogan to be the first to use the phrase 'art therapy' in an effort to convince professionals of its medical benefits. In those early days there were overlaps for Hill too, 'As soon as I was fully recovered, I started canvassing for likely talent, visiting the "bedders", giving talks and doing demonstrations on the blackboard to the "up" patients" – showing reproductions and generally getting the Sanitorium Art conscious' (Hogan 2001).

Edward Adamson was an artist who started visiting the Netherne hospital to lecture on specific art works brought to the hospital by the British Red Cross Society (BRCS) in 1944 where there were patients recovering from a range of battle injuries and operations. Following their arousal in interest in the paintings discussed, many said they wanted to try painting for themselves and Adamson was appointed 'art master' at the Netherne hospital in 1946. Adamson had a range of titles in his new job, which demonstrates the amorphous state of his role at that time. It is amazing to read that in 1948 Adamson had a purpose built art studio built in the grounds of Netherne. Even though this was a converted army hut, could we imagine the NHS agreeing to such a project these days? Adamson already had strategies in place that supported confidentiality such as keeping artwork filed away and not displaying it. Each patient had a standard set of equipment and did not work to a set theme. There is no mention of any time-limited work in Hogan's descriptions, as patients could access art therapy for the duration of their stay in the hospital. The facility was well subscribed and there was some tension about whether Adamson was influencing the images while Adamson felt he should not make interpretations of the patient's work for other medical professionals.

In the current economic and political climate and increasing job scarcity in public services, NHS art psychotherapy jobs being cut and a general limited understanding about this comparatively new profession, I was struck by this part of a description from the BAAT website and I identify with parts of it because even though time has passed by there are still ambiguous associations with what do we do, should we be paid and by whom? Other art psychotherapists, who are employed, seem to be under constant threat of cuts to services.

'Between the 1940s and 1960s, many interested artists and art teachers offered their services to hospitals and clinics. Sometimes they encountered a Consultant Psychiatrist or a Medical Superintendent who was enthusiastic about the value of art in treatment; they were then taken onto the staff and paid under whatever establishment was available' (BAAT website 2013 http://www.baat.org).

By contrast, in my case clinical and managerial supervision is provided regularly and I have access to the NHS training facilities and support to increase my knowledge in relation to therapeutic knowledge. In these difficult times, time-limited art psychotherapy is a way of showing results as well as enabling increasing numbers of the mental health population to access limited resources for art psychotherapy that are available.

When I started co-facilitating the group, I was introduced to the service users in the latest cohort for the group that had already met for two sessions. This was because I joined the group post-assessment. The group was time-limited for cycles of 15 weeks before individual reviews were carried out and the membership reassessed.

The group consisted of five people who we shall call Lucy, Kate, Barry, Bonnie and Bob. At one point during the cycle of the group, Barry left the group and Neil joined as a new member. The group met once a week for one and a half hours. When everyone had used the art materials as much as they wanted for image making, which was around the first half of the session, the second half was for discussing individual's images as a group.

Case vignettes

The group membership was made up of a core of five service users initially, who came from a range of different circumstances. Lucy suffered from depression and this was made worse by the loss of her mother who had moved away from the area. Lucy lived with her boyfriend and from her descriptions, he sounded quite controlling. Kate had a history of drinking and drug-taking, abusive relationships and had been raped when younger. Bob had been subjected to what he described as ritualistic sexual childhood abuse and had indicated that he himself had abused. He had reported the incidents but it is unclear whether all had happened as his sense of place and time is largely confused or absent from these narratives. Barry was suffering with psychosis, which caused him to hear voices and feel disorientated from his surroundings. Bonnie was an artist. She had been in a 15-year on/off abusive relationship and was self-harming. Later, Barry left the group, just before the first review, because he wanted to find a job and return to being employed. This left a space for Neil who became a new member. Although comparatively young, he had been undergoing treatment for alcohol abuse, had recently been involved in violence toward his then girlfriend and was constantly vulnerable to a pattern of violence from his step-father. During the period of time I co-facilitated the group, the membership's ages ranged from 19 to 62.

Lucy attended the group erratically, sometimes sending a message to let us know why she could not come and often not letting us know until we saw her again. This caused some anxiety for us as we had concerns about the extent to which her boyfriend would go to control her attendance. Letters that had been sent to her address, notifying her about the group and her review appointments, had mysteriously disappeared. Lucy often seemed as though she had the persona of a little girl and in general her images carried this impression through. They were brightly coloured and childlike.

At one session she announced her engagement, which formed the foundation of the group's conversation during that session. Lucy described the theme for her wedding as 'Alice in Wonderland' (from the novel by Lewis Carroll published in 1865), in which she would wear a blue Alice dress and have her hair in pigtails. When talking about her images, Lucy made references on more than one occasion to the tunnel that Alice fell into, and disappeared,

> Either the well was very deep, or she fell very slowly, for she had plenty of time as she went down to look about her and to wonder what was going to happen next. First, she tried to look down and make out what she was coming to, but it was too dark to see anything; then she looked at the sides of the well, and noticed that they were filled with cupboards and book-shelves; here and there she saw maps and pictures hung upon pegs. She took down a jar from one of the shelves as she passed; it was labelled 'ORANGE MARMALADE', but to her great disappointment it was empty: she did not like to drop the jar for fear of killing somebody, so managed to put it into one of the cupboards as she fell past it.
>
> (Carroll 1865)

Lucy's wish to disappear or her feelings of being lost and separate from her mother were contained in her analogies with falling down the tunnel like Alice.

Kate was more mature in years and could take on a maternal role within the group at times. She had experienced a series of abusive relationships and for the duration of the group she was involved in a relationship with a man who had moved into her home near the start of their relationship. As Kate became more familiar with her own emotional needs and more assertive about expressing them, she made adjustments to this relationship by allowing him to continue living in her house but only as a lodger, then serving him with notice of eviction. She then continued the relationship while they lived at separate addresses, but it seemed she could not take the final step of leaving what she conveyed as an unhappy relationship. Kate's images developed over time and at the beginning of the group's existence, her images resembled a page of scattered, individual doodles. Later on, she produced images that were more integrated into a whole. A landscape theme frequently ran through her images. Her landscapes often contained recurrent elements such as; a river, trees or a single tree and sometimes animals and birds. The trees she drew were in varying states of existence; sometimes bare, sometimes in pairs or groups, united by a shared system of branches or covered with an abundance of leaves and apples. Kate sometimes gave advice to other members of the group about relationship difficulties or related stories of her own experiences. She referred to one of her images as 'Freddie Kruger'. This drawing contained a representation of a threatening farmer/land-owner and seemed to be related to her own abuse and rape, not put into words but which lurked in the wings of her ideal landscape and now had a name attached to it to identify this narrative and experience.

Bob was in his early sixties but the sexual abuse he described being subjected to as a child had affected his whole life. He said he had difficulty speaking due to a throat condition and quite literally, he struggled to speak at the beginning of the group's existence. This seemed to be the dilemma he faced of managing expression and profound trauma and at other times unable to suppress its horror. It was interesting how his images followed a format in their layout and over the duration of the group, the format developed and changed, which appeared to parallel a development in Bob's increased self-esteem and ability to talk about what had happened to him. When he first attended the group, Bob only drew around the edges of the paper. A theme close to his heart was his allotment and he used image making to show the safety he felt when working on his allotment. Ordered rows of vegetables and preparations for hanging baskets were detailed in Bob's images.

After just a few weeks he began to work on images that could be viewed from the top or the bottom. For example, from one direction he portrayed an image related to his childhood abuse that he would keep covered with a pencil box from the art materials and from the other direction, the picture would usually show something connected to his work at the allotment or something that had happened to him during the preceding week. In this way Bob was very gradually able to show and share with the other group member's something about his life, both present and past. Near the end of the group, Bob's images became less diagrammatical and more about exploring different ways of mark-making, using the compositional space defined by the four edges of the paper and the emotional content embodied the image itself in a new expressive way. In between these two approaches to his images, Bob also explored the possibility of using a diagonal composition on the rectangular paper space a few times, something that he could have observed from how some of the other group members used the materials, but if this was the case, it helped him to change his rigid approach to image making. This also shows the benefit of a group when working in a time-limited way as the members are influenced to some extent by each other's work. Havsteen-Franklin

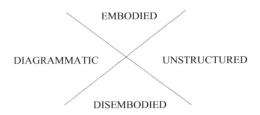

Figure 6.1 Havsteen-Franklin's diagram showing different types of images

(2008) writes about Schaverien's concepts on embodied and diagrammatic images and says that there is an indication of her not intending these concepts to be completely rigid. Havsteen-Franklin (2008) posits that there can be two other types of image, unstructured and disembodied, which his reproduced diagram shows in Figure 6.1. Havsteen-Franklin's paper (2008) and Schaverien's concepts (1991) do lend themselves to a more in-depth reflection in regard to Bob's images but this is a complete subject in itself. The idea of these four different types of images as put forward by Havsteen-Franklin (2008) is especially applicable to the manner in which parts of the images were unrevealed to the group unless the group or Bob felt it was right to refer to them or show them. Havsteen-Franklin writes that an image may be the result of alternating or combining the embodied image, the disembodied image, the diagrammatic image and the unstructured image. The narrative contained in Bob's earlier diagrammatic images showed past events from his childhood and also the previous week. Those image parts that were initially concealed by pencil boxes became something from which Bob was disembodied in order for them to be tolerated and processed by him and the group. In this way, Bob could make small and gradual changes in his thinking through his use of different types of images (Diagram taken from D. Havsteen-Franklin 2008).

Accompanying this change, Bob's willingness to talk in the group increased over time. His sense of being held by the group and facilitators seemed more robust as his interaction with other group members improved. Although he felt vulnerable, he spoke of growing to trust the group and seemed over time to become emotionally supported within it. Bob made reference to the time when I had first joined the group as co-facilitator and how this had made him feel apprehensive because he did not know me and had not met me before. However, given time to get to know me, Bob grew to trust me as part of the group too. Gradually, within the group environment Bob was enabled to talk, if he wanted to, about some of his past as well as his current worries. Bob's life was enriched by his engagement with art psychotherapy after such difficult life experiences; he was able to trust the group experience enough to refer to what had happened to him and also speak about moving on in terms of what he would do when the group finished. Bob had also been able to prepare for this in his one-to-one art psychotherapy, which he had before starting to attend the group.

So it seemed the process of getting to know and trusting was an ongoing process for Bob and part of trusting his care pathway. In the art psychotherapy group, Bob developed his strategy to tentatively explore trust and safeness of the group as shown by the degree to which he let the other group members view totally, partially or not at all, the narrative images of his childhood. Bob's images of his early damaging experiences of an alleged paedophile ring were explicit and diagrammatic and their content was a chilling contrast to those images on the opposite edges of the paper that showed his allotment, alive with seasonal colour and the care of nurturing. These were generally the format of the majority of Bob's images until towards the end of this cohort's group's existence his images took on other qualities such as the use of expression in the type of mark-making used and composing the image as a whole entity within the four edges of the paper. When Bob found he was creating this type of embodied image, which was a new departure for him, he was quite lost for words as there was no narrative as such. Some of these new images were about his future plans for his allotment and he liked these images. Havsteen-Franklin (2008) writes about the content of the embodied image being as a form of unspoken, in-depth communication:

> [It] has its own language differentiated from words and therefore to some degree the word and the embodied image remain irreconcilable. Therefore according to Schaverien (2003) verbal conscious recognition or enquiry fails to acknowledge the depth of content as it is revealed in the experience of the image at the time of making.

Bob's childhood experiences were treated sensitively by the group members and childhood sexual abuse referred to objectively, especially when the late TV presenter, disc jockey and charity worker Jimmy Savile's story of predatory paedophilia became news. Bob's drawings and the work he carried out at his allotment during the different seasons of the year were for Bob, and also over time became for the group members, related to elements of the life cycle. During discussion about Bob's work, the use of metaphor related to going back to the ground and the start of a new beginning sometimes occurred, not only by the facilitators but also by one or two of the group members. I'm not sure whether Bob himself had taken in these comments on a conscious or subconscious level but the change in the images themselves indicated that something in his thinking was changing. In the group, Bob had an opportunity to continue to process his terrible childhood and focus on other aspects of his life with what might be regarded as a new set of thoughts because of the psychological holding of the group. The images contained some of his story and it was enough for the group members and facilitators to accept them without focusing on explicit details and for Bob to talk about 'sorting out the rubbish on his allotment' and 'making preparations for a new season'.

The dynamics within the group developed during the life of the group. The support felt within the group and the safety of the group space was commented on sometimes by the group members. However, some individual issues remained unspoken; for example Kate, Bonnie and possibly Lucy, never actually spoke about their abusive relationships openly but they offered each other advice on improving their relationships with men and protecting themselves and situations arising from relationships. They also spoke about families and how to approach difficult topics that required tackling.

Bonnie was an artist who had been involved in an on/off relationship for 15 years. She seemed to have had a controlling mother and father and she self-harmed and experienced anxiety and depression. She was of mixed nationality and her father was a medical professional. Bonnie spoke of being in the shadow of her sister who had rewarded her parents by making the sort of life choices they could be proud of while Bonnie always felt she disappointed them. Bonnie's job did not really compare to the perceived success of her sister. She was buying a house but could not afford the repayments and had rented it out and gone back to live at her parent's house where they had built a studio for her in the garden. Bonnie had been a swimming teacher when the group started but at one point she decided she did not want to continue with that work and gave it up.

While Bonnie was a group member, her relationship broke up twice. During these periods she was able to explore her feelings about her sense of self. As an artist, Bonnie was a painter but in the group she chose to use clay. Her paintings explored the movement of water paints and oil paints on a 2D surface she told us and occasionally she engaged with the paints in the art psychotherapy group. For the majority of her images she used clay in a way that involved kneading, stroking and using a similar flowing technique that she used in her painting. She produced a series of 3D forms throughout her time in the group. In some ways they resembled Henry Moore's or Barbara Hepworth's abstracted natural forms. These were more about Bonnie being led by the clay, coaxing and smoothing the creation of these pieces. The clay images varied in size from about two centimetres to about 15 centimetres across and often they would have one or more holes through them. Sometime Bonnie would make another smaller piece from the clay that was removed to make the hole and the resulting images were seen by her as a pair. Her work and the way in which she produced it reminded me of the erosion of stones in water and also of the type of work produced by sculptor Anish Kapoor who has an interest in black holes, blank mirrors and other phenomena. In an exhibition catalogue of Kapoor's work and his intention to produce a 'sublime' piece of 3D work which resonated with the clay pieces Bonnie has been exploring, Van Winkel quotes Kapoor as saying;

> The void has many presences. Its presence as fear is towards the loss of self, from a non-object to a non-self. The idea of being somehow consumed by the object, or in the non-object, in the body, in the cave, in the womb etc. I have always been drawn to a notion of fear, toward a sensation of vertigo, of falling, of being pulled inwards. This is a notion of the sublime which reverses the picture of union with light. This is an inversion, a sort of turning

inside-out. This is a vision of darkness, of which the eye is uncertain, towards which the hand turns in hope of contact, and in which only the imagination has the possibility of escape.

(Van Winkel 1995)

The idea of finding the sublime, which is about experiencing one's own insignificance amidst the vastness of the forces of nature, was linked by Bonnie, looking at her own vulnerability. Bonnie had spoken of trying to find a way through her problems and with reference to a dip or a depression in the clay she used the phrase 'explore the depression'. However, she was not always willing to talk about herself. She said she felt others would not be interested to hear anything about her. Other members in the group always showed a liking for Bonnie's clay images and would see different objects or creatures in them, often imagining where they would like to sit or hide in them if they were large scale sculptures, thereby sharing their appreciation of her work and changing and adding to her sense of connection to the group members.

Bonnie also explored the fluidity of glazes and underglaze colour. The clay pieces were to be transported to and from another site for both biscuit firing and a second time for glaze firing as we did not have a kiln and Bonnie would ask if her pieces were back from firing. Due to the glazing process having an element of unpredictability in the resulting effects of adding colour it seemed that Bonnie enjoyed discovering exactly how the pieces looked when they had been glazed fired. Toward the end of her time in the group Bonnie started to add a word to each clay piece written in a place where it was not immediately seen. For example, the first word she wrote on one of her pieces was, 'kindness'. Perhaps these words, or qualities, related to her increased level of hope in finding them in herself and in others. One of Bonnie's ambitions was to work with clay on a larger scale.

After one of the breaks and when the group was at the beginning of a new cycle, they were joined by Neil, a 19-year-old young man with an alcohol problem. He lived with his mother, two younger brothers and his step-father who he described as violent. Neil himself led quite a disordered existence. Within his chaotic family Neil made spasmodic efforts to reach outside for a more stable, accomplished and respectable sense of self and often this was sabotaged by Neil himself or was superseded by family dynamics.

Neil's behavioural problems had first begun in school, resulting in him being unable to take part in normal lessons except for the art lessons. It seems his art teacher had accommodated Neil's need to work alone on independent projects and let him express himself by creating an observational drawing of a highly decorated and embellished jacket that belonged to the teacher and creating 3D work using the teacher's chair as a foundation for these pieces. Even though it had been maybe two years since Neil was in school, he still carried photos of his school artwork on his phone and showed these proudly to the art psychotherapy group members and facilitators. The teacher's acceptance and facilitation of this work supported Neil to feel seen and identified with his creativity.

Neil liked to talk in the group. At times he became the 'annoying pupil in the class' by his propensity to reading texts or texting on his phone. He knew the rules and challenged them as if he might have done if he was in school revealing the potential for non-conformity as an expressive vehicle. Neil was quite resistant to image-making when he first joined the group and he was reluctant to even acknowledge his difficult feelings let alone talk about them. He showed us photos of his previous art work made at school and he copied a couple of cartoon characters from his phone. He brought in his sketchbook, which contained more copied cartoons again revealing themes of individuation and independence in the safety of cartoons and typical adolescent conventional iconography. However, later on he created a clay structure but the scale was far too demanding for the clay to support its own weight and Neil became disillusioned with this clay tower as if the boy was struggling to grow like the tower. With Neil, I felt a mix of roles between an art teacher in the transference as well as art psychotherapist, I felt it to be a useful blend of skills and was able to encourage Neil to start image-making, as he had mentioned he wanted to be involved in making something in 3D by offering to supply some materials for the following week if he wanted to make a design for a piece of 3D work. Neil asked me if I could get some Modroc (plaster impregnated bandage) for an object he wanted to start making. He had drawn the design in his sketchbook and discussed how he would form an armature from cardboard tubes. In a concrete way, he was able to follow through with an idea with my assistance and not be sabotaged. With my facilitation, Neil as able to make a successful object and during the making process I felt I was supporting Neil's self-esteem as well as with practical aspects of the project.

The next week, Neil came to the group with numerous rolls of kitchen roll from a pound shop and donated the carrier bags of surplus tissue to the materials cupboard so that he could use the tubes inside the rolls. We used a generic meeting room for the group, but Neil was conscientious enough to prepare his work area by protecting the table and surrounding area with plastic sheeting and there were minimum traces of plaster finger prints on the furniture to wipe off by the end of the project thus revealing his responsible role in relation to others when not over-riding others. He worked for several consecutive weeks on creating the object he had planned. This was to be a sculptural idea generated from a computer game (Kingdom Hearts) in which the player gained power through winning and possessing a giant key that also doubled as a weapon to use against opponents (a keyblade). Different colours and designs of keyblades indicated different powers contained within the keyblades. The one that Neil had chosen to make was wielded by the main character in the story of the game and was used to protect and fight creatures called the 'Heartless'. Neil painstakingly created the inner structure of the key by stuffing the tubes tightly with tissue from the kitchen roll and joining the tubes with cuts that slotted together. His conversation was sprinkled richly with bravado and tales of his rebelliousness and unbounded social life as he related how he had become barred from numerous bars and pubs. In the art psychotherapy group, Neil considerately created little mess and made the keyblade in sections so we would not have difficulty storing it with the rest of the group's art work. He made good use of the Modroc to join the sections and build up layers. Each layer added extra strength to the keyblade as Neil smoothed out the plaster when he applied it. Neil's keyblade became invested with its own power and strength because of the care he took over making it.

At the beginning of the project, he spoke kindly of making one for his younger brother for Christmas when this one was finished. Then he decided to give this one to his younger brother. As the group progressed it became more clear how powerless Neil felt over many aspects of his life and how he also identified with, and worried about his younger brother. When finished, the keyblade was very strong and we wondered as facilitators and at our supervision, what Neil would do in the group now the keyblade was complete. He painted it grey, yellow and blue and these colours also represented specific super powers and characteristics in Kingdom Hearts. Figure 6.2

Figure 6.2 Neil's keyblade before painting

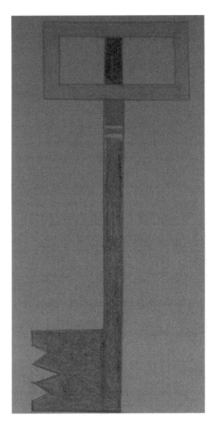

Figure 6.3 Author's diagrammatic representation of how Neil painted his keyblade (also see colour plate section)

is a photograph of Neil's work before he painted it and Figure 6.3 is a diagram of the colours used on the finished piece. After the keyblade was finished, Neil copied some cartoon characters that had more serious expressions about them and in addition, some haunting, charcoal drawings that depicted ambiguous, crow-like creatures, which although they had a sense of movement were not exactly birds, but the imprint marks a bird might leave when attempting to take flight. At the end of the group Neil was due to go on to the Mind Expressive Arts group (a group piloted between art psychotherapists and MIND at a local community venue) for a while, before he took up a university place in the autumn and our hope was that he had taken in some of the protection and power of the keyblade to take with him from the time-limited art psychotherapy group.

We held reviews within the group session and members were asked to select one or two pieces of work created during the time in the group. The selected pieces were spoken about by the members comments from the others in the group were made about their work and progress in the group, usually of a supportive nature. Some group members had already spoken about leaving the group and this was explored further in the group review. Some members had been attending for a year and were not ready to leave. As a general guide they would receive this group intervention for a year. End of group reviews, which signified the end of a part of the cycle of one group and the beginning of the new one starting, were carried out individually. For these reviews, the group would not meet and instead, service users had individual appointments for that week. These reviews were at approximately four-month intervals and the service users discussed their progress with us, the group facilitator. Another topic of discussion with service users at their individual appointments was whether they were moving toward the aim of their therapy and what they were going to do next if leaving the group.

The reviews were an important part of the art psychotherapeutic process. Reviews were also important because the group was time-limited and this review process supported service users by working with them to ascertain whether they had worked toward their therapeutic aims and assess whether they were ready to leave. Waller and Gilroy (1992) write about 'brief' art psychotherapy and emphasise the need to have a theoretical structure that focuses on the beginning, middle and end as a foundation of the group. In this way time becomes a 'dynamic factor in the therapy' and a 'time frame determines what may be dealt with in the sense that a realistic focus must be established'. Waller and Gilroy (1992) list four elements that are common to time-limited therapies but in the group I write about, the element that I would consider to be the most important and forms part of the important group's structure is, 'anticipating the ending in a concrete way throughout the therapy' hence reviewing the group on a group basis and an individual basis.

Part of the time-limited recovery based programme was to set up a community pathway using art psychotherapy. Kate Frederickson, an art psychotherapy student on a training placement with us, developed a project in which she liaised with Mind and began an 'Expressive Arts Group' that was run locally, on Mind premises. This group was co-run along art therapeutic principles but there was also be a taught element in which attendees would learn techniques to enhance their image making skills. This was by agreement as Mind Network's remit is for education. I believe this was useful because it provided a smaller, interim step in between the art psychotherapy group ending and the outside world. I feel the service users would make good use of this type of group. They had been exposed to image-making as a form of expression and on some occasions they had practical questions from time to time in the art psychotherapy group about technical aspects of their work such as, in which order under paints and glazes should go onto fired clay pieces, did I know of any art courses at local colleges and how to achieve certain effects with water colours.

The Expressive Art group was subject to some delays as it was a pilot scheme but it was a good concept for those that left the art psychotherapy group to go onto for those that needed it. During the service user's individual reviews at the end of therapy each member had remarked that even though they were finishing in the group, they were pleased to have the opportunity to be moving on as a group to the Mind Expressive Art Group because they were with people they knew. It seemed to give the service users confidence about being able to deal with life without the art psychotherapy group. They had spent time in the group building up trust and confidentiality as one entity and it would be easier for them to move onto some-thing new with some of this element already in place, but in different surround-ings and with some other new members joining the Mind group.

Conclusion

Although art psychotherapists are under pressure, as many people who work for an employer are, in as much as they have to fit in more actual 'work' into what feels like less time, and at no extra cost, I believe this makes us even more accountable for using time effectively by having structured aims. Not all service users are ready to leave the group but it is helpful for them to see how far they have travelled in terms of recovery and in some cases they are able to continue in the art psychotherapy with a new or adjusted aim. The care pathways structured around the needs of the client to recover are created to help and support the service user as well as fulfilling limits on time.

The concept of engagement with individual art psychotherapy, moving onto group art psychotherapy and moving on physically to an Expressive Art Group parallels the first phases of life where we are with our primary care-giver (mother/ therapist) and developing thoughts and feelings. Later moving into family group dynamics, as Yalom says, 'Corrective recapitulation of primary family group – experiencing transference relationships growing out of primary family experi-ences providing the opportunity to relearn and clarify distortions' (Yalom 1995). The opportunity to grow and leave home could be seen as equivalent to moving onto the Expressive Arts Group, as we venture into the outside world.

Bibliography

BAAT: Website (2013) A Career in Art Therapy, Historical Information. http://www.baat.org.

Havsteen-Franklin D. (2008) The Composite Image: an exploration of the concept of the 'embodied image' in art psychotherapy. *International Journal of Art Therapy: Inscape* 13(2). Abingdon, Oxon.

Hogan S. (2001) *Healing Arts: The History of Art Therapy*. Jessica Kingsley Books. Lon-don and Philadelphia.

Royal Academy of Arts (2009) Anish Kapoor Exhibition catalogue. Van Winkel (1995).

Shavenien, J. (1991) *The Revealing Image. Analytical Art Psychotherapy in Theory and Practice*. London and Philadelphia. Jessica Kingsley Books.

Waller D. and Gilroy A. (1992) *Art Therapy: A Handbook*. Open University Press Psycho-therapy Handbooks Series. Buckingham.

Yalom I.D. (1995) *The Theory and Practice of Group Psychotherapy*, 4th edition. Basic Books. New York.

Chapter 7

Evidence for the use of imagery in time-limited art psychotherapy, emotional change and cognitive restructuring

Gillian Solomon

> The great complexity of being human is that we are two 'selves' that do not necessarily get along . . . One communicates in words, the other through the sensor motor channels of the body. The resolution of the dilemma of our emotionality lies not in privileging one stream over the other but integrating the two.
>
> (Greenberg, L., 2002)

Introduction

Since the publication by Gilroy, Tipple and Brown on art psychotherapy assessment (Gilroy, Tipple, & Brown, 2012), discussing best practice, we have been placed under further pressure to conform and provide evidence and information about the efficacy of what we do. However uncomfortable this change is, it offers an opportunity for investigation of the efficacy of time-limited work with people suffering from anxiety and depression, using current guidelines issued by the National Institute of Clinical Excellence (NICE) that will allow us as art psychotherapists to integrate our work into the formal theorised field of current clinical psychotherapy practice.

This chapter suggests a way of utilising new cognitive research data, produced over the past decade, which provides strong evidence of how particular *mental* imagery is linked to emotion and memory across psychological disorders (Holmes, Hackmann, & Bennet-levy, 2011b; Stopa, 2009). This research has led to the use and understanding of the role internal imagery plays, showing how it might be used to provide evidence of psychological change and cognitive restructuring.

The advantage of access to Cognitive Behavioural therapy is its words, in assessments, though self-report questionnaires (PHQ9 and GAD7) in evaluation of disorder, and risk. This allows access to short-term interventions that can be measured. This chapter shows how this enables evidence of how intrusive mental imagery, seen in the mind's eye, maintains disorders, and how we might document maintenance cycles. This allows them to be evidenced and gives access to NHS treatment according to schedules of care, allocating number of sessions in short-term care so it can allocate the appropriate scale of fees.

Art made in psychotherapy consists of images, made by hand. Up to now we haven't developed a reliable model of assessment , with which to measuring or show the disorder or to document psychological change in a systematic way. Greenberg's quote at the beginning of the chapter highlights the split between our cognitions, as thoughts or images that together with experiences, memories and emotions, are all part of the self.

Making an image directly is a behaviour. Art psychotherapy and cognitive therapy, in using images, are both focused upon how behaviour, and behavioural change can be observed and measured. The act of re-drawing, and re-painting (re-scripting) can be described as a behavioural experiment that causes psychotherapeutic change and allows a shift in perception of self and others. Creative, art psychotherapy, believes that self-expression is healthy, a concept that must be informed by a structured set of (SMART) goals that target and show how this therapeutic change happens.

How we document and observe what happens in art psychotherapy practice helps us understand, how, at each stage, directly made art (images) as opposed to *indirect imagined ones*, cause affective change, and are qualitatively and practically different than images seen in our imagination and then described in words.

This task requires careful observation, so that art can be properly described and become explicit prepositional code. Images and words are formally quite different, a difference that makes images emotionally accessible. It's not enough to know art psychotherapy works, we have to show how and why what we do works, as Roth and Pilling (updated, 2007) and NICE require.

NHS guidelines from Roth & Pilling briefly describe an evidence-based method for identifying competences, and present a competence model for cognitive and behavioural therapy (CBT).

This organises the competences into five domains:

- Generic competences – used in all psychological therapies.
- Basic cognitive and behavioural therapy competences – used in both low- and high-intensity interventions
- Specific cognitive and behavioural therapy techniques – the core technical interventions employed in most forms of CBT
- Problem-specific competences – the packages of CBT interventions for specific low and high-intensity interventions
- Metacompetences – overarching, higher-order competences which practitioners need to use to guide the implementation of any intervention.

The report then describes and comments on the types of competence found in each domain, and presents a 'map' which shows how all the competences fit together and interrelate.

In line with these NHS requirements this chapter suggests that self-report questionnaires, Learning Theory and Micro-formulation, can help art psychotherapists identify and describe distinct themes that are the manifestation of a number of psychological disorders. A practice that need not detract from the essential subjectivity and expressive understanding inherent in art psychotherapy.

Positive imagery

Images are inclusive; they show us both positive and negative aspects of self at once. Words formally are strung linearly, and they access either negative or positive aspects one at a time. This formal difference, between image and word, causes art psychotherapists to dislike narrow assessment and diagnosis, as it limits the description of the image in verbally negative one-dimensional terms. This prejudice seems not to have been informed by practice, but is an intuitive resistance to the limitations, which words impose. It is important that we examine our prejudices to document these formal differences as critical examination will enable understanding and documentation of what we find, so we can become 'scientist practitioners'. Art psychotherapy has positive advantages. The role and function of images and how their formulation can visually show points of change is vital to evidence of psychotherapeutic change.

There is much conflict about the role of art in therapy and that of art, which shows us universal gestures of despair, for example Picasso's *Guernica*. Picasso's work transcends individual grief in its ability to use the formal means of art to communicate anguish in a universal way over time. What *Guernica* has in common with other images that use visual means to express distress, is that it shows us how trauma caused by violence is an aspect of the common dilemma of being human, and how loss in our capacity to express and communicate those feelings appropriately is a common human problem. All images are idiosyncratic to the maker, no matter for what purpose they are made. However imagery produced in therapy requires no aesthetic ability or skill, its purpose is to help us understand the function and role the image serves in perpetuation of the unhelpful thoughts feelings and behaviour of its maker. Art psychotherapy needs to understand the difference between imagery in clinical practice and art made for aesthetic means, between the social function served by art intended for public view in galleries, and the functional analysis of the behaviour maintained by images produced as a manifestation of psychological distress. Beck's insight that cognition causes suffering, is correct. However thinking about thinking isn't going to help us. Words divide us in two and perpetuate dualism, they return us to suffering, to comparisons that make us seem not good enough.

The power of imagery is its lived exposure in the here and now. Art psychotherapy is about getting out of cognition and suffering back to 'the self' through imagery, in the here and now, a mindfulness practice, in which we are directly witnessed, accepted and good enough. A process that is compared to the maternal gaze.

Imagery making allows exposure to distress so it can be voluntarily externalised, an act that often reveals implicit knowledge, that can then be made explicit, consciously understood. This behavioural experiment enables us to re-draw our preferred reality in what cognitive therapy calls 're-scripting'. Art psychotherapy therefore is a process of creating a tangible object that separates the client from the presenting 'problem', making it visible and credible in a way words do not, as 'seeing is believing' and the 'prohibited' may be given 'voice'.

The advantage creative production has is its ability to show the lived situation from many aspects at once (Rice & Rubin, 2011) in ways that words formally cannot, so that 'schema' can be seen in the past, present and future in common with cubist painting, or sculpture.

In this chapter I use clinical examples of *directly made art psychotherapy images*, to show how common themes, as well as idiosyncratic meaning, are useful in case formulation, showing us manifestations of disorder, that when formulated lead to cognitive restructuring and increase a sense of personal agency.

The use of imagery in clinical psychology

The use of images in dreams conducted by Freud that provided a foundation for Beck's research on depression (1976) has recently developed into a body of cognitive and neuropsychological scientific investigation of the brain. Imagery has become regarded as an active and essential component in understanding clinical disorders. Cognitive therapy research argues that the exploration of mental imagery represents a new and important arena within clinical psychopathology (Holmes et al., 2011b; Holmes & Hackmann, 2004; Holmes & Mathews, 2010; Pearson, 2007).

This new research shows how images play a key role in various psychological disorders, including Post Traumatic Stress Disorder (Grey, Young, & Holmes, 2002) Social Phobia (Hackmann, Clark, & McManus, 2006), Prospective Imagery in Schizophrenia (D'Argenbeau, Raffard, & Van Der Linden, 2008) and Depression (Patel et al., 2007).

Images are addressed in clinical psychology in two different ways:

- *Cognitive Therapy* asks what is seen in the in the 'mind's eye', from imagination, from short- or long-term memory.

and in

- *Art psychotherapy*, which, on the other hand, is an active process when a direct manifestation of distressing imagery is created as a picture, drawing, sculpture or other art objects, often in a non-directive way.

In addressing PTSD, research has shown (McAvinue & Robertson, 2007; Kosslyn 1980, 1994; Kosslyn, Ganis, & Thompson, 2001) that involuntary and distressing images are experienced in relationship to the recall process, as a flashback, a dream and nightmares or as a frequently recurring and reported memory. These 'mental images' are a manifestation of disorder and subject to assessment demonstrating evidence of anxiety, trauma or depression, in a negative maintenance cycle (Holmes, Hackmann, & Bennett-Levy, 2010). Cognitive Therapy attempts to validate mental imagery, through verbalising, imagined images and asking questions to discover if this image is a fantasy or a memory. This is useful, however it limits the intervention, to ask what we think about what we feel. The act of describing though directly making imagery allows distress to be experienced, felt, seen and transformed, as well as witnessed. This exposure to the trigger of distress, allows a learning process to take place and then the behavioural experiments that enable transformation through showing why and how anxiety and depression are being maintained can take place.

Art psychotherapy in working with distorted, 'unconscious' images of the self that are experienced first-hand, allows implicit unprocessed, perhaps negative images to become expressed, and this allows us to see in what way they are causing distress. Here the term unconscious is not used in the narrow Freudian sense but means that which is not yet explicit. This imagery is found to trigger memory and affect, in a way words cannot, because words are formally exclusive; one-dimensional and emerge one at a time. Formally words allow a limited access to the self, whereas images made directly during art psychotherapy, foster liberation from the tyranny of internalised negative thoughts because of the process of externalisation, sharing and exploration of unconscious implicit representation visible.

Art allows us to see the problem from all sides

Cognitive researchers Rice and Rubin (2011) conducted two studies in which they asked individuals to describe the perspectives they experienced when they imagined situations visualised from an external vantage point. Results showed a wide variation of experiences that differed from first- to third-person perspective, noting that 'out of body' experience, may be more common than previous studies have demonstrated. They discovered that the viewpoint from which we see situations depended on the emotional load of the event being recalled. This research proposes image making facilitates creative problem solving as it shows us aspects of self from all sides at once, as David Edwards schema therapist goes further when he observes (personal conversation);

a schema is shaped by the past so reflects past experience, it shapes perception of the present (often distorting it) so it is very much in the present when activated, and of course it shapes the future as it guides our plans and we try to shape the world based on our schemas, showing four aspects at one time. This provides support for the proposition that imagery when directly has the positive advantage of facilitating creative problem solving by showing us aspects of self from all sides at once.

Why it is positive to see ourselves in a nuanced way?

Art comprises two-dimensional images that are flat, and traditionally allude to classical three-dimensional perspectives. Cubism was revolutionary as it showed us that this is not the way we experience the world. The abstract paintings made by Picasso and Braque alluded to the fact that we experience the world from three dimensions. Hence the painted shadows on the surface of a cubist painting are a visual pun that allude to three dimensional space. This is reflected in research conducted by cognitive therapy that says we are selves within a context of psychological meaning, with a self-schema. Schema that, when formulated longitudinally by (Beck & Clark, 1997) shows how our past experience predispose us to certain rules for life, or core beliefs, and how a recent incident may have triggered our current distress, that this may influence the way we view our future. Art psychotherapeutic use of direct images, through drawing and painting, processes those often distorted images, allowing access to and expression of these unhappy memories and feelings caused by previous difficult life experiences. The production of such images is therapeutically transformational. Cognitive therapy evidences how we 'see' ourselves indirectly, through questionnaires and words, asking us what we see in our minds eye. It gathers evidence about the intrusive image that is maintaining depression or anxiety and how that imagery perpetuates the associated safety behaviours. However the formalities of word are unable to express affective truth. Words can only tell us about that which is logical and one dimensional, I am depressed, present tense. I can't go out, is conjugated formally in specific way in language.

> The drawn image formally reveals self by showing multiple perspectives that are subtle and nuanced. This reveals the contradictions we experience in the world through the body, perceived in three dimensional space, from all directions, all sides of the self. The negative self, and the positive self, and the one that doesn't know how to speak, all at the same time.
>
> Words on the other hand reinforce depression and anxiety as they only permit crude logical access to one side of the self at a time. Words only reveal one thing at a time, the depressed side, or the anxious side, which causes us to compare and contrast one with the other causing rumination and suffering. Mindfulness cognitive therapy is correct, mind is the cause of suffering and mindfulness can lead to alleviation of suffering through being in the here and now by use of positive imagery.
>
> Art images directly made show us ourselves from all sides at once. Since the task of psychotherapy is to liberate us from affective conflict and not to reinforce it, it seems that words and logic reinforce narrow access to the self in ways that direct imagery, or does not. This is why imagery helps us problem solve; it shows us solutions we haven't thought of yet. Implicit creative solutions that can then become consolidated through articulation.

The function of using directly made images rather than imagined ones is that we are able to see the manifestation of a disorder with clients and through therapeutic means resolve conflict, bringing about both emotional and cognitive change. Cognitive Therapy research has shown us how 'mental' imagery is indeed both positive and necessary; this evidence has important utility for art psychotherapy practice in allowing us to extend this evidence to show how direct imagery is what makes images a positive problem solving tool.

The manifestation of themes across disorders

The Introduction of Access to Psychological Therapy (IAPT), has been a radical health care initiative that has caused controversy and misunderstanding. This ambitious and visionary initiative has utilized Beck's model of cognitive therapy (Beck & Emery, 1979), to train therapists to use a practical step-wise model that can be monitored through data collection to show results.

Whilst currently, some art psychotherapists elect to monitor case work through the use of data, such as the Beck Depression Inventory (BDI; Beck, 1961) this is not an aspect of standard practice. The vital first step in recording the disorder and in showing how distress is being maintained, and is an important in motivating for access to treatment, which is expensive and needs to show its efficacy on order to continue to justify its use of public funds.

Case formulation

At present Art Psychotherapy practice is encouraging clinicians to research, which could be linked to art psychotherapy training though the standardisation and professionalisation of skills in structured clinical assessment diagnosis and treatment in line with NICE best practice guidelines. If these become linked to real world applied placement in mental health care, then we will be able to structure art psychotherapy in ways that are considered acceptable to the service we hope to serve. The development of our own skills of structured assessment will enable a deeper understanding of the role of images in maintaining disorders and this will enhance collaboration with clients through mapping of subjective experience, in a more structured way.

Patients may not report imagery unless explicitly asked about them, and art psychotherapists have very unique skills, and knowledge of the subtle and complex nonverbal meaning that are linked to memory and feeling about the past, that causes distress as well as physical and emotional affect. We are aware that verbal restructuring doesn't necessarily change these stored meanings, which may not be understood and often reflect early experiences that need to be updated through being remade. We have a level of visual literacy unusual in psychotherapy that must be used to showing our understanding the role imagery plays in the dual processing of thoughts, feelings and behaviors. We need a model that demonstrates how somatic symptoms are being experienced, evidencing why intrusive images are problematic, so we can use disorder specific models as a guide to content showing how they may be understood and changed.

> An understanding of imagination, seen in the mind's eye, can be made directly, and evidence or map, how images form a functional analysis of behavior. This shows function the image plays in the maintenance of the problem. Which in turn allows the development of goals for treatment that can be shared. This subjective map need can become focused as a collaborative case formulation, helping the understanding of lived experience. Which permits the identification of how each aspect of the problem, the mood, feelings, thoughts and behaviors contribute to the overall maintenance of depression or anxiety. It *also allows* similarities in themes to become identified, as a differential diagnosis.
>
> In order to use disorder specific models as a guide to the content of imagery art therapy must assess for images that represent self, and show us memories of the past as well as what is called future 'flash forwards' images seen in depression and suicidality.
>
> (Holmes, Crane, Fennell, & Williams, 2007)

The diagram below shows a *verbal description* of what clients saw or imagined in each case, in assessment. Demonstrating how mental imagery provides a way of identifying common themes, and anticipates the kinds of unhelpful images (and cognitions) that maintain the problem.

Examples of cases across disorders

Disorder	Beliefs & Concerns	Content of Intrusive Memory/image	Documented Examples
Depression, as defined through the Beck's Depression Scale (BDI). (Beck & Emery, 1979)	Feeling low, a sense of loss and failure. Feeling alone and abandoned humiliated and guilty, as if they had let themselves and others down.	Negative images of letting themselves and others down. Of running away and being a coward, and of being bullied. Imagining themselves as a helpless, victim. Unable to do anything, being passive, lying still, and sleeping forever.	Past experiences such as own or significant other's illness or injury, threatened or actual assault, and interpersonal problems (Patel et al., 2007; Reynolds & Brewin, 1999). Suicide-related, future-oriented flash-forwards (e.g. jumping in front of a train, slashing the wrists, seeing own funeral while being in the coffin) (e.g. Holmes, Crane, Fennell, & Williams, 2007). Images of wanting to escape, and sleeping forever. Of not waking up. Being engulfed by a black shape/ and falling into a dark void.
Social Phobia (Clark & Wells, 1995; Stopa, 2009)	Appearing small diminished, a little person who was foolish, red faced, tongue tied and struck dumb.	Image of oneself as a very small person, who had no physical power, diminished, like a child.	Worst fears about one's behaviour in social situations being realised (e.g. blushing intensely, appearing stupid or awkward) (e.g. Hackmann, Clark, & McManus, 2000; Hackmann, Surawy, & Clark, 1998).
Social Phobia (Hodson, McManus, Clark & Doll, 2008)	Appearing abnormal deranged and mad to others.	Picture of self at centre of a whirlwind, caught up and out of control.	Self as social object (Clark & Wells, 1995).
Panic disorder (Clark et al., 1997)	Fear that a disaster will happen. Imagining recurrent catastrophes, motor-car accidents and others.	Image of self-falling down, collapsing ill, and crawling on the ground unable to rise, in demise.	

Disorder	Beliefs & Concerns	Content of Intrusive Memory/image	Documented Examples
Agoraphobia (Arntz, 2012) (Beck & Clark, 1997)	Being trapped in a place from which one cannot escape.	Imagines being lost in the back aisles of a large supermarket being jostled engulfed, shoved & unable to breathe.	Physical or mental catastrophes, disorientation, lack of ability to cope with agoraphobic situations, panic (e.g. passing out while in public, being stuck in a place with no escape) (Day, Holmes, & Hackmann, 2004; Hackmann, Day, & Holmes, 2009).
Obsessive compulsive disorder (Rachman, 1997; Salkovskis, 1985)	Fear that one will harm others or will be harmed, or contaminated.	Image of child blue in the face, poisoned from ill prepared food. Images of a mangled body shape on the road, injuring or killed a pedestrian. Image of poison, contaminating people. Fungus from soil on bottom of shoes, floor and causing disease.	Images/sensory impressions related to obsessions and compulsions, such as seeing the oneself covered in faeces and urine (Speckens, Hackmann, Ehlers, & Cuthbert, 2007).
Phobia (Ost, 1986)	Fear of an object that is perceived as dangerous, for example meat, spiders, feathers, blood needles, birds.	Image of injury caused through irresponsibility or negligence.	Image of injury caused from needles or glass. Sounds and screams of pain.
Post Traumatic Stress Disorder (Steketee & Foa, 1987; Brewin, Lanius, Novac, Schnyder, & Galea, 2009)	A threat, danger to the physical or psychological self.	Images of person being physically harmed. Sexual or physical assault, and smell of body odour	Brief sensory fragments of the trauma, such as having a gun pointed to the head or hearing the sound of glass shattering (e.g. Grey & Holmes, 2008; Hackmann, Ehlers, Speckens, & Clark, 2004; Holmes, Grey, & Young, 2005).

(Continued)

Disorder	Beliefs & Concerns	Content of Intrusive Memory/image	Documented Examples
Health anxiety (Warwick & Salkovskis, 1990)	Fear of contracting a physical illness or ailment, will became ill or die.	Image of oneself with weeping sores. Skin itching. Image of humiliation.	Fears related to health and death (e.g. being accidentally buried or cremated alive, being kept in hospital against one's will with no visitors until death) (Wells & Hackmann, 1993).
Eating disorder (Fairburn, Cooper, & Shafran, 2003; Fairburn et al., 2003)	Being obsessed with one's physical appearance.	Seeing one as misshapen and distorted.	Seeing oneself as with bulging eyes and nose and a misshapen and distorted face.
Psychosis		(e.g. being hurt or tortured), traumatic experiences (e.g. being assaulted),	Feared events associated with paranoia or persecutory delusions perceived sources of auditory hallucinations (e.g. spirits of friends), content of auditory hallucinations (e.g. stabbing someone) (Morrison et al., 2002).
Body Dismorphic Disorder (Lambrou, Veale, & Wilson, 2012)	Exaggerated and distorted beliefs about one's physical self and appearance.	Perceiving oneself, in the mind, with rolls of fat, being obese and ugly. Feeling disgusted and ashamed. Too large to go through the doorway.	Exaggerated pictures of and sensations such as tingling in the body parts of concern (e.g. skin, hair, teeth) (Osman et al., 2004).
Bulimia Nervousa			Pictures of the self being overweight and unattractive, sensations of clothes being tight and feeling bloated & heavy (e.g. Hinrichsen, Morrison, Waller, & Schmidt, 2007; Somerville, Cooper, & Hackmann, 2007).

This overview shows how important common features of many psychological conditions are as intrusive images and memories that can be linked with disorders (Reynolds & Brewin, 1999).

(Lipton, Brewin, Linke, & Halperin, 2010).

We can see that there are themes associated with events, and this shows us how disorders can be identified by themes, which may help in showing the type of disorder.

Whilst art imagery is always an idiosyncratic self-expression of that theme, in the form of colour, mark, size shape, which is subjectively experienced through memory or feelings that are triggered by anxiety or depression. These subjective images can be explore through Socratic questioning to elicit further images and explore meaning that shows the context and significance of the image to the individual who makes it. This individualised self-expression can become formulated and provide information that may not yet be explicit, but that can once accessed directly can then be articulated using words.

So whilst art psychotherapy is about understanding the mind, through nonverbal means, and being able to represent ideographically a functional analysis of the role images play in maintaining distress, as a manifestation of disorder. This use of imagery can clinically help us problem solve, as recent research conducted shows (Pearson, Deeprose, Wallace-Hadrill, Burnett Heyes, & Holmes, 2013a; Morina, Deeprose, Pusowski, Schmid, & Holmes, 2011). Holmes asks for a guiding framework for this work:

> a thorough assessment of mental imagery in clinical psychology will help advance understanding of underlying mental imagery processes across a range of psychological disorders, and this in turn will help drive forward advances in both theory and treatment.

Art psychotherapy training could contribute to this new framework, and become included in new written scientific research, that shows why direct imagery has distinct advantages over words, and contribute to the growing understanding of the important role of imagery in psychotherapy scientifically. Currently the only direct images used in cognitive therapy are from computers which are being employed therapeutically (Holmes, James, Coode-Bate, & Deeprose, 2009).

Case example

Depression

Depressed patients working with art psychotherapist David Thorne (Thorne, 2011) illustrate how depression has recurring themes of being trapped and overwhelmed. They show themselves being overwhelmed by a black mood. Falling into a void, or vortex, and being trapped, overwhelmed, being stuck and unable to escape from difficulty, as well as being alone and abandoned, and feeling that something bad is about to happen. Illustrated with the following five images (Figures 7.1–7.5):

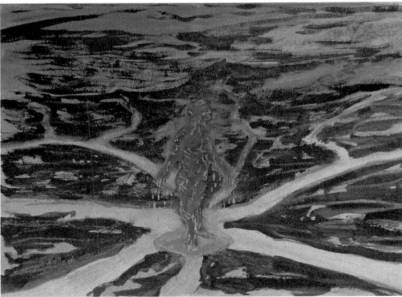

Figures 7.1–7.5 Depression paintings (also see colour plate section)

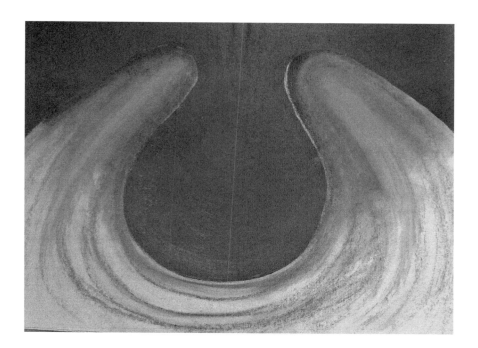

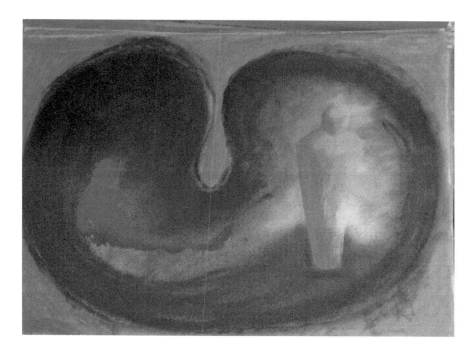

Figures 7.1–7.5 (Continued)

Figures 7.1–7.5 (Continued)

We can see the 'storyboard' of recurring themes assist us in understanding and exploring the specifics of each individuals feelings and memories, through the way each image contains a theme common to depression. This could be used as diagnostic tool that supports and brings theory of disorders to the day-to-day practice of self-expression, and may allow us to distinguish between individual mood, cognition and self-expression that drives unhelpful depressed or anxious behaviours that are making life difficult. Art images have not been explored in this way; however they could assist us in clarification as well as classification of disorder. Thorne asks for assistance in the discrimination and recognition of the manifestation of disorders as art images, in support of case assessment and formulation.

Images give us access to vital aspects of memory and emotions that drive unhelpful suicidal cognitions, that cannot be verbalised, and could help us in our risk assessment. This is important as art psychotherapy shows many individuals' internal world and gives us access in unique ways to this cognitive process (Pearson, Deeprose, Wallace-Hadrill, Burnett Heyes, & Holmes, 2013b):

There are currently not enough 'images in psychiatry,' in either clinical assessment or treatment that check the presence of suicidal flash-forwards imagery, not just 'suicidal ideation', but those that could aid risk assessment, and a clinical focus, that disregards imagery which is such a crucial aspect of many individuals' internal world and a cognitive process is critically linked to dysfunctional emotions.

Art psychotherapy must use research provided by cognitive therapy to show how images give better access and understanding about emotional events. Especially when working with suicidal depressed clients whose involuntary memory and flashbacks can be seen as both images and through verbal questionnaires. This would allow us to consolidate our treatment targets and goals. To develop our practical knowledge of assessment and formulation. This links to Thorne's request and highlights and corroborates recurring themes he sees in collection of data that would permit him to evidence, structure and provide clarity in collaboration for use with his patients, in order to bring about therapeutic change, and support him in the difficult task of motivating his often suicidal depressed clients. This structural clarity through articulation of practice would allow us to consolidate our targets and goals so that our practical knowledge of assessment, formulation and treatment to bring us in line with the wider therapeutic community, and motivate for a familiar professional language and a differential diagnosis that allows a sensitive identification of what is individually unique and different at the same time.

The use of learning theory in art psychotherapy

'Psychopathological images tend to be highly intrusive, distressing and repetitive.'
(Hackmann, 1998)

The process of using learning theory in the form of Kolb's Circle, through experience, observation, expression and reflection (Kolb, 1984) when used with images serves to shift our understanding of the fact that words provide an understanding of negative cognitions. Imagery is positive and able to show both resilience and distress. In this way images provide concrete evidence, for emotional change and cognitive restructuring.

Art-making in its focus on complex emotional goals, allows visualisation of change through the re-making or re-scripting of the directly made image. This serves a number of goals, it is a rehearsal for the future during which the desired therapeutic outcome can be felt and experienced as a behavioural activation. It can be tracked by using David Kolb's experiential learning theory (ELT) to show how we learn new behaviours in response to situational demands, as a practical means of linking feelings, reflection on those behaviours and how we change (Kolb, 1984). This is guided by the formulation, which is flexible and can be

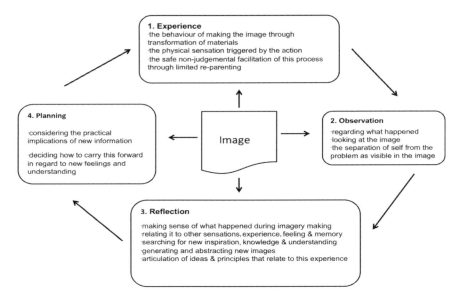

Figure 7.6 Kolb's Learning Circle in Psychotherapy

adjusted to reflect new needs, and it enables goal setting and targets to be reached so cognitive restructuring can take place in treatment.

The component parts of Kolb's learning circle (Kolb, 1984) are;

1   **Experience:** exposure to real or imagined cues that trigger the imagined situation as imagery

2   **Observation:** objective awareness of aspects of this image, including what triggered it, sensory components, emotions, meanings of the content, appraisals made of the significance of having the image, behavioral interactions etc.

3   **Reflecting:** analysing, making sense, relating the experience of the image to the formulation, to current and past experience, knowledge and ideas, and experiments formulating new perceptions in the present.

4   **Planning:** considering the practical meanings of this imagery and the implications or meaning of the wider perspective.

The use of Kolb's Learning Circle (Kolb, 1984), through experience of creating art, provides a paradigm in which to examine our images, reflect on their importance to us and we can see how the image makes sense of our day-to-day experience. It is then possible to see how practical attempts to re-script[1] the problem becomes changed, both in the mind and as the drawing or art is produced. Changes made to the image reflect an updated view of experiences that have occurred as a result of the changes in feeling and cognition hence cognitive restructuring is both felt and seen, and can be articulated.

Seeing the bigger picture

We have seen how art shows a 'bigger picture' allowing access to both positive as well as the negative memories and feelings simultaneously. Direct imagery is holistic it gives us access to detail that becomes evidence, that can become a journal of data. New evidence based practice needs us to show how image maintain disorders first, before we process those images.

Cognitive Behavioural Therapy (CBT) begins from the assumption of a 'mental' image, which is unprocessed, and shows the client how negative images contribute to the maintenance of disorder and contributes to psychological difficulties. These 'unprocessed' mental images contain aspects of unexamined assumptions, because the actual made image is not open to scrutiny.

During art therapy the consequence of the image to the maker is discussed, exploring how this recurring image maintains depression or anxiety, by linking it to historical and autobiographical experience. The emphasis on negative words rather than positive imagery, is something art psychotherapists are unaccustomed to, they believe it can polarise therapy if not balanced by a resilience-based techniques.

Micro-formulation of images

Micro-formulation is offered by Holmes, Hackmann, & Bennet-Levy (2011a) to allow imagery to be contextualised as memory, dream or fantasy, so their emotional impact can be felt and identified by the client and to show how unprocessed negative imagery may provide evidence of the disorder and maintains it. This process enables the documentation of both mental and directly made images in art psychotherapy.

The method displays the role of imagery in the maintenance of psychological problems, when micro-formulations of individual parts of images can be made, by the therapist in order to:

1   Bring the image into awareness. Discussing it as an event that happened or a daydream or nightmare, or a past incident.
2   Observing and reflecting, about what the image is, and means.
3   Linking aspects, and parts of the same image.
4   Asking what one aspect means when seen together with others: the relationship between aspects of the image.
5   Regarding the interaction between multiple aspects of the same situation from new perspectives.

In the process of art psychotherapy active transformation of subjective negative imagery is possible through art making, which brings about new insights and changes as the image is processed and changed over time. This re-scripting process shows three things;

• How the disorder was maintained, through micro-formulation.
• The way the imagery is changed (re-scripted) or altered through the act of making, termed Imagery Rescripting (Holmes, Arntz, & Smucker, 2007). A collected series of works forms a journal of evidence, which can be used as data.

Hackmann offers a cognitive therapy diagram that illustrates and show how notes can be made of the journey around the image as a micro-formulation, which demonstrates a maintenance cycle (Butler, Fennell, & Hackmann, 2010):

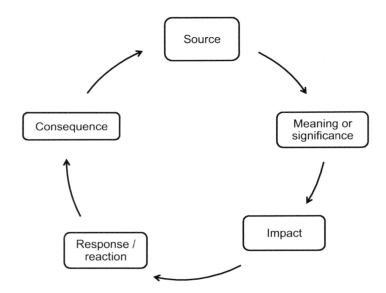

Figure 7.7 Micro-formulation of imagery

(Hackman, Holmes, & Bennett-Levy, 2010)

Micro-formulation currently shows what is imagined in the mind's eye, however, when applied to art psychotherapy, the act of making art that shows intrusive distressing feeling and memory may illustrate how schema are shaped by our past, and reflects past experience and in being re-made, that shapes perception of the present (often distorting it).

Micro-formulation of art images

The micro-formulation of directly made images allows us to observe and experience feeling and memory of past experience through the complexity of colour, form, shape and line:

> **The source** of the image: arises from the maker's experience, in the past, a memory of feeling depressed. For example David Thorne's client's images show us their experience of isolation, oppression and being stuck, in a dark cave or black void.
>
> **The significance of the image** in the present when described in words is to tell how one sees oneself. At the centre of a dilemma, in a trap, unable to think clearly or see the way forward, in a circle of confusing paths, in a dark and ominous place. In cognitive therapy micro-formulation of images is about the consequence of the image in the mind's eye, and how that image reinforces negative behaviours that perpetuate the problem.
>
> **The consequence** of the image when seen in the mind's eye, when described in words is to say how one sees one negative aspect of self. This articulation because it is negative can perpetuate the experience of feeling stuck and depressed. The purpose of micro-formulation in cognitive therapy is just that, to show how this image is a maintenance factor in depression or anxiety.

Seeing ourselves this way in our minds eye confirms our thought that we are indeed stuck (in our own head).

The function of direct imagery making, in art psychotherapy, is to process the image, through the act of making. However if we are to gather evidence we need to do this before we process experience. We must ask and evidence maintenance factors and then process the image afterwards. This is asking art psychotherapy to first assess the function of the negative image.

In making art we access experience through the feeling and memory of an event in the past, as it becomes re-constructed as an art work in the here and now. This art is a separate object, and as it is made, that process of making is witnessed by the client and therapist together. This is a form of limited re-parenting, when the individual experiences themselves held through a reliving process over time. Seeing and enacting this experience of being held allows us to feel contained and safe, it is a metaphor. It allows light in . . . At the front, of the drawing, as it were, since whilst this process of creation happens it is experienced in a multidimensional way. From all sides, in the here and now, whilst it contains affect and memory from past present and is the future in process. Art images show us schema from all sides, and are a rehearsal for future change.

The creative act delineates a point of entry (into the past) from memory that separates who we are, here and now, in the present, from the event that happened in the past. We put the trauma behind us, in the past by making an image, and in doing so we experience our memory of the past event. Then the observation and reflection of its meaning to us can be articulated.

We can then re-script the image to make it as we might prefer.

The astute therapist could now ask Socratic Questions that are about resilience, and document this showing evidence of cognitive restructuring.

How was this image achieved?

Where did the courage come from to make this one exception, to trust someone (the self, who avoided and the therapist who is a stranger) to see this image?

The witnesses are the art maker, who has avoided the situation and is now confronted with it.

This is why traumatic imagery is often so hard to contemplate.

This self of the maker is now become a mindful witness to an event that might become witnessed compassionately anew, one is no longer alone with the experience.

Could other exceptions be made to allowing trust and allowing oneself to be seen?

What would the conditions for that exception have to be?

If life is so dark and obscure, how is it we can see what is in the image?

What do we see?

The consequence of having made an art image is very different than that of describing the situation in words. When I say 'I see myself in a black hole,' present tense, I reinforce the negative logic of being stuck.

When I make an image the consequence of that making directly changes that self-perception. It is shows what was, in the past, as well as what is, in the present. Making an image in the here and now allows a re-living of past experience. That experience can then be evidenced as both negative in the past and positive in the present. Making the image that taps into implicit feeling and memory of the past that is painful. This is seen directly, witnessed as an exposure to how difficult life is and has been. Re-experiencing of this kind takes courage and is a rehearsal for future behaviour, as it is a departure from safety behaviours that maintain the problem. The re-scripting example given shows how re-making an image allows change that can be seen.

This step-wise process is an important aspect to evidence gathering in art psychotherapy.

Step one: client could access negative imagery and create an understanding about historical events perhaps from childhood, and make links between that experience and the way life is experienced in the here and now.

Cognitive therapist Luisa Stopa quotes one of her patients as saying that:

'You need to go to a safe place in your head, well that is already impossible for me if it must be positive. If it is negative I don't get it out of (?) my head. I also feel like I'm talking bullshit because I really find it difficult and don't see it for my eyes.'

Step two: the physical act of making art in therapy allows us to the re-make or re-script situations in our lives, over time in a journey that has the potential to help us to become who we might be (Taylor & Stopa, 2012).

Making images as re-scripting

Recent interest in the use of imagery re-scripting with traumatic memories includes the seminal work of Arntz and Weertman (Arntz & Weertman, 1999; Weertman & Arntz, 2007) and Smucker with colleagues; art psychotherapy, with its understanding of the process of artistic creation, provides what Arntz calls

> *a multi-level framework for changing 'self-image' over time, in ways that assist clients to visualise creative alternatives, allowing multiple perspectives and alternative 'rehearsals for the future', which are more functional than the ones which were creating conflict and making life difficult for the client.*
>
> (Arntz, 2012)

Arntz believes that imagery re-scripting (IR) is a powerful technique, which lacks a theoretical base, and he calls for a return to an analysis of individual cases in a multi-level framework, such as we see with Learmonth and Gibson (2010). This allows us to unravel the mechanisms that enable psychotherapists to use images effectively, in the way art psychotherapy does, this means we must be able to see the image, on paper and not simply imagine it in our head.

'This will open out the process of creating "whole sense change" and elicit information from clients in session feedback and longitudinal follow up.'

The act of making imagery allows transformation by action, from feeling into cognition, and this shows how art imagery makes visible parts or aspects of the direct image, showing us how they relate to one another, as the memories and feelings evoked promote an emotional response. This behaviour leads to changes in mood and to connection between past and present that maintain the problem. It shows possibilities for future change. As we see cognitive research shows us how to collect these images and then formulate them.

Art psychotherapy is an act of sensory re-living, through the creation of a tangible object. Making art shifts our perception of ourselves in the past, out of personal history, grounding it in the present. This re-scripting creates a new context for it in the here and now, a perceptual updating that shifts the problem out of the past as it was experienced, allowing it to emerge and be experienced anew. It becomes evidence as it can be witnessed and observed.

Patients are assessed as able to benefit if they are able to discriminate between imagery and reality, and able to transform old imagery and appraisals, in order to create new imagery, and new meanings. The basic procedure of imagery re-scripting is as follows:

Stage 1 Bring into focus the aspect of the image that is problematic

Stage 2 Ask what the problem is and what might be done to understand it

Stage 3 Try experimenting (BE) with aspects of the image to resolve the problem

Stage 4 Experiment with solutions and re-draw the image

Figure 7.8 Imagery re-scripting example

Figure 7.8 is an example of how an image becomes re-scripted, by using a photograph and drawing on it, to show what happens.

Re-scripted image

This image[2] is seen in two stages:

The first stage of this image example is a photograph that shows a one-dimensional view of a girl alone on a jetty with her dog, looking out to sea. Then lines have been drawn in transforming the photograph showing another child sitting beside her and boats on the horizon. This re-scripting in action example demonstrates how a one-dimensional photograph can be changed by hand, in a way that suggests change over time. After the photograph is drawn upon we can anticipate a positive resolution – the arrival of the boats. The added lines create a positive shift (or re-scripting), and show the concept of change over time, which is the difference between one point perspective and multiple viewpoint perspective. This allows alternative schema to be experienced in the past present and future. The photograph shows us the past, and like cognitive therapy is concerned with the logic of the maintenance cycle, which doesn't imagine change, as for that to become possible we must imagine over time, moving through the past and memory, and our lived experience. This subjective visualisation is important as it anticipates psychological change. It also gives an explicit rationale for working with art using directly made images. This provides the theory Arntz is seeking through understanding the client's higher implicational meaning, through the exploration and transformation of materials, making sense of abstract concepts allowing evidence to be gathered, shown and reflected upon, so that data can be recorded and assessment carried out across clinical sessions, showing evidence of change.

Evidencing change and cognitive restructuring

New NHS commissioning frameworks embedded in a modernist world view that value rationality, objectivity and pragmatism (Woolfolk & Richardson, 1984) such that cognitive therapy has been criticised as insensitive because of its use of unfortunate pejorative terms such as 'maladaptive thinking' and 'dysfunctional behaviours', which seemed to view self-criticism as maladaptive thinking to be recognised, controlled and eliminated (Messer & Winokur, 1984). It appears that more recent use of imagery in cognitive therapy, like art therapy encourages acceptance of self-expression in order to explore subjective distress, to understand and share experience. In order to learn how to make cognitive changes and understand ourselves better in line with democratic practice that values choice.

Cognitive re-structuring in art psychotherapy could be introduced to enable both emotional processing and enhanced functional understanding towards carrying out therapy in a more strategic and time-limited way.

Reconciling our two 'selves'

It seems that cognitive therapies focus on words, as cognition has created an unexplored gap that might be filled by direct imagery making used in art psychotherapy that shows how our emotions sometimes are automatic, an impulse, allows us to identify and link body states with their associated thoughts. This dual processing framework outlined by Strack and Deutch demonstrates how a two systems model can show that behaviour results from two cognitive processing systems, a reflective system deliberate and intentional, and an impulse system that is fast intuitive and effortless (Strack & Deutsch, 2004). The illusive defining feature of direct images is that they capture experience in ways that words do not. Art utilises the implicit in a fast intuitive and impulsive way. Imagery is free of the bottlenecks provided by cognitive processing or words, for this reason making direct images draws attention away from the deliberate controlled process, as well as from depression and rumination. Theorists (Preston, Buchanan, Stansfield, & Bechara, 2007) speak of an 'impulsive amygdala – dependent system' that signals pain or pleasure associated with short-term immediate outcomes speculating that this impulse is more difficult to override.

The futures of art psychotherapy are to harness and bring about affective change. We haven't said how we might achieve this, but the use of multi-level theories (Teasdale, 1997) have been articulated to show us how body states in the form of visual auditory, gestatory and other nonverbal information is experienced, asserting the need for holistic ways of collecting data. It is up to art psychotherapy to show how behaviour seen through making imagery directly links us to the primary nature of how clients become stuck. Images have a special relationship that helps us access impulse, so we can understand and change signals that are otherwise difficult to pin down. It seems that we are able to use imagery, to access information directly, that cannot be identified through words or explicit self-report, that help us understand why our clients continue to try and dull pain caused by childhood trauma, that repeatedly shows up as depression and anxiety. If we can chart implicit behaviour through micro-formulation, to gain access to specific themes, we can identify risk not revealed in other ways, as well as develop a disorder specific model, that can be used to get access to treatment in short-term art psychotherapy, for depression and anxiety.

Notes

1   Dr. Mervin Smucker began clinical experiments with imagery rescripting as a clinical associate professor at the University of Pennsylvania, where he also served as Director of Education and Clinical Training. Working closely with Prof. Aaron Beck at the Center for Cognitive Therapy. In 1994, his first scientific publication on Imagery Rescripting appeared, which detailed its clinical application with trauma and PTSD. Mervin Smucker spent the next 20 years developing and refining his treatment – today known as Imagery Rescripting & Reprocessing Therapy (IRRT) – and its clinical applications not only with trauma-related material, but with other clinical disorders and distressing symptoms as well. Today, Imagery Rescripting & Reprocessing Therapy is one of the leading internationally recognized treatments for clinical symptoms relating to trauma.
2   Photo provided by Helen Kennerly at the Oxford Cognitive Therapy Centre in a workshop.

References

Arntz, A. (2012). Imagery rescripting as a therapeutic technique: Review of clinical trials, basic studies, and research agenda. *Journal of Experimental Psychopathology*, *3*(2), 189–208. Retrieved from http://jep.textrum.com/index.php?art_id=74#.UwoJJ_RdV8E

Arntz, A., & Weertman, A. (1999). Treatment of childhood memories: Theory and practice. *Behaviour Research and Therapy*, *37*(8), 715–740. Retrieved from www.ncbi.nlm.nih.gov/pubmed/10452174

Beck, A., & Emery, G. (1979). Cognitive therapy of anxiety and phobic disorders. Retrieved from http://scholar.google.co.uk/scholar?q=1979+a+beck+and+emery+&btnG=&hl=en&as_sdt=0,5#4

Beck, A.T. (1961). An inventory for measuring depression. *Archives of General Psychiatry*, *4*(6), 561. doi:10.1001/archpsyc.1961.01710120031004

Beck, A.T., & Clark, D.A. (1997). An information processing model of anxiety: Automatic and strategic processes. *Behaviour Research and Therapy*, *35*(1), 49–58. doi:10.1016/S0005-7967(96)00069-1

Beck AT, Ward CH, Mendelson M, Mock J, Erbaugh J (June 1961). "An inventory for measuring depression". *Arch. Gen. Psychiatry 4* (6): 561–71.

Beck, A. T., Rush, J. A., Shaw, B. F., & Emery, G. (1979). *Cognitive therapy for depression*. New York: Guilford Press.

Brewin, C.R., Lanius, R.A., Novac, A., Schnyder, U., & Galea, S. (2009). Reformulating PTSD for DSM-V: Life after Criterion A. *Journal of Traumatic Stress*, *22*(5), 366–373. doi:10.1002/jts.20443

Butler, G., Fennell, M., & Hackmann, A. (2010). *Cognitive-Behavioral Therapy for Anxiety Disorders: Mastering Clinical Challenges* (p. 224). New York: Guilford Press. Retrieved from http://books.google.com/books?id=2QvoM5tBoN8C&pgis=1

Clark, D. M., Salkovskis, P. M., Ost, L., Breitholtz, E., Koehler, B.E., A., W., . . . Gelder, M. (1997). Misinterpretation of body sensations in panic disorder. *Journal of Consulting and Clinical Psychology, 65*(2), 203–213. doi:10.1037/0022–006X.65.2.203

Clark, D. M., & Wells, A. (1995). A Cognitive Model of Social Phobia. In R. G. Heimberg, M. R. Leibowitz, D. A. Hope, & F. R. Schneier (Eds.), *Social Phobia: Diagnosis, Assessment and Treatment* (pp. 69–93). New York: Guilford.

D'Argenbeau, A., Raffard, S., & van der Linden, M. (2008). Remembering the past and imagining the future in schizophrenia. *Journal of Abnormal Psychology, 117*, 247–251.

Deeprose, C., Malik, A., & Holmes, E. A. (2011). Measuring intrusive prospective imagery using the Impact of Future Events Scale (IFES): Psychometric properties and relation to risk for bipolar disorder. *International Journal of Cognitive Therapy, 4*(2), 187–196. doi:10.1521/ijct.2011.4.2.187

Fairburn, C. G., Cooper, Z., & Shafran, R. (2003). Cognitive behaviour therapy for eating disorders: A 'transdiagnostic' theory and treatment. *Behaviour Research and Therapy, 41*(5), 509–528. doi:10.1016/S0005–7967(02)00088–8

Gilroy, A., Tipple, R., & Brown, C. (Eds.). (2012). *Assessment in Art Therapy. Art Therapy* (Vol. 30, p. 228). Routledge, London. doi:10.1080/07421656.2013.787220

Gosden, T., Morris, P.G., Ferreira, N.B., Grady, C. and Gillanders, D.T. (2014). Mental imagery in chronic pain: Prevalence and characteristics. *Eur J Pain.* 2014 May; 18(5):721–8.

Greenberg, L. S. (2002). *Emotion-Focused Therapy: Coaching Clients to Work through Their Feelings* (p. 337). Washington, DC: American Psychological Association. doi: 10.1037/10447–000

Grey, N., Holmes, E. "Hotspots" in trauma memories in the treatment of post-traumatic stress disorder: A replication. *Memory (Impact Factor: 2.09). 09/2008; 16*(7):788–96. South London & Maudsley NHS Trust, King's College London, UK.

Grey, N., Young, K., & Holmes, E. (2002). Hot spots in emotional memory and the treatment of posttraumatic stress disorder. *Behavioural and Cognitive Psychotherapy.* Retrieved from http://scholar.google.co.za/scholar?hl=en&q=holmes+grey+and+young&btnG=&as_sdt=1,5&as_sdtp=#9

Hodson, K. J., McManus, F. V., Clark, D. M., & Doll, H. (2008). Can Clark and Wells' (1995) Cognitive Model of Social Phobia be applied to young people? *Behavioural and Cognitive Psychotherapy 36*, 449–461. doi:10.1017/S1352465808004487

Holmes, E. A., Arntz, A., & Smucker, M. R. (2007). Imagery rescripting in cognitive behaviour therapy: Images, treatment techniques and outcomes. *Journal of Behavior Therapy and Experimental Psychiatry, 38*(4), 297–305. doi:10.1016/j.jbtep.2007.10.007

Holmes E.A., Crane C., Fennell M.J.V., Williams J.M.G. Imagery about suicide in depression—flash-forwards? *Journal of Behavior Therapy and Experimental Psychiatry. 2007;38*(4):423–434. [PMC free article] [PubMed]

Holmes, E. A., & Hackmann, A. (2004). A healthy imagination? Editorial for the special issue of memory: Mental imagery and memory in psychopathology. *Memory 2004;12(4):387–388. [PubMed] Hove England* doi:10.1080/09658210444000133

Holmes, E. A., Hackmann, A., & Bennet-Levy, J. (2011a). *Mental Imagery and Formulation in Cognitive Therapy* (p. 233). Oxford: Oxford University Press. Retrieved from http://books.google.com/books?hl=en&lr=&id=ngajYg3K8I8C&pgis=1

Holmes, E.A., Hackmann, A., & Bennet-Levy, J. (2011b). *Oxford Guide to Imagery in Cognitive Therapy* (p. 233). Oxford University Press. Retrieved from http://books.google.com/books?hl=en&lr=&id=ngajYg3K8I8C&pgis=1

Holmes, E.A., James, E.L., Coode-Bate, T., & Deeprose, C. (2009). Can playing the computer game 'Tetris' reduce the build-up of flashbacks for trauma? A proposal from cognitive science. *PloS One, 4*(1), e4153. doi:10.1371/journal.pone.0004153

Holmes, E.A., & Mathews, A. (2010). Mental imagery in emotion and emotional disorders. *Clinical Psychology Review, 30*, 349–362. doi:10.1016/j.cpr.2010.01.001

Kolb, D. (1984). *Experiential Learning: Experience as the Source of Learning and Development.* Englewood Cliffs, NJ: Prentice Hall.

Kosslyn, S.M., Ganis, G., & Thompson, W.L. (2001). Neural foundations of imagery. *Nature Reviews. Neuroscience, 2*, 635–642. doi:10.1038/35090055

Lambrou, C., Veale, D., & Wilson, G. (2012). Appearance concerns comparisons among persons with body dysmorphic disorder and nonclinical controls with and without aesthetic training, *Body Image, 9*(1), 86–92. doi:10.1016/j.bodyim.2011.08.001

Learmonth, M., & Gibson, K. (2010). Art psychotherapy, disability issues, mental health, trauma and resilience: 'Things and people.' *International Journal of Art Therapy, 15*(2), 53–64. doi:10.1080/17454832.2010.523880

Lipton, M., Brewin, C., Linke, S., & Halperin, J. (2010). Distinguishing features of intrusive images in obsessive-compulsive disorder. *Journal of Anxiety Disorders, 24*(8), 816–822. Retrieved from http://discovery.ucl.ac.uk/125588/

McAvinue, L., & Robertson, I. (2007). Measuring visual imagery ability: A review. *Imagination, Cognition and Personality.* doi:10.2190/3515–8169–24J8–7157

Messer, S.B., & Winokur, M. (1984). Ways of Knowing and Visions of Reality in Psychoanalytic Therapy and Behaviour Therapy. In H. Hall (Ed.), *Psychoanalytic Therapy and Behaviour Therapy* (pp. 63–100). Springer US. Retrieved from http://link.springer.com/chapter/10.1007/978-1-4613-2733-2_5

Morina, N., Deeprose, C., Pusowski, C., Schmid, M., & Holmes, E.A. (2011). Prospective mental imagery in patients with major depressive disorder or anxiety disorders. *Journal of Anxiety Disorders.* doi:10.1016/j.janxdis.2011.06.012

Morrison A.P. Beck AT , Gledworth D Dunn H. Reid. G.S. Larkin W. *Behavior Research & Therapy. Imagery & Psychotic symptoms Preliminary studies.* (2002) Pubmed.

Osman, S., Cooper, M., Hackman, M., & Vegle, D. (2004). Spontaneously occuring images and early memories in persons with body dysmorphic disorder. Body Image, 1, 113–125. *Encyclopedia of Cognitive Behavior Therapy* pp 83–86.

Patel, T., Brewin, C.R.C., Wheatley, J., Wells, A., Fisher, P., & Myers, S. (2007). Intrusive images and memories in major depression. *Behaviour Research and Therapy, 45*(11), 2573–2580. doi:10.1016/j.brat.2007.06.004

Pearson, D.G. (2007). Mental imagery and creative thought. In *Proceedings of The British Academy, 147*, 187–212.

Pearson, D.G., Deeprose, C., Wallace-Hadrill, S.M.A, Burnett Heyes, S., & Holmes, E.A. (2013a). Assessing mental imagery in clinical psychology: A review of imagery measures and a guiding framework. *Clinical Psychology Review, 33*(1), 1–23. doi:10.1016/j.cpr.2012.09.001

Pearson, D.G., Deeprose, C., Wallace-Hadrill, S.M.A., Burnett Heyes, S., & Holmes, E.A. (2013b). Assessing mental imagery in clinical psychology: A review of imagery measures and a guiding framework. *Clinical Psychology Review, 33*(1), 1–23. doi:10.1016/j.cpr.2012.09.001

Preston, S. D., Buchanan, T. W., Stansfield, R. B., & Bechara, A. (2007). Effects of anticipatory stress on decision making in a gambling task. *Behavioural Neuroscience, 121*(2), 257–263.

Reynolds, M., & Brewin, C. R. (1999). Intrusive memories in depression and posttraumatic stress disorder. *Behaviour Research and Therapy, 37*(3), 201–15. Retrieved from http://dx.doi.org/10.1016/S0005–7967(98)00132–6

Rice, H. J., & Rubin, D. C. (2011). Remembering from any angle: The flexibility of visual perspective during retrieval. *Consciousness and Cognition, 20*(3), 568–577. doi:10.1016/j.concog.2010.10.013

Rice, H. J., & Rubin, D. C. (2009). I can see it both ways: First- and third-person visual perspectives at retrieval. *Consciousness and Cognition: An International Journal, 18*(4), 877–890.

Rice, H. J., & Rubin, D. C. (in prep). Visual perspective during autobiographical retrieval across time periods.

Roth, A. D., Pilling S. and Turner, J. (in preparation) Therapist training and supervision in CBT in major trials for depression and anxiety.

Rubin, D. C. (2005). A basic-systems approach to autobiographical memory. *Current Directions in Psychological Science, 14*(2), 79–83.

Somerville, K., Cooper, M., & Hackmann, A. (2007). Spontaneous imagery in women with bulimia nervosa: an investigation into content, characteristics and links to childhood memories. *Journal of Behavior Therapy and Experimental Psychiatry, 38*, 435–446. PubMedCrossRef

Stopa, L. (Ed.). (2009). *Imagery and the Threatened Self: Perspectives on Mental Imagery and the Self in Cognitive Therapy* (p. 280). London & New York: Routledge. Retrieved from http://books.google.com/books?hl=en&lr=&id=8R59AgAAQBAJ&pgis=1

Strack, F., & Deutsch, R. (2004). Reflective and impulsive determinants of social behavior. *Personality and Social Psychology Review: An Official Journal of the Society for Personality and Social Psychology, Inc, 8*(3), 220–247. doi:10.1207/s15327957pspr0803_1

Taylor, K., & Stopa, L. (2012). The fear of others: A pilot study of social anxiety processes in paranoia. Retrieved from http://journals.cambridge.org/production/action/cjoGetFulltext?fulltextid=8701388

Teasdale, J. (1997). The relationship between cognition and emotion: The mind-in-place in mood disorders. Retrieved from http://doi.apa.org/psycinfo/1997–97380–004

Thorne, D. (2011). Images on the void: An enquiry into the nature of depression through reflections on five commonly presented images. *International Journal of Art Therapy, 16*(1), 20–29. doi:10.1080/17454832.2011.570275

Veale, D., Ennis, M., & Lambrou, C. (2002). Possible association of body dysmorphic disorder with an occupation or education in art and design. *American Journal of Psychiatry, 159*, 1788–1790. http://dx.doi.org/10.1176/appi.ajp.159.10.1788

Warwick, H.M.C., & Salkovskis, P. M. (1990). Hypochondriasis. *Behaviour Research and Therapy, 28*(2), 105–117. Retrieved from www.sciencedirect.com/science/article/pii/000579679090023C

Weertman, A., & Arntz, A. (2007). Effectiveness of treatment of childhood memories in cognitive therapy for personality disorders: A controlled study contrasting methods focusing on the present and methods focusing on childhood memories. *Behaviour Reseach and Therapy, 45*(9), 2133–2143.

Woolfolk, R. L., & Richardson, F. C. (1984). Behavior therapy and the ideology of modernity. *American Psychologist, 39*(7), 777–786. doi:10.1037/0003–066X.39.7.777

Chapter 8

Notes on service design for art psychotherapists working in time-limited group programmes on adult mental health inpatient wards

Kate Rothwell and Sheila Grandison

Introduction

The increasingly fast throughput of adult patients in acute mental health settings is integral to how we have defined time-limited art psychotherapy treatment for the purposes of this chapter. At the time of writing, the average length of stay on an inner London acute mental health admissions ward is 27.3 days.

With the duration of admissions on acute wards averaging less than four weeks, and given the implausibility of setting a therapeutic contract due to the unpredictability of the patient's discharge date, we are not attempting to discuss art psychotherapy within a contracted time-limited model of a kind more suitable for outpatient work. Furthermore, how the art psychotherapist supports patients with high levels of emotional disturbance whilst on the ward, to begin a positive attachment to the therapist in the here-and-now, may not be identified as formal 'therapy' in the patient's mind.

Engaging with patients in acute states of mind in the interests of establishing meaningful contact is the remit of all members of the multidisciplinary care team, and not only the art psychotherapist. However, unlike ward-based nursing colleagues, for example, art psychotherapists can work towards establishing a therapeutic relationship that need not end at the point of discharge from the ward.

Acute, complex, and enduring mental health presentations may not move in a simple linear direction between inpatient and outpatient community services. The progress towards recovery may be interrupted through, for example, relapse and multiple admissions, changing needs and circumstances, and whether engagement in treatment is voluntary or is compulsory under the Mental Health Act. How acute and community art psychotherapy service provision can be designed *flexibly*, what it might look like, and what is required of the art psychotherapist, is what we describe in this chapter.

In addition to the therapeutic skills required for working with patients in acute states of mind, our attention is on what else is required of the art psychotherapist when working in the acute sector. What we are emphasising is a consideration of what needs to be held in her mind, with a view to *ongoing work*, and when the patient has developed more ego strength. From our experience, as Heads of NHS Arts Therapies Services in Adult Mental Health and Forensics Directorates, for this thinking to be able to happen, a carefully designed plan for the service delivery of integrated acute and community provision, one which enables *the continuity* of art psychotherapy between acute and community settings, has been found to be essential.

Such a service plan needs to be informed by the overall trajectory of psychic recovery, such as put forward by Pamela Fuller (2013). That is, from working with a patient's lack of a consistent, cohesive sense of self during an acute admission (undifferentiated sense of self), to an emerging sense of self, through to a more stable sense of self (differentiated self).[1] Transitional input between acute and community provision of art psychotherapy can be integrated into a flexible service delivery plan that broadly follows a psychodynamic model of movement towards self-definition. Within a dynamic model, *the active transitioning of the patient in the art psychotherapist's mind*, can then parallel the patient's *actual movement* through mental health acute and community services.

Due to the increasingly short duration of admissions, a model of art psychotherapy in acute settings may constitute a very short piece of work that takes place over three to four weeks, and conflates assessment and treatment. How, as art psychotherapists, do we regard these briefer-than-brief short periods of work in relation to longer term benefit for the patient? In order not to let patients down at the point of discharge from the ward, working towards developing and maintaining a therapeutic relationship is paramount. For the patient's transition from acute to community service provision to be effective, the art psychotherapist's thinking and sensitive consideration of care planning further along the patient's recovery journey is required. Such thinking keeps in mind the effective engagement of patients in a positive therapeutic alliance along *the patient's* care pathway to recovery.

Referring to the treatment of psychosis specifically, the updated guidance from the National Institute for Health and Care Excellence (NICE) acknowledges:

> Engaging people effectively during an acute schizophrenic illness is often difficult and demands considerable flexibility in the approach and pace of therapeutic working. Moreover, once engaged in a positive therapeutic alliance, it is equally necessary to maintain this relationship, often over long periods, with the added problem that such an alliance may wax and wane.[2]

Such challenges for therapeutic engagement, together with the impact of stigma and social exclusion, may be said to be applicable to sufferers of all acute, severe, complex, and enduring mental health difficulties, irrespective of diagnosis.

The framework of evidence-based practice

All art, music, drama, and dance movement psychotherapists working within the environment of inpatient mental health wards find themselves working with psychosis and psychotic processes, as well as other complex mental health difficulties and trauma. At the time of writing, the updated guidance from the National Institute for Health and Care Excellence (NICE) on *Psychosis and Schizophrenia in Adults* (2014) remains very relevant, in that arts therapies are included as psychological therapies that should be considered for all patients with a diagnosis of schizophrenia, and for the treatment of negative symptoms in particular. In the UK today, in order to provide and adhere to evidence-based practice, compliance with NICE guidelines is expected.

With a small empirical evidence base for the arts therapies, the research recommendation by NICE for more randomised control trials in arts therapies to enhance the emerging evidence, may be outside the resource and funding capability of small arts therapies services. However, what is more likely to be within the resource capability and financial budget of a small arts therapy service is the recommendation by NICE, in the guidance for psychosis and schizophrenia in adults, that specifies *continuity of care* from acute through to community provision, and calls for arts therapy intervention to be primarily group-based. The two NICE guidelines are as follows:

- When psychological treatments, including Arts Therapies, are started in the acute phase, including in in-patient settings, the full course should be continued after discharge without unnecessary interruptions.
- The intervention should be provided in groups unless difficulties with acceptability, access and engagement indicate otherwise.

We have taken the NICE guidance for continuity in patient care, and the significance of the effective engagement of patients in a positive therapeutic alliance, as a general principle for informing sound and innovative service design when delivering an integrated acute and community art psychotherapy service. Regarding group-based therapeutic provision, Irvin Yalom's theory of group work (2005)[3] provides a helpful frame regarding the important task of beginning a sustainable attachment to the art psychotherapist in the here-and-now, and developing it beyond the here-and-now. Yalom's theory is underpinned by the significance of the therapist being mindful of the three stages of beginning, middle, and end when working in groups. When working with groups in acute settings, Yalom gives emphasis to how, in an open, revolving membership acute group, the working through of the three stages is compressed and may need to be completed in one session, whereas in a longer-term, fixed membership community group, the three stages develop gradually over time.

On the acute ward, art psychotherapy can provide an entry point for patients who may not be able to engage in other psychological treatments due to their high levels of distress. The art psychotherapist's holding in mind of the patient's overall recovery journey, held in the interests of sustaining attachment from acute through to community, can similarly be conceptualised using a beginning, middle, and end model such as Yalom's. That is, to think simultaneously about assessing for the suitability of art psychotherapy during the early, beginning stages of recovery on the ward, in relation to moving through a range of group-based art psychotherapeutic interventions during the middle transition from acute to community, and on to worked through endings in the wider community provision of the patient's treatment and care plan. Through innovative partnerships with outside agencies, art psychotherapy can provide a range of interventions from inpatient wards to community therapy groups that connect, for example, with mainstream culture and education sectors, for full *social recovery*, with a view to enabling an active and responsible life within the familial and cultural contexts of patients. Just as the artistic medium in art psychotherapy can be used as a bridge to verbal dialogue within therapy sessions, so a range of carefully designed group-based art psychotherapy interventions can increase access and provide the bridging role in the service delivery of a socially inclusive integrated acute-community programme.

Further general principles for effective service design can be taken from NICE Guidance. From the guidelines for psychosis and schizophrenia in adults, the following recommendations for the delivery of groups are useful for utilising what is usually a small resource:

- The intervention is delivered by one therapist in groups of 6–8 people
- The average duration of the group is one hour
- The average length is 12 weeks of therapy[4]

Due to the inability to set fixed time-limited therapeutic contracts with patients, and in the interests of good practice in acute settings, the alignment of NICE treatment guidance with NICE quality standards for patients in adult mental health, their families, and carers, emphasises the human experience at the core of all we are doing when working with highly vulnerable people. Quality standards included in the NICE guidance on *Service User Experience in Adult Mental Health* (2011) include:

- People using mental health services, and their families or carers, feel they are treated with empathy, dignity and respect.
- People using mental health services, and their families or carers, feel optimistic that care will be effective.
- People using community mental health services are normally supported by staff from a single, multidisciplinary community team, familiar to them and with whom they have a continuous relationship.
- People in hospital for mental health care have daily one-to-one contact with mental healthcare professionals known to the service user and regularly see other members of the multidisciplinary mental healthcare team.[5]

We have found that through our integrated acute and community services being informed by the NICE guidance for psychosis and schizophrenia and the NICE service user quality standards, not only are they together very pertinent to our art psychotherapy work, they represent good practice in a way that is understandable to patients, managers, and commissioners alike. Outlined below are notes that go towards putting integrated acute and community service design into practice.

Working on an acute inpatient ward

Here the skills required of the art psychotherapist are used to work effectively with the multidisciplinary team in the knowledge she alone has no final say over patient discharge. Where the art psychotherapist positions herself within the team to undertake early intervention work is important in order to be able to assess patients from the outset. From this strategic platform within a multidisciplinary team, designing a service beyond the acute ward, and how to refer on to other agencies or taking the patient through the service is vital.

The art psychotherapist's own narrative about the distress and difficulties of working with the acute client group can change on a daily basis. In Forensics for example, art psychotherapists new to working on a Low Secure Unit Specialist Learning Disabilities ward are advised to learn quick and effective ways of addressing patient issues, as the demand is relentless. There is a sense of dependency from the patients that puts staff in the parental role. The patients infantilise themselves in the process, no doubt in an effort to be looked after and cared for. The patients need parental 'noticing', but with the added element of risk on a secure ward it is vital for the art psychotherapist to be psychologically minded in order to maintain and sustain the thinking mind, to understand the polarities, paradoxes, dichotomies, and fast-moving extremes in patients' behaviour and the emotions *impacting on staff*.

Traditionally art psychotherapists give sessional input to acute wards and are trained to understand and weather such disturbance. Through training the capacity to differentiate between potentially meaningful, and destructive, patient communication is fostered. Over time art psychotherapists, whether in training or qualified, learn to sustain and develop resilience through experience when working with high levels of active psychosis and emotional disturbance. Given this backdrop, how do art psychotherapists function to hold their thinking to get their groups started, often without a formalised referral system, and often with the felt experience of being seemingly invisible to other staff more involved in daily ward tasks.

Referral systems for brief group work on an acute ward: Assessment to recovery

Art psychotherapy in acute settings is combined assessment and treatment and requires a specialist way of working and thinking. On an acute ward art psychotherapists work with blanket referrals rather than a referral system, that is, open to all patients and without a waiting list. Any referral system would very quickly bottleneck and become unmanageable due to the fast through-put and limited art therapy resource. We have developed a needs-led service model that considers the acute admission ward as the first phase of recovery. It is a model that keeps patients' recovery and wellbeing central beyond the immediate ward environment into post-discharge to maintain and advance therapeutic progress and a successful transition. That is to ensure positive therapeutic engagement is not truncated abruptly.

When admitted to an acute ward, the patient finds him/herself in a place where they can be positioned on a pathway to recovery, given there may be breakdown, inconsistency, or waiting lists elsewhere in community provision. Given the specialism of art psychotherapy in acute settings, it is necessary to reconsider how the art psychotherapist communicates clinical information to staff in an environment where there may be insufficient time for her to write an assessment report for each patient outlining the aims of their therapeutic interventions.

The art psychotherapist needs to show quickly and effectively, and in an accessible way, that coming into the art therapy room, being in the room with an art psychotherapist, and accepting of what the therapist has to offer by way of using art materials, is of use or benefit to the patient. Conveying the levels of willingness shown by the patient to communicate with another, is also showing that art psychotherapy is more than an activity, and is a form of interpersonal engagement. Seeing art psychotherapy as a useful first step for the patient is a means of finding a place for them to move from a narrow field of preserving their defence systems to the possibility of opening up a psychological window, no matter how small.

The art psychotherapist's observational skills and attention to detail is needed to ensure the multidisciplinary team does not miss significant communication. In acute forensic services, such assessment practices may be re-labeled as 'pre-pre-therapy' and 'pre-therapy', though one may run seamlessly into the other without a specific time-limited frame.

Acute settings and the risk of psychic assaults: The 'pre-pre-therapy' engagement group

In brief acute art psychotherapy work the care pathway holds the patient in mind giving continuity of provision by positioning the therapist correctly in the service from acute to recovery in the community. To not consider transitional groups would be to collude with the attacks on linking. When we consider the fragmentation of personality that often emanates from deprived and abusive experiences of care, it is important that the 'pre-pre-therapy' group exists. Its role is to support the patients to develop a capacity to link thoughts, feelings, and experiences and to manage dissociation or outbursts derived from internal trauma triggered by current events.

Acute settings can bring about the risk of psychic assaults, described by Gordon and Kirtchuk (2008) as follows:

> The link (attachment) between the patient and other people; between the patient and his own thoughts, feelings, experiences and history; between the patient as an individual and the social group – including the ward milieu – to which he belongs: *these links are all seriously disturbed, distorted, attacked or obliterated.*[6]

Coming to work each day on an acute ward

Art psychotherapists on an acute ward cannot remain isolated but need to get stuck in and be part of the whole, to become familiar with the everyday comings and goings, and find a balance between alertness, noticing, and acceptance. Yet some experiences cannot be pre-empted. To take this into our stride requires us to know that we will not really know what waits for us every morning. What is necessary is to contextualise rather than personalise each experience.

As art psychotherapists, we work with people who need looking after, they need to be cared for and feel cared for. Our role is to form a therapeutic relationship that takes into consideration that we matter to our patients and they may need us to do more than purely sit in a room or go on to the ward once a week.

What are the skills required of the art psychotherapist on the ward?

In our service model we have found it important to establish our working relationships quickly by being visible and part of the ward community. It is helpful to be willing to join in and useful to the smooth running of the ward to be a kind human, using plain language in the service of enhancing everyone's understanding, as an invitation for others to contribute to our thinking about how to understand the needs and communications of patients better.

By art psychotherapists owning their thoughts, and voicing them in the team to support the work our patients have engaged in, the building of trust and willingness to use our services is enhanced. We recommend having an active involvement in the Care Programme Approach (CPA) to patient care, being pro-active, showing we have contributed to treatment and can hold a valid opinion on the patient's progress.

An art psychotherapist's perspective on managed transition of care from ward to community

With the NICE guidance and developments in practice the therapeutic work does not end when patients are discharged. We are using the term 'care pathway' to describe the *patient's* pathway to recovery, and therefore the therapeutic journey, as distinct from HONOS clustering of diagnoses into specified care pathways. On this definition, we have found it important to consider transitional work that is time-limited and focused. As such, the patient is moving clearly through a developmental recovery pathway with clear aims and objectives. The length of treatment is not specified from the outset, but can be reviewed at certain points in different phases of the work, and which may be ascertained, for example, through patient-led goal-orientated outcome measures such as GAS (Goal Attainment Scoring).

When first engaging with individuals in acute settings, the service model requires us to consider if we have got the makings of a new group in the community post-discharge. To be able to hold this thinking, it is necessary to know what the group provision is, its capacity, and what else is out in the community to link up with, for example in the voluntary sector. We know who our colleagues are and will encourage referrals whilst also referring to ourselves if we identify an unmet need, though at times we have to be prepared to argue against premature termination of our work.

Examples of groups from the inner London NHS Foundation Trust in which we both work, include a range of different levels, durations, and frequency of groups designed to move the patient through from 'pre-pre-therapy' (which may be individual work) to post-discharge work. Inpatient groups may include ward-based open groups, cross-ward, off-ward, combined arts modality groups, access to gallery-based groups, cross-ward out-of-hours Saturday groups. Community groups may include early intervention groups, transitional groups, diagnostic specific groups, mixed-diagnosis groups, open studio groups, womens' groups.

Some initiatives for expanding the therapeutic frame

From this range of groups, the Saturday Living Gallery Group is one component of a broader Adult Mental Health partnership for innovative practice with Tate Modern, London, set up as a social inclusion initiative for patients on acute wards, together with their ward-based nursing staff. The 'Thinking about Looking' partnership takes place within the public spaces of a large London art gallery, Tate Modern, and the inpatient wards of the acute mental health unit. For the patient participants, the group study days, facilitated jointly by an art psychotherapist and a Tate curator, are de-stigmatising, providing the opportunity for being and learning in a public space as equal members of the public. For enhancing patient experience, all patients accessing the programme have returned 100% satisfaction rates for enjoyment and shared experience in a group. Central to the group days are the visual art dialogues and creative interactions facilitated in the gallery by patients with their nursing staff for building forms of shared meaning. These dialogues are developed through both looking at, and making artworks together, and are exported back to the wards for further development there in the context of the care planning process. Work that begins at Tate Modern is continued back on the wards at the mental health unit in a co-operative and collaborative way. Patient participants have the opportunity to continue in the project through volunteering schemes post-discharge.

The Saturday group provides an in-between space back at the mental health unit for patients who were unable to visit the Tate, but can be with others on their wards who were able to visit, to look together at selected art works from the gallery through projected images. The Saturday Living Gallery Group is held off the ward in a room used on weekdays for management meetings, and not usually used by patients. It is, however, the room that connects the wards on either side of it, thereby making use of the architectural design of the mental health unit as a symbolic in-between space.

Examples of groups from the Forensic Arts Psychotherapies service are designed and facilitated by drama and music therapists as well as art psychotherapists. The Early Intervention Screening Service (E.I.S.S) is a model based on a similar service and adapted to fit with the overall strategy of the Trust where we practice. The E.I.S.S is a care pathway, which helps give access to all new patients who are referred to the forensic services via the arts psychotherapies, and put into practice on the wards with all new admissions. Newly admitted patients often feel disorientated and defensive and many struggle to communicate their feelings verbally. They may also be required to answer lots of questions by staff and can be resistant to treatment. The arts therapies offer a contained and non-intrusive space where relationships with staff and other patients and the experience of working with the art materials can gradually develop as an orientation to further treatment.

Despite the limited resource available, one art psychotherapist and one dramatherapist, the majority of admissions coming through the E.I.S.S service in the Forensic Directorate actually come into contact with introductory groups facilitated by an arts therapist. Introductory groups in art psychotherapy are widely used to enable potential participants to have taster sessions to enhance the patient's awareness of the approach and to experience art psychotherapy prior to making a commitment to the group. Here the therapist works flexibly, is open to answering relevant questions and takes a mindful and accepting stance to encourage the service user to explore through the medium, including use of the sand tray, image cards, and the dramatherapy Communicube, whilst also using the opportunity to assess the patient's ability to use the group or individual therapy, or a combination of both.

How do art psychotherapists translate the visual image into information that is useful to others so that multidisciplinary team members can also support the ongoing programme?

If the context is that an art psychotherapist working within Forensics with patients whose admission, for whatever reason, is longer term, be they heavily medicated, seen as untreatable, a high risk and difficult to place, then the aim of art psychotherapy is to give patients resources they can use during the next developmental stage of the work.

Perhaps there needs to be a brief period of pre-therapy to prepare the patient for therapy work. Prior to patients entering into a specific government approved programme, for example, sex offender treatment, anger management, and thinking skills, there may be the need for a structure to enable patients to focus on positive aspects of the self, where they are not required to discuss what brought them into the programme in the first place. This may help build ego strength to manage the next phase of treatment. The default position may be making use of and engaging with something to get started. Time-limited work can help build ego strength as it functions very much in the here-and-now, it is more containing as the group has a specified time-scale so they know when the work will end. It is less regressive developmentally and more about making an attachment. There is a developmental stage into the next phase and less likelihood to activate defences that can cause the patient to resist the work.

Art psychotherapy through the pre-therapy experience goes some way in providing a sense of safety. A patient requesting a book to draw from may be the starting point, thereby using the art materials in itself as an indicator of allowing trust to develop in a therapeutic relationship, that is, can make use of art materials and with the potential for progression. Similarly in adult mental health, the art psychotherapist may be using the creativity of the therapeutic relationship itself when, for example, she reads a newspaper with a patient, through participation in which she may be paving the way for working with words and images together at a later stage.

This gently unfolding assessment process and therapeutic relationship builds the rudiments of a basic psychotherapeutic language, without complex theorising. It is important not to use language that alienates multidisciplinary colleagues who are working from a different knowledge base.

During these early stages of contact there is no need to describe what is on paper, however the process has established the art psychotherapist's role as a psychologically minded colleague who can discuss and de-mystify the work without having to try and translate the workings of a visual image to others. But the art psychotherapist does have an image and the patient is connected in a personal way, which is workable within the therapeutic alliance still to be built.

In the role of art psychotherapist we use the visual image to provide a conduit to arousing the curiosity of colleagues but without necessarily sharing with them patient narratives. The professional role is maintained not by going into an interpretation, but by sharing the curiosity by saying, for example: 'yes it will be interesting to see how this develops from here'. We can be in a position of helping staff to re-connect and re-kindle empathy towards very difficult to engage patients as we may be holding a different part of the patient who is able to make use of the art psychotherapeutic relationship and reveal narratives usually hidden verbally due to the early privations and traumas in their lived experience.

Being a needs-led service model the art psychotherapist may be able to slow things down to help maintain a thinking stance in the work, and the image is part of a process. It is this aspect that makes the NICE guidance, of beginning treatment within the acute phase and continuing the full course after discharge without unnecessary interruption, so very important, as is working at a pace suited to the person.

How art psychotherapists contribute to multidisciplinary teams

We have found it useful to pursue any possibility of collaborative working at the outset, for example inviting co-facilitators as a means of being transparent and to be seen to be willing to share expertise and to train others up to work with the art psychotherapist. It is very significant for patients to be able to see that the art psychotherapist is part of the multidisciplinary team. Art psychotherapists are of course clinicians who have a specialism, and through our specialism are specialists at helping the wider care team to think.

Ever since the Department of Health document Mental Health: New Ways of Working for Everyone: Developing and sustaining a capable and flexible workforce (NIMHE, 2007), a best practice implementation guide, emphasis in the workforce has been given to flexible ways of working in a move away from professional isolation. Produced by the National Institute for Mental Health in England (NIMHE) National Workforce Programme, the report builds on previous guidance and promotes a model where distributed responsibility is shared amongst team members and no longer delegated to a single professional such as the consultant.

Exotic pet or flexible team member?

We have found it is important for the art psychotherapist to work as a support for the team with a clinical contribution that helps others to understand their patients. It is important that she communicates actively her thinking regarding patient care, being clear that art psychotherapy does not suit all patients and contra-indicators may include patient refusal and the use of actively risky behaviour.

Health organisations want patients to have less dependency on their services. This invariably means less money to be spent. Therefore it would be foolhardy for an art psychotherapist to argue in a CPA that more time is needed with the patient on the ward when the economic urgency is to discharge as soon as possible. Commissioners need to hear that art psychotherapists are flexible, adaptive in being able to provide something for each individual patient, requiring clear information on how patients are discharged from the ward and how care will be continued in the community if, where, and when it is appropriate.

As highly trained staff with particular expertise needed for the monitoring of quality standards, in the current climate it is necessary to bear in mind that not everybody will be able to make use of art psychotherapy during their admission and might not be ready for art psychotherapy at this early stage of their recovery. The art psychotherapies require us to think where it is best to position any intervention. For example at the following stages:

- Pre-therapy
- Orientation work

- Treatment or transitional work in pre- and post-discharge groups
- Social inclusion recovery groups

This shows we are thinking of where best in a patient's clinical episode might we pick up time-limited phases of work.

In anticipation of diagnostic specific care pathways, it remains to be seen whether the patient's needs-led recovery care pathway will survive the diagnostic specific groups through HONOS clustering currently being introduced nationally. The adaptability and patient-focused nature of art psychotherapy practice in meeting patients' needs as they progress through mental health services is essential for patients who do not fit neatly into economically driven health categories.

The wider mental health configurations require art psychotherapies to be more specific, not only about therapeutic aims but also working towards clearer goals be it:

- Re-integration into the community
- Employability
- Referring on to another part of the service
- Using the art work to help the wider team understand a complex patient
- Helping the service user to formulate their own end goals, for example to visit an art gallery or to exhibit their art work, be it at a multidisciplinary team treatment review, or the wall of a ward, or the wall of an exhibition space.

It is unrealistic to think that only the art psychotherapist can work with an individual at any one time. In an acute ward setting there will be many professionals working with the same patient, as the nature of the work requires this level of intensity, just as a surgeon, nurse, and physiotherapist might all work together with the same road accident patient. It cannot be the work of one person at the beginning of an acute admission, though it may become so as the patient develops through their recovery.

We recommend participation in team forums wherever possible. We have found that in order to be able to advise on clinical need we need to be there. We also consider bringing the artwork to a ward-round or staff forum, where patients have the opportunity to speak to their own image. Once a working alliance has been developed with a patient, it is essential to get explicit consent from the patient and prepare them for such meetings, and for the art psychotherapist to be mindful of how this sharing could damage the therapeutic alliance or derail the internal working through for the patient. Timing is key with these interventions and links with the overall aim of the building of ego strength previously discussed. At the end of treatment we hold a review, which may comprise of putting on an exhibition of the patient's work when this is not likely to re-traumatise and is more likely to support their self-esteem.

Evaluating art psychotherapy intervention

To date, there is no outcome measure specific to art psychotherapy but we have been collaborating on qualitative measures to run alongside, for example, CORE (Clinical Outcomes in Routine Evaluation), which has become the most frequently used outcome measure in psychological services across the UK. Given the compound nature of art psychotherapy, in its utilisation of visual and verbal expression, for qualitative initiatives to capture data about the patient experience, it has been necessary to create our own means of measuring such as the AIR (audio-image recording), or the use of postcards at the beginning and end of sessions, or looking for a development over time of an individual visual vocabulary, for example from fragmentation to integration between the first and last image made and how this reflects improved mental health. Audio-image recording is used to emphasise the patient's voice and their personal journey through art psychotherapy, whilst the single session postcard evaluations capture change and experience over one session.

Conclusion

Our therapeutic endeavour is simultaneously holding the acute and community experience in mind, and at times concretely, to keep open on-going therapeutic potential. We have emphasised continuity of therapy from acute to community, and working at a pace suited to the individual patient, to ensure that all our work is in the interests of a positive developmental therapeutic experience. Personalised recovery journeys and narratives are at the centre of the recovery model ethos.

We have used short-term work in the sense of working without a set contract, whereas time-limited defines work where the end date is agreed at the beginning of a specific therapeutic intervention. We have used short-term art psychotherapy in the sense of:

*   sometimes briefer than brief acute assessment
*   brief time-limited evidence based practice group interventions in acute mental health and secure settings
*   transitional holding between acute and community pre- and post-discharge.
*   positioning art psychotherapy work to be embedded within mental health teams that require effective multidisciplinary working and design of care pathways.

Attention to care pathways ensures the art psychotherapy intervention happens at the right place, in the right time, and for the right people without prematurely stopping or being abruptly cut across.

Economy of working in groups

In our definition of care pathways as explained above, it is essential to design a set of different groups so that patients are able to move seamlessly between assessment and screening groups into time-limited treatment groups, both short-term and longer-term. In addition, our recovery groups are out-of-hours. This is positive as it enhances optimism and hope and manoevres the patients back into the community. The overall therapeutic aim is of art psychotherapy as a vehicle for social recovery. This aim chimes with one of Yalom's primary therapeutic factors for working with groups, that of instillation of hope. That is, encouragement that recovery is possible.

Notes

1 Fuller, P. R. (2013) *Surviving, Existing, or Living: Phase-Specific Therapy for Severe Psychosis.* Hove: Routledge, Table 1:1.
2 National Collaborating Centre for Mental Health (updated edition 2014) *Psychosis and Schizophrenia in Adults: The NICE Guideline on Treatment and Management.* National Clinical Guideline Number 178, p. 209. www.nice.org.uk/guiance/cg178.
3 Yalom. I. (2005) *The Theory and Practice of Group Psychotherapy.* London: Basic Books.
4 NICE (2014) *Psychosis and Schizophrenia in Adults,* p. 219.
5 National Institute for Health and Care Excellence (NICE) (2011) *Service User Experience in Adult Mental Health.* NICE Clinical Guidance 136, p. 7. www.nice.org.uk/guidance/cg136.
6 Gordon, J. and Kirtchuk, G. (2008) *Psychic Assaults and Frightened Clinicians: Countertransference in Forensic Settings.* London: Karnac Books, pp. 7–8.

Previous publications (Kate Rothwell)

Hutchinson, L. and Rothwell, K. (2011) Hiding and being seen: the story of one woman's development through Art Therapy and Dialectical Behavioural Therapy in a forensic context. *The Online International Journal of Art Therapy (ATOL)* London: Goldsmiths.
Rothwell, K. Entry: Images used to convey the 'action of violence' in Wood, C. (Ed) (2011) *Navigating Art Therapy: A Therapist's Companion.* London: Routledge.
Rothwell, K. What Anger? Working with acting-out behaviour in a secure setting. Chapter 7 in Liebmann, M. (Ed) (2008) *Art Therapy and Anger.* London: Jessica Kingsley Publishers.
Rothwell, K. (2008) Lost in translation: Art psychotherapy with patients presenting suicidal states. *International Journal of Art Therapy* (formerly *Inscape*). 13.1 2–12.

Previous publications (Sheila Grandison)

Fuirer, M. and Grandison, S. (2012) Drawn to Dialogue: Nouns and Verbs, *engage*, no. 30, pp. 86–98.

Hardcastle, M., Kennard, D., Grandison, S., and Fagin, L. (Eds) (2007) *Experiences of Mental Health In-Patient Care*. London: Routledge.

Chapter 9

Time-limited art psychotherapy in a community mental health team

Individual work

Marian Liebmann

Introduction

I work for the Central Recovery Team, a community mental health team based at Brookland Hall in the inner city of Bristol, an area of considerable diversity including white British people, immigrants from Europe, Asia, Africa, the West Indies and the far East, and their children born in Bristol. As a port, Bristol has had minority ethnic people settling there for several centuries.

The community mental health team is multi-disciplinary and includes psychiatrists, community psychiatric nurses, mental health workers, psychologists, liaison workers with other agencies and a part-time art therapist (me). Several staff are from minority ethnic groups, with knowledge of many languages. Clients are visited at home or in counselling rooms at the team base. My art therapy room doubles as a multi-purpose room when I am not there. From time to time I run theme-based groups on specific topics (see Chapter 10), but most of my work with service users is with individuals, usually weekly appointments for one hour, sometimes fortnightly.

Rationale for short-term work

Working in a community mental health team means working under pressure for much of the time. It is good that art psychotherapy is now much more well-known, but the result is often too many referrals for the capacity available. When art therapy was less well-known, art therapists could work for many years with the few referrals who came their way. They worked with people until they were able to cope on their own and lead meaningful lives free of mental health symptoms, often taking many years. This is no longer the case. Art therapy is now also offered to a much wider range of service users, as the benefits have become better known, and sometimes other treatments have had little impact.

When I started work in my community mental health team, I was aware of a short-term counselling service in the inner city, attached to primary care, offering up to 12 sessions of counselling, mainly for mental health problems around life events, such as bereavement, divorce, unemployment and so on. Ours was a secondary service, for those whose needs could not be met by the primary service. Clearly I needed to offer more than 12 weeks – but if I offered an open-ended contract, I was aware that, after accepting the first handful of service users, I could be booked up for years. I therefore offered individual service users a year, which could be renewed up to two years. This was useful in sorting out those who proved capable of using the service well, and those for whom it was not achieving very much.

The latter group of service users included people who failed appointments to the extent that work with them lost coherence; those who hardly used the art materials (of course using art materials every session is not obligatory, but if someone does not find them at all useful, they would be better off being referred to verbal therapy); those whose needs turned out to be far from art therapy, e.g. sorting out practical problems week by week; and those who just did not seem motivated to make any changes in their lives, looking for a ready ear to repeat their story. I did not turn these people away, but when the agreed year was up, we simply finished our work and reviewed what they had done and what they needed next – work on alcohol or drugs; a community care worker; advice on voluntary work and so on. However, if someone was working hard and making progress with their issues, I offered them another six months, and maybe a further six months. Some of the most successful work has taken two years, occasionally more.

With the pressure of referrals, these times have been revised downwards, and I now am able to offer only six months in the first instance. Again, some people finish their six months, and I do not offer more, as they do not seem able to use the space or the medium in a constructive way. Some I offer another three or six months, then we finish after a year. Occasionally we continue for more time, but this is discouraged in our Psychological Therapies Service, unless we make a case for longer-term work. We now see our work as providing 'episodes' of treatment, working as part of a multi-disciplinary team, rather than seeing a person through to the end of their treatment on our own.

We are also now much stricter with people who fail appointments. There may be many good reasons why people cannot keep appointments, but with the pressure of referrals, we need to work with those who are able to come. So there are several people who are referred but never show up. This is probably more of an issue in our inner city team than the other teams, but it is a problem there too. Generally two (or occasionally three) appointments are offered, then if they do not make contact, they are taken off the list.

Sometimes I am asked to do a short-term piece of work with a service user, around a particular issue, for instance anger; or relapse prevention; or looking at sexuality using art therapy; or work issues (for the few service users who are in work). Then I agree with the service user to offer eight to 12 sessions, and we keep to that. This was the case with the service user I will describe.

Cathy: Work issues

Cathy was in her early 50s and had been sacked from her job as a nurse for making a mistake with medication, and was trying to come to terms with the end of her career and livelihood as a nurse and midwife, and find a way forward. She had asked for assessment by a psychologist, as she had not had one before, and felt this might help. However, the psychologists were booked up, so I offered her 12 sessions of art therapy. Although somewhat dubious, she agreed to give it a try, as it seemed to be the only thing on offer.

Cathy told me something about her background. She described her problems starting when she was born, and said she had been depressed from the age of 14, receiving little help and support as a child. She had a brother two years younger, and said that he had similar problems, being unable to communicate, resulting in aggression and violence. The family moved to Wales when Cathy was aged six, and at the age of 12 she was sent to boarding school in Oxford, because it was the school her mother went to. Her brother stayed at home and she was jealous of him, and felt excluded from the rest of the family. But she enjoyed boarding school, and felt she was better off there than at home, because of the tensions with her parents and brother. Her mother was very authoritarian, resulting in many arguments; even now that she was in her late 70s, it was clear that she had a lot of power over Cathy.

Despite this shaky start, Cathy had tried to make a go of her life. She had trained initially as a nurse and then as a community midwife, working in a variety of places, with some periods of unemployment, during which she had returned home. She had then attempted a degree in environmental management, but had left after the first year. A more recent job had been with a drug and alcohol team in Birmingham, where she had felt unsupported and succumbed to anxiety and depression. She had received nine months' counselling, which had given her the strength to carry on. But the depression and fatigue ultimately led her to resign from the job. She applied for the job in Bristol because it sounded good, with adequate support – but the reality had been different. She experienced the same lack of support and crashed into depression. She made the mistake with medication while under extreme stress. She took extended sick leave and was in the process of being dismissed when she resigned. Later she decided she had been 'constructively dismissed' and went to an employment tribunal. At the time of my involvement, she was waiting for this, and also taking advice from MIND, and writing to her MP.

Art therapy assessment

We discussed the issues Cathy was facing. I often give service users two forms, which they can fill in, or ask me to act as their secretary. The first one lists problems and how severe they are, giving each a score out of 10 (where 0 is terrible, and 10 is fine) (see Form 1 at the end of this chapter). Cathy's list was as follows:

1   Coming to terms with what has happened as regards mental breakdown (8).
2   How I am going to live because I've lost my livelihood (0).
3   Worry as regards elderly parents as they are supporting me at the moment and their health is not too good (8).
4   Worry about losing my flat due to loss of income and having to move in permanently with my parents (6).

5   Stress outside my control as this can lead to fatigue which is the route to depression. Fear that medication might stop working (2–4).

Top of Cathy's list was clearly her loss of income, followed closely by stress leading to fatigue and depression.

The second form has a 'future focus' and is more orientated towards solutions (see Form 2 at the end of this chapter). I asked Cathy to say how she would know when she was better. She wrote:

1   Being able to cope again despite depression which I might always be suscep-tible to.
2   As the months go by and being on medication I can feel the difference – I can feel 'lighter and brighter'.
3   I remember how bad I was when my mental health broke down.
4   I'm able to remain calmer for longer under stress (reasonable). I don't with-draw into myself so much.
5   Coping skills are returning and this time are becoming more positive and changing somehow.

Finally I asked her what strengths/ personal qualities she had that helped her cope with difficult things. She wrote:

•   Inner strength and resilience
•   The ability to search out information and beaver away in an attempt to under-stand my breakdown
•   Gardening – having created a garden out of the jungle that had become my garden.
•   Ability to withdraw in a positive way – going for long walks, gardening.
•   Finding ways to rebuild my life through social history projects, as a conse-quence of walking and tree-gazing

I usually find that the more someone can say how they would know they are better, the more likely they are to achieve that. Many service users cannot do this at all. The fact that Cathy could do so was an optimistic sign.

Art therapy sessions

Session 1

Cathy talked about her current state of mind and her anxiety about getting depressed again. She used pencil and felt-tip pens to draw four windows showing this (see Figure 9.1):

Top left: plain green – representing normality/ nature
Top right: plain light blue – representing peace/ sea

Figure 9.1 Current state of mind
(Author's sketch based on Cathy's picture)

Bottom left: black downward spiral on grey, surrounded by black – representing depression

Bottom right: black coals and orange flames, surrounded by red – representing turmoil

Between the windows, she filled in yellow between the green and blue, and grey between the rest.

I asked Cathy if she was aware of any signs of looming depression, and she said she withdrew. She thought other people could see this, but they had not responded as she had hoped (e.g. asking how she was, a kind word or sympathy) and Cathy had felt hurt by this. I wondered if she had considered the many possible responses to someone withdrawing, depending on the other person's state of mind – this seemed a new idea to her.

Session 2

Cathy asked to look at the previous week's picture and started tracing with her finger what led to what. This led on to her next picture (see Figure 9.2).

Figure 9.2 Depression cycle (also see colour plate section)

Cathy used coloured pencils, felt-tip pens and oil pastels, which she enjoyed for the variety of textures they could portray. She used elements of her first picture, but showed more clearly how one state led to another. She again drew a block of light blue for calmness (top centre), which could get upset and ruffled (different shadings of blue, and blue spiral), leading to a black downward spiral finishing in black depression at the bottom left. But somehow Cathy usually managed to find her way to emerge through fiery flames and 'phoenix rising', through a tunnel back to blue calmness (bottom right). I remarked that she must be a tough survivor, and dealt with some difficult situations – to which she responded, 'That's what everyone says.' I wondered if we could find a way of interrupting the cycle whereby she doubted herself and spiralled into depression when things went wrong. I also wondered if she could find ways of asking for support in such a way that she was more likely to receive it. Cathy said that doing the picture was useful in helping her to focus, as she could see more clearly what was going on.

Session 3

We looked through the picture from Session 2 to try to find clues how to break the cycle, but Cathy was adamant that there were none. She then mentioned the 'green space' from Session 1 as a place/ state she never reached, so I suggested she might focus on that. She chose light green paper and drew a rural scene with a house, a barn, a church, birds, animals, trees, meadows, hills, the sea, a fence and a gate. It was a real place, where friends of hers lived. She was quite tearful while doing this, as she felt it was an inaccessible dream that had been dashed time and again. She told me she was waiting to hear about a course on administration – she had spotted a 'gap in the market' of admin workers in health settings with medical knowledge. She had seen that the turnover of admin workers was quite high, so thought she might get a job in medical administration without too much difficulty, if she re-trained in admin work. She had also received a date for her employment tribunal.

Session 4

We looked at the previous week's picture again. Cathy noticed that there was little connection between the blue and the green, so her next picture set out to explore this connection. It included some of the black square too. She used broad strokes of felt-tip pens to draw a scene of hills, meadows, sun and sea, then added details of a village using coloured pencils (see Figure 9.3). The connection seemed to be the sea and a boat connecting the two halves of the picture, and we discussed how this might be a metaphor for life – navigating the flowing and unpredictable waters, with rain clouds above (top right). Cathy also talked about the special quality of light in estuaries, as she was a keen photographer. She had been offered a place on the admin course, so we needed to renegotiate the times of our sessions.

Figure 9.3 Connecting green and blue (also see colour plate section)

Session 5

Cathy had started her admin course, and was feeling positive about it. It finished at 3 pm, so we arranged our sessions for 4 pm. Cathy did not do any art work in this session, but looked through her pictures again, and talked about her family, especially her mother, and how to fend off her mother's negative comments, as she homed in on Cathy's problems. Cathy had reframed these with, 'No, I don't have problems, I have solutions.' and seemed optimistic about devising her own 'virtuous circle' to replace the vicious cycle of negative events leading to depression.

Session 6

Cathy seemed well, and had recognized the patterns of communication from her mother, and was detaching herself from it. She was also beginning to recognize triggers to depression and deal with them differently. She drew two pictures, using soft pencil. The first was of a tangled ball of string, signifying the tangled state she had got into, but with a thread pulled out and laid neatly in folds to show issues clarified and dealt with. She added arrows and a hammer near the tangled ball, to show the pressures she had experienced in the 'knotted-up' state. She started a second picture using coloured pencils to draw a positive scene of sea, sun and hills.

Session 7

Cathy was enjoying her course, although there were a lot of new things to take in. She reflected that admin work did not carry as much responsibility as medical work, so she was less worried about it. She completed the picture she had started in Session 6, paying great attention to detail, and enjoying the colours of the sea, sun, clouds and varied mountains. She was very engaged in doing the art work.

Session 8

Cathy had not slept well and was tired. She reported an incident on her course, in which she had failed to complete a task in the approved way. This led her to feel that her brain wasn't functioning, and in turn led her to withdraw. She felt things were falling apart again 'in the same old way', but I encouraged her to think of it as a gift, because we had the opportunity to examine what was going on in a real-live situation. So we tried to pick the incident apart. Cathy wrote down her feelings in capital letters in boxes, with arrows showing how one thing led to another. She included: attacked/ stupid/ trying too hard/ rigid & alone/ withdrawal/ shut down/ judged/ should be doing better/ fear/ anxiety/ failure/ others being better/ assumptions/ competition (see Figure 9.4). We discussed strategies she could use, such as deep breathing, and telling herself that she could take her time, that she was not stupid, and that she could do it.

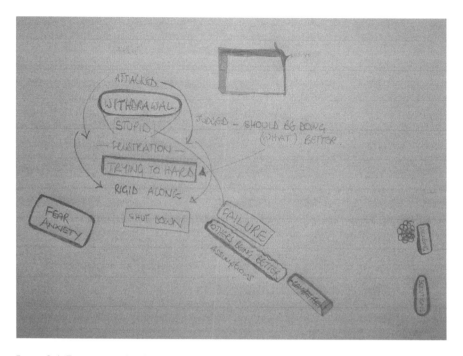

Figure 9.4 Examining what happened

Session 9

Cathy brought a drawing she had done, of the effect of stress, showing herself split between serenity and stress. We then focused on more incidents on the course, this time looking at ways of stepping back to think what's going on, using 'I-statements' to ask for help, instead of spiralling downwards into depression. Cathy worked out an I-statement for one situation: 'When you go too fast, I feel lost because I can't take in the information at that speed.' Cathy also remembered a childhood incident, at the age of 10, when she felt stupid because she didn't understand something, and thought that everyone was looking at her, especially a particularly bullying teacher. She made a pencil drawing of this, with arrows showing pressures on her. This link provided a very useful insight for Cathy, who commented that previous counselling had not got 'beneath the surface' in this way.

Session 10

Cathy was fine, almost wondering if things were going too well. But the intervening time had been quite eventful. She had experienced another crisis shortly after the previous session, when she had felt bad but forced herself to attend, came unstuck with a computer package, and 'flooded' with feelings of inadequacy and hopelessness. But this time, instead of withdrawing into depression, Cathy went to see the university counsellor, and then talked things through with the course tutors the next day. She was surprised and pleased to receive a lot of support, because she had managed to ask for it in a more direct way. She also managed to talk herself down from anxiety and feeling that she was stupid and everyone else was better – realising that her slow and meticulous approach would pay off in the end, rather than rushing through things in a 'quick and sloppy' way. She also received a boost in confidence from a writing course she attended at the weekend, and from the way she had represented herself at the first hearing of her employment tribunal.

Session 11

We looked at the forms Cathy had completed at the beginning of our sessions, and reflected on Cathy's progress. For two of the items there was no change (coming to terms with what had happened; worry about elderly parents), but for the other three (livelihood; worry about flat; stress leading to depression), there was substantial movement, 2–5 points in the direction of 'not a problem'. Looking at 'How will I know that I'm better', Cathy realised she had achieved many of these. Cathy said the art therapy sessions had been very beneficial. We made a list of achievements, tools, challenges and risks, outlined below.

Progress made:

- Understanding the process of how you became depressed
- Coming to terms with the realisation of it
- Exploring the connections between different states of mind
- Making sense of the cyclical nature of your depression
- Finding a sense of hope once more
- No longer feeling so overwhelmed, so that you are able to stay in control of your emotional state
- As a result of this, coping better with problems as they arise, without beating yourself up
- Coping better with your mother's emotional response to you
- Learning to ask for support in such a way as to receive it (something you have not experienced in the past)
- Handling the preliminary case conference for the tribunal on your own, doing it well and achieving a positive result

Tools developed:

- Stop, calm down, get focused again
- Keep thinking my way through things
- Take things one step at a time

- Back off, go out, take a break
- Talk to someone, talk things through
- Cup of tea and relax
- Remind myself not to beat myself up
- It's OK to fail, it's not the end of the world

We listed the challenges ahead (re-engaging with the world of work, a further tribunal hearing, achieving stability, coming off medication at the right time) and the risk of relapse.

Session 12

In our last session Cathy seemed fine. We said our goodbyes, and Cathy took her pictures home. I'm sure she will have encountered further challenges.

Conclusion

This piece of work shows how it is possible to use art psychotherapy to do a time-limited piece of work, accomplishing some insight and progress. I am sure that Cathy will have experienced further challenges, but hopefully with the help and support from our 12 sessions, she will be better equipped to cope with these. One of the great benefits of using art psychotherapy in this case was the opportunity for Cathy to show the cycle of depression so that she could see it, focus on it, and derive further images from it, leading to developing some new strategies to interrupt the process.

Art therapy evaluation (1)

We are being asked to evaluate our work – to see if it helps. If you can outline the problems you would like help with, we can see if art therapy has helped. Please write in your problems and how you see them:

Name   Date

My problems are	All the time or terrible	Often or very bad	Sometimes or quite bad	Occasionally or a bit of a problem	Never or not a problem
1					
2					
3					
4					
5					

Thank you!

Art therapy evaluation (2)

Date: Name:

A)   How will you know
                when you are better?

1.

2.

3.

4.

5.

B)   What strengths/personal qualities do you have which help you
                cope with difficult things?

Chapter 10

Time-limited group work in a community mental health team

A short-term art psychotherapy group for Asian women

Marian Liebmann and Lynne Francis

Introduction

This piece of work took place in the Central Recovery Team, a community mental health team based at Brookland Hall in the inner city of Bristol, an area of considerable diversity including white British people, immigrants from Europe, Asia, Africa, the West Indies and the far East, and their children born in Bristol. As a port, Bristol has had minority ethnic people settling there for several centuries.

The community mental health team is multi-disciplinary and includes psychiatrists, community psychiatric nurses, mental health workers, psychologists, liaison workers with other agencies, a part-time art therapist (Marian) and often a trainee art therapist (Lynne at that time). Several staff are from minority ethnic groups, e.g. Europe, Asia, Africa, black British, with knowledge of many languages. Clients are visited at home or in counselling rooms at the team base. The art therapy room doubles as a multi-purpose room when art therapy is not taking place. Most work with service users is with individuals, usually weekly appointments for one hour. From time to time it is possible to run theme-based groups on specific topics.

This group came about in response to Marian's offer to run an art therapy group for the team, if there was an identified need. Nazlin, an Asian Specialist community care worker/transcultural counsellor in the team, asked for a group for some Asian women who had been in the mental health service for a long time and were quite stuck. She thought an art therapy group might help them to move on. Following discussion with Nazlin, it was agreed that the theme would be 'moving on', that it was to be a closed group of eight Asian women who already knew each other and who were well known to Nazlin, and that help with translation would be provided by Nazlin.

The 'moving on' group

We therefore planned a series of six sessions around the theme of 'moving on', co-facilitated by Marian and Lynne, and helped by Nazlin, who acted as translator and role model. We planned two sessions looking at the past, two at current concerns and two looking towards the future. The series was as follows:

1   Introductions. My start in life.
2   An event in childhood or adolescence that had a lasting impact on my life.
3   Problems I have encountered in my life.
4   Things that have helped me move on.
5   The future I would like – and one personal goal.
6   Review of pictures – and one strength I have. Evaluation and closing.

After each session we reviewed how the group had gone and planned the next one in detail, making any amendments we thought necessary. In our initial discussions about the group we agreed that we as facilitators would also participate in the art-making, as we hoped this would encourage group members.

The group consisted of six women who were mental health service users, an extra Asian women's worker and the three of us as facilitators. This meant we had four workers and six service users, who all participated in the making of art together and in the sharing afterwards. The group ran for six sessions over an eight-week period, in the art therapy room at Brookland Hall. Each session ran for two hours, including a short period for coffee or tea at the beginning and a shared lunch together at the end. Art materials were provided in the art therapy room: paper, paints, brushes, pencils, pastels, oil and wax crayons and coloured felt-tip pens. All the different art materials were used over the duration of the course.

Cultural issues

Although all the women were originally from Asia, they did not necessarily share all aspects of culture or language. We started the group by together devising our own ground rules and an introductory round where everyone introduced where they originally came from. Including ourselves, this covered India, Bangladesh, Pakistan, Kenya and the UK. As we did this exercise, women also spontaneously introduced their religion – Islam (at least two varieties), Hinduism, Christianity, Buddhism, Sikhism – so we discovered we had most of the major religions in the world present. It was also a very mixed group in terms of background and economic status. The women had very varying degrees of ability in English – some were fluent, whereas others still struggled, despite having lived in the UK for many years.

We were very grateful to have Nazlin's help with translating from English into several different Asian languages and vice versa. It was an enormous amount of work and quite draining. She had hoped that the women's English would be good enough for that to be the medium of exchange. The fact that the group's communication had previously been in Asian languages may have made it difficult to switch to English. But it has also been found that in intercultural therapy situations, people often need to use their emotional language, which is usually the one they grew up with (D'Ardenne and Mahtani 1989; Thomas 1995).

Attendance

Attendance was excellent at 83 per cent, with all women bar one attending all or most sessions. This was helped enormously by Nazlin working hard at encouraging them beforehand and reminding them between sessions.

The following account of the group sessions is divided into reflections on the sessions focusing on the past, then current concerns, then moving towards the future. A case study of one member of the group is interwoven into the account.

The past: Images of the natural world

Session 1: Introductions. My start in life

In our first session people were slow to start painting and seemed to find it difficult to share information about themselves. In all the women's pictures, images of the natural world stood out – flowers and trees were present in almost everybody's pictures. One woman painted a large blue sky with clouds and birds; another painted a yellow sun, birds, a red sunset and two flowers from her homeland; another picture depicted flowers, a buffalo and an orange tree. Another woman painted herself as a child with a flower, and added a moon and a butterfly. Several others painted flowers and trees that they remembered from childhood. Houses and living rooms from the women's childhoods were also depicted, and they remembered chalk boards they had drawn on in school. Several women also put themselves and their families in their pictures. Many pictures were evocative of rural life and climates very different from that in the UK, with hot skies and colours, something now missing from their lives.

Rashida

Rashida was the eldest of nine, with five brothers and three sisters. She got married in Pakistan and then came to the UK with her husband. Her parents remained in Pakistan. Her husband was the Imam of the Muslim community, she accompanied him to prayer meetings. She had been married for 16 years and had seven children, four daughters and three sons, all living with their parents in a three-bedroom council house. One of her daughters was especially supportive in helping to build up Rashida's confidence.

Rashida had a long history of depression, especially in winter, with some psychotic symptoms. She had problems with sleep, and had dreams of snakes and dead or naked people. These dreams kept her awake. She became anxious and panicky in unfamiliar places or crowds. At times she was housebound due to severe headaches. She felt there was an insect in her brain, moving about and causing her pain. She felt her eyes were burning and was sometimes tearful. At times she felt she was going to die.

Figure 10.1a My start in life (also see colour plate section)

She also suffered from physical problems, especially arthritis, giving her constant pain in her joints. She had had a hysterectomy, and this had led to stress incontinence and urinary infections.

Rashida spoke Urdu and Punjabi, and some English, although she found it difficult to express herself in English, finding it easier to make herself understood in Urdu. She had poor memory and concentration, often jumping from one thing to another in conversation. She was grateful for the support of mental health services.

She attended all six sessions of the art therapy group.

In her first session, Rashida was not shy about using the art materials and chose paints (see Figure 10.1a). Her picture shows her grandmother's orange tree in Pakistan on the left, two flowers (top left and bottom right) a black buffalo (top right), which they used for milk, and her own face in faint pencil (bottom right), looking quite sad. At the top she painted a moon and stars, and the sun at the very top right – a theme that was repeated in several of her pictures.

Session 2: An event in childhood or adolescence that had a lasting impact on my life

In this session there were several pictures of childhood homes, family members and traditional cooking implements – plates and beds, domestic tasks, large families, landscapes and plants. Most people had depicted happy times from childhood.

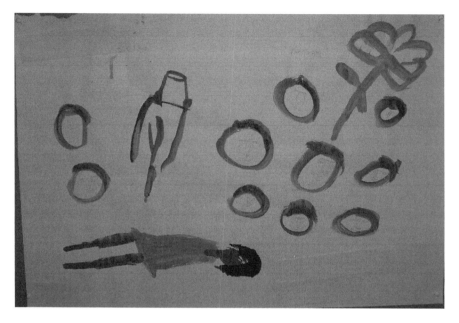

Figure 10.1b An event in childhood with a lasting impact (also see colour plate section)

These were tinged with an element of sadness because they were from times they could not go back to, and countries they no longer lived in. Again, things from the natural world figured in most people's paintings – skies, moons, flowers, birds and butterflies.

Most of the women found it difficult to talk about their pictures but were drawn out a little by others' questions and comments. The atmosphere soon became quite lively and some had to be reminded not to interrupt others. At first we were tempted to interpret this as individuals not having heard the ground rules or misbehaving a little, but in supervision afterwards we considered whether this was a Western expectation of how to behave. In some cultures interrupting and talking over others is an accepted norm (Tannen 1990). We also discussed the preponderance of natural world images. This had also occurred in another art therapy group that Marian had run for Asian clients, where plants and animals were common features in their paintings (Liebmann 2002 and 2004).

Almost all the scenes depicted were of everyday life as they grew up, and it was not clear what impact this had had on their lives, so we asked them. Some seemed sad that things had changed but found it hard to explain how it had affected them. However, two members in the group shared the sadness from childhood of a close family bereavement and the impact that it had had on their lives. One member cried when she shared the memory of her mother's death but was able to talk about it and be supported by the group.

In supervision we discussed how most women seemed to be finding it difficult to express feelings and thoughts about the past. We wondered whether this was because they had not understood the theme or whether there was a constraint in Asian culture concerning talking about problems. We also thought it could be because the group was very new or we were very new to them. We also remembered the tendency for many immigrants to 'put their previous lives in a box' to enable them to deal with their new lives – sometimes this box can become inaccessible.

As facilitators, we had all thought carefully about what to share about our own histories in the group. Lynne selected something about her father's mental health background, to facilitate others. Marian chose to share an early family bereavement, which felt difficult but formed a common bond with some of the women in the group. It also enabled Nazlin to use us as role models and explain that even therapists encounter problems and find it difficult to share feelings at times.

Rashida used paints again, with pencil for the detail of the faces (see Figure 10.1b). She depicted her mother and father on the left, and said that her mother was cooking. The stove is next to them. On the right she painted circles for her eight brothers and sisters, and a large flower. She painted herself lying down sleeping. She said this was a happy memory, but she was sad because she was not together with her family any more. She said she dreamt nice dreams of this period of her life, and preferred these dreams to reality.

Current concerns: Developing common ground

Session 3: Problems I have encountered in my life

During this session, when people were painting, the atmosphere felt quite weighty. When we shared our pictures later, things started to spill out and the atmosphere lifted. Common themes arose as several women talked about feeling lonely, sad, crying a lot, with family difficulties and problems with children. We seemed to have established some common ground that acknowledged the difficulties of bringing up children even amongst those that did not feel able to share. It felt to us that the group had broken down barriers, and despite our different cultures we had found some universal themes for women. The group ended as usual with us sharing lunch together. Discussions that had started in the group spilled into lunchtime, which began to feel like an extension of the art therapy group.

In supervision we agreed the group had gone very well and was starting to gel. However, the initial plan for us to facilitate the sharing of information, and Nazlin to translate, had become blurred. Although all the women spoke some English, they seemed to find this difficult in the group, and Nazlin had to translate more than she had initially expected. The translation task itself was very complex – Nazlin explained that she had to translate not only from Bengali into English, and vice versa, but also translate between some of the women who spoke other Indian languages. This was complicated further by the fact that Nazlin knew the women well and fell naturally into a facilitation role, taking the lead. It was often difficult for us to tell whether Nazlin was talking to people because they found it hard to speak English or because she was trying to encourage them to move on. At times when discussion became animated, the task became almost impossible for Nazlin, and the discussion was very difficult for us to follow. In a brief conversation after the group, Nazlin said that she was finding the pressure on her in the group very hard, so we arranged to meet before the start of the next group to see what we could do.

The meeting with Nazlin proved very useful. She said she was surprised how much the women were depending on her to speak for them, and she was finding the translation between so many different languages so hard that she 'felt as if her head was going to explode'.

She was also getting rather frustrated with a few of the women for not talking more in the group about their problems, as she was concerned about them and wanted them to move on.

We suggested that Nazlin should try to let Lynne and Marian do a bit more, and ask the other Asian worker to help by making teas and helping with translating at times. Nazlin agreed with these suggestions and before the next group told us that she had asked another Asian worker to join us for more support.

Rashida used coloured pencils for this picture (see Figure 10.2a). She showed herself crying (top right), a bed with a pillow (top left), a house (mid-left), a large sun with a face (mid-right), a blue moon below that, and a garden at the bottom. She also drew some strange creatures (monsters and gravestones) from bad dreams, and a knife (lower left), with which she had tried to kill herself. She talked about having seven children and two miscarriages, and described herself as 'crying for 10 years' while having them. She also remembered being beaten for being late for prayers, and for being late for school, where she had been bullied.

Session 4: Things that have helped me move on

In this session, leaving their original homes featured strongly in women's individual stories, as did accounts of loneliness and isolation when they first moved to the UK – and the relief they experienced when people helped them learn English. Religion and prayer were also things that helped them when things were difficult, and this was common to all the religions in the room.

As it happened, at the beginning of this session, Nazlin was taken up with one member of the group who was very upset, so one of the support workers naturally stepped into the gap and made the teas. We agreed to start the group without Nazlin and the Asian worker translated for us. Although some of the women were initially concerned about Nazlin's absence, they seemed to relax once we reassured them she would arrive soon.

Figure 10.2a Problems I have encountered

Figure 10.2b Things that have helped me move on

We then introduced the theme 'Things that have helped me move on – people, events, courses, activities, personal qualities.' This week the women needed little prompting to get started and when Nazlin came in soon after, she found people working intently in a calm and quiet atmosphere. It seemed some women were now worrying less about what they were doing and starting to use materials more freely, which was lovely to observe. The woman who had been upset also joined us but did not participate in any artwork, just sat with the group.

Religion was mentioned by nearly everybody as a form of support. A trip to Mecca, reading a holy book, a prayer group, meditation on their own, prayer to God, prayer to the sun, moon and stars – all were mentioned by different women.

In this session Rashida used felt-tip pens and coloured pencils (see Figure 10.2b). She drew herself crying again (top centre and top right), when she had her children. We tried to find out what she meant by this, but she did not elaborate. She drew symbols of prayer and going to Mecca on the left (top and centre – the black square represented the Ka'aba at Mecca). In the centre she drew herself sleeping in bed, and reading magazines and books. At the bottom right she drew the sun, moon and stars, and said she prayed to them. She drew flowers at the bottom of the picture. She said all these things helped her, as did learning English. She also spoke about helpful friends.

Thinking about the future

In the last two sessions, the concept of 'moving on' and the future seemed to cause some problems for people. We were not sure if this was a mental health issue or a problem of translation between languages – or even cultures. We wondered if the whole idea of 'individual goals' and 'moving on' was too much of a Western concept, which might not always mesh with the acceptance of the present expressed in many religions (Fernando 1991). The women's acceptance of their lives and discussion of the present could also be seen as a realistic assessment of their circumstances.

Session 5: The future I would like – and one personal goal

People started their artwork and worked intently and quietly again on their own pictures, showing even more engagement with the materials than last week, some people's pictures becoming more elaborate. At the end of the art-making time we shared our hopes for the future together.

Rashida used brightly coloured felt-tip pens to draw all the things she wanted to include in her life: a tree and flowers (top), a jungle (bottom), which she worked on in detail, and a house with a big garden by a river (see Figure 10.3a). She hoped it would be in Pakistan, as she said she liked living in hot countries. She added that she wanted to catch the 'genie causing suffering' and put an end to it. Possibly the little shape on the right might be the genie.

Figure 10.3a The future I would like (also see colour plate section)

Figure 10.3b Review and a strength (also see colour plate section)

Session 6: Review of pictures – and one strength I have. Evaluation and closing

The last session seemed to come round all too soon. There was quite a lot to cover in this session. The first task was for all of us to individually review our work by looking through all the pictures we had done. We asked the women to look for any recurring themes and also to look for strengths or things they could appreciate about themselves, their circumstances or their lives. There was quite a lot of chatter and bustle as people looked through their work and seemed genuinely surprised by how much they had done. We then asked them to do a final image that gathered these things together, and also to try to identify one strength.

As before, it seemed difficult for the women to identify a strength, but they were able to explain what it was they wanted to do to move on. One woman painted a picture of her dream house with carefully selected fireplace curtains and flowers – we suggested that her strength was her arrangements of form and colour. Another woman did a picture of the past with an Indian bed and a Tandoori oven – she explained that she had recreated the past in her imagination, as this was a place she could no longer go to in real life. Most women included flowers and fields or gardens in their pictures. Two women's pictures had big gardens as gardening was something they enjoyed. One of these women described 'working on her husband' as something she needed to do, in order to leave the past behind. One woman put herself in the picture for the first time and another did a dynamic image of herself 'more happy' and moving on, quite different from pictures she had done before.

Rashida used the bright felt-tip pens again, and completely filled her paper (see Figure 10.3b). She drew a house with a big garden (centre right), a river (top and centre right), the sun (bottom right), flowers (at the bottom and all around the picture), the genie (centre), animals, village life, and herself (bottom right), but not crying this time. She was surprised by the review to see how much she had done. She talked about her love of gardening as her strength, and other members of the group pointed out her strength in bringing up her children.

Evaluation

We did this verbally with the group, as Nazlin suggested this would be more appropriate than written evaluations. We asked four questions:

1   *What did they enjoy?*

   Responses included: being in the group, doing the artwork, an opportunity to look inside themselves, developing insight, getting things out on paper, looking at the past and the future, sharing in other women's lives.

2   *Did the sessions help, and if so how?*

   The women said the group had helped them try to deal with things, given them ways of managing themselves, enabled them to think about the past, to remember their skills and to face things on paper.

3   *Was there anything you would have liked to be different?*

   The only things mentioned were: bigger paper, more space and more time (it was true that it had been a squash for 10 people to get round the table in the art therapy room).

4   *Is there any way you would like to take this forward?*

   The women suggested some possibilities: do art at home, be referred for individual art therapy and arrange another group.

Engagement with art materials

It was noticeable that the women started off very tentatively with limited materials, unsure how to use them or to express themselves. Over the six sessions they began to experiment with a greater variety of media, and their pictures became fuller and more interesting. Some women who still found it hard to talk, nevertheless gained a lot from being able to express themselves through the art materials.

Conclusion

It was a lot of hard work for all of us to plan, organise and facilitate this themed art therapy group, including the difficulties involved in translation. But it was very worthwhile in providing an avenue of expression not available through words – as evidenced in the colours, the shapes, the enjoyment, the tears, the engagement with the art materials and the group.

The theme of 'moving on' proved an interesting theme to work with. It was not always clear that the women fully understood some of the components that we had used to make up the overall theme. On some occasions the focus of the session seemed to go a bit astray and we seemed to be working on the topic of the previous session. Even so, each session still seemed to provide a valuable forum in which to work. However, more research could be done (with more time) into what 'moving on' might mean in Asian culture. It is also difficult to know what can be expected and achieved in a six-session group, but by the end Nazlin (as group facilitator in the longer term) felt she had a clearer idea about what the women in the group needed next.

For ourselves, we felt we had been given a rich insight into the positive aspects and the difficulties of some Asian women's lives. It gave us a better understanding of how difficult it can feel to leave somewhere you think of as home, travel a long way away, and try to adjust and settle somewhere completely new and alien. We learnt about the barriers that some women have to overcome in order to express themselves even a little – economic barriers, those of gender, cultural language, prejudice, stigma and lack of confidence. We also learnt how satisfying it can be to see such women gradually gaining in confidence, and how a little change can seem to go a long way.

References

D'Ardenne, P. and Mahtani, A. (1989) *Transcultural Counselling in Action.* London: Sage.

Fernando, S. (1991) *Mental Health, Race and Culture.* London: Macmillan.

Liebmann, M. (2002) 'Working with Elderly Asian Clients', *Inscape, the Journal of the British Association of Art Therapists*, Vol. 7, No. 2, 72–80.

Liebmann, M. (2004) 'Working with Elderly Asian Clients', *Generations Review, Journal of the British Society of Gerontology*, Vol. 14, No. 2 (April), 8–11.

Tannen, D. (1990) *You Just Don't Understand: Women and Men in Conversation.* London: Virago.

Thomas, L. (1995) 'Psychotherapy in the context of race and culture: an inter-cultural therapeutic approach'. In S. Fernando (ed) *Mental Health in a Multi-ethnic Society: A Multidisciplinary Handbook.* London: Routledge.

Index